# Yiddish

# Yiddish

## *Biography of a Language*

JEFFREY SHANDLER

OXFORD UNIVERSITY PRESS

OXFORD
UNIVERSITY PRESS

Oxford University Press is a department of the University of Oxford. It furthers the University's objective of excellence in research, scholarship, and education by publishing worldwide. Oxford is a registered trade mark of Oxford University Press in the UK and certain other countries.

Published in the United States of America by Oxford University Press
198 Madison Avenue, New York, NY 10016, United States of America.



Library of Congress Cataloging-in-Publication Data
Names: Shandler, Jeffrey, author.
Title: Yiddish : biography of a language / Jeffrey Shandler.
Description: New York : Oxford University Press, [2020] |
Includes bibliographical references and index.
Identifiers: LCCN 2020007938 (print) | LCCN 2020007939 (ebook) |
ISBN 9780190651961 (hardback) | ISBN 9780190651985 (epub) |
ISBN 9780190651992
Subjects: LCSH: Yiddish language—History.
Classification: LCC PJ5113 .S532 2020 (print) |
LCC PJ5113 (ebook) | DDC 439/.1—dc23
LC record available at https://lccn.loc.gov/2020007938
LC ebook record available at https://lccn.loc.gov/2020007939

1 3 5 7 9 8 6 4 2

Printed by Sheridan Books, Inc., United States of America

שלמהן—
נאָך אַ מאָל און אַלע מאָל

*For Stuart—*
*once more and ever more*

# Contents

# Acknowledgments

I thank the School of Arts and Sciences at Rutgers University for providing me with a sabbatical and a fellowship leave, which were essential to completing the research and writing of this book. During this period, I benefited greatly from my term as a Harry Starr Fellow at the Center for Jewish Studies of Harvard University and am especially grateful for the thoughtful intellectual engagement I enjoyed with David Stern, director of the Center for Jewish Studies, and the other members of the fellowship group. And I am most thankful to my friends Emily Lichtenstein and John Minahan for their generous hospitality during my stay in Boston.

For their kind assistance during the course of my work on this book, I thank Zachary Baker, Ayala Fader, Zev Feldman, Raphael Finkel, Paul Glasser, Stefanie Halpern, Paul Hanebrink, Jordan Kutzik, Rafi Lehmann, James Masschaele, Michael Miller, Holger Nath, Anita Norich, Samuel Norich, Chaya Nove, Rebekah Pejsova-Klein, Derek Penslar, Eddy Portnoy, Alyssa Quint, Rukhl Schaechter, Gitl Schaechter-Viswanath, Naomi Seidman, and Vital Zajka.

My most heartfelt thanks go to Stuart Schear, my partner in life and intrepid fellow adventurer in Yiddishland.

# Author's Note

Standard Yiddish, as established by the YIVO Institute for Jewish Research beginning in the 1930s, provides the basis for the Yiddish grammar, lexicon, orthography, and phonology presented in this book. All Yiddish terms are romanized, in italics, using the YIVO system and reflect Standard Yiddish pronunciation, except when demonstrating dialect variants. In some cases, accepted scholarly spellings of certain terms (e.g., Haskalah) are used and are not italicized. Romanizations of Yiddish that appear in citations preserve their sources' spellings.

Some Yiddish terms also appear in this book in the Jewish alphabet (i.e., the *alef-beys*) when this is relevant to the discussion. Except where noted, these terms are spelled according to YIVO Standard orthography, and they are also romanized. Hebrew and Russian terms are romanized using the Library of Congress system, minus diacritics. Yiddish, Hebrew, and Russian names of people and organizations are romanized according to their own preferred spellings, when known (e.g., Sholem Asch, Bais Yaakov). When a preferred spelling is not known, an authoritative version (per the Library of Congress catalog or *YIVO Encyclopedia of Jews in Eastern Europe*) is used; otherwise, names are romanized according to one of the aforementioned systems.

Endnotes indicate when translations of cited works are by the author; otherwise, they are per the sources cited.

# Introduction

It is remarkable how often people have spoken about Yiddish as if it were a kind of person. They variously characterize the language as a mother, an orphan, a maidservant, a seductress, a deviant, a muse, a laborer, an invalid, a foreigner, a magician, even a ghost. What are the implications of this wide range of portrayals? How do they inspire—and complicate—relating the story of Yiddish as the narrative of a human being, as a biography?

A biography of Yiddish—or, for that matter, of any language—is an intellectually provocative concept. It anthropomorphizes something that, while not human, depends on humankind for its existence. Language is not only entirely the creation of humans (though religious traditions may teach otherwise) but also an attribute widely regarded as distinguishing humans from other beings. Moreover, language use figures extensively in differentiating among national, regional, ethnic, religious, class, gender, sexual, generational, educational, ideological, and professional groups. Therefore, approaching a language as the subject of a biography, a genre conventionally reserved for the study of an individual person, draws attention to the relationships of a language with its speakers and with the cultural practices that people realize in or in relation to the language.

These issues are especially fitting for a book about Yiddish, the foundational vernacular of Ashkenazic Jewry (that is, the diaspora Jewish people generally understood as originating in northern Europe). The language is closely identified with particular Ashkenazic populations, their activities, mores, convictions, and sensibilities. Moreover, the scope of discussions of Yiddish regularly expands to address the nature of these Jews and their cultural practices. This interrelation among people, language, and culture is a central concern for the study of Yiddish, as are its speakers' complex internal diversity and their long, varied history of contact with speakers of other languages.

In order to probe both the possibilities and the challenges posed by the notion of a biography of a language, this book is not organized according to chronology, geography, activity, or ideology but instead offers a series of short thematic chapters that follow the rubric of a biographical profile: date and place of birth, family background, residence, and so on. Each chapter integrates an examination of some aspect of the development, form, or characteristics of Yiddish with part of the range and dynamics of the language's role in Ashkenazic life, from the Middle Ages to the present, and in locations on every continent where Yiddish speakers have settled. These chapters also probe the symbolic meanings that Jews and others have attributed to Yiddish over time, which are key to understanding the varied perceptions and valuations of the language. For example, the chapter "Name" both enumerates the different terms used over the centuries to identify the vernacular of Ashkenazic Jewry and considers what each name that people have given to the language now generally referred to as Yiddish reveals about their understandings of its use and its significance.

This book's structure enables an innovative approach to relating the story of Yiddish by integrating an account of its development over time with examinations of how the language has been discussed as a subject of interest in its own right. Therefore, rather than starting with a presentation of one or more theories of the origins of Yiddish, as is often the case in studies of the language, the chapter "Date and Place of Birth" first considers the relatively recent context in which theorizing the language's origins emerged. The chapter then examines various models for the beginnings of Yiddish not only to present this range of possibilities but also to analyze their different assumptions regarding the value of the language and its speakers.

The implications of anthropomorphizing Yiddish receive particular attention throughout the book—for example, in the chapters "Health," which examines how the language has been pathologized by its detractors and championed by its defenders, and "Personality," which considers various attributions of a distinct character to the language (and, implicitly, its speakers) as a whole. Probing these discourses calls attention both to the problems that arise from likening Yiddish to a human being, especially as this notion readily conflates linguistic concerns with other issues, and to the enduring attraction of this comparison. In these discourses, language is both the subject of scrutiny and the means of its discussion. The tension resulting from the inevitable involvement of language at both levels resembles a tension that is inherent in relating the story of Yiddish as a biography, a genre that grapples with the difference between a life lived and a life narrated. Awareness of this distinction enables critical insights into how the story of a language has been told. For example, the rubric of biography implicitly endows Yiddish with the integrity and continuity of a human life, a notion that should not go unquestioned. At the same time, it is important to recognize the value invested in this conceptualization of the language.

While this book is organized thematically, the history, geography, activities, and ideologies of Yiddish and its speakers do figure within this book's structure, though not in a conventional way. Rather, key phenomena recur in multiple chapters according to their particular thematic focus. These phenomena include the earliest Yiddish manuscripts and printed books, the settlement of Ashkenazic Jews across northern Europe, their development of new intellectual movements (such as the Haskalah) and religious movements (such as Hasidism), relationships between Yiddish and German and between Yiddish and Hebrew, the emergence of modern Jewish political movements, the efflorescence of modern Yiddish literature and culture, the development of Yiddishism as the ideology of a secular Jewish nationality, the mass immigration of Yiddish speakers beyond Europe, the advent of the field of Yiddish studies, and the impact on the language of the Holocaust and the creation of the State of Israel.

This book offers readers who have little or no familiarity with Yiddish an introduction to its significance within multiple scholarly perspectives, including European studies, Jewish studies, diaspora studies, and immigration studies, as well as language and culture studies. As this book is written for readers of English, sources cited are in that language wherever possible, as a guide to further study. For those readers conversant with Yiddish and the field of Yiddish studies, this book's format presents new ways of understanding familiar phenomena and scrutinizing conceptualizations of the language, its speakers, and their cultures. The notion of a biography of Yiddish invites all readers to engage the topic at hand creatively, as an edifying adventure.

• • •

Several principal observations about Yiddish are fundamental to this book's approach. To begin with, Yiddish has an unrivaled reach in the history of Jewish language use, as a vernacular once employed widely by generations of Ashkenazim. Though the origin of Yiddish is, like most languages, modest in scope, its speakers grew in number and geographic reach over time. By the eighteenth century, Ashkenazim had become the world's majority Jewish population, surpassing the number of Jews living around the Mediterranean and throughout the Middle East who spoke other Jewish vernaculars. The presence of Ashkenazim expanded further during the following century, as they began emigrating in large numbers from Europe to the Americas, South Africa, Palestine, and Australasia. At the same time, some of the practices that traditionally distinguished Ashkenazic Jews changed, including their vernacular language. Though they now comprise approximately 75 percent of the world's Jewish population, most Ashkenazim today do not speak Yiddish.[1] Many of these Jews are removed only by a generation or two from ancestors who were Yiddish speakers, and many Ashkenazim profess an attachment to Yiddish, even though they have limited or no knowledge of the language.

Given this history, examining the dynamic relationship between the instrumental uses of Yiddish as a vernacular with the symbolic values that people have invested in the language is central to this book. A vernacular, or demotic, is not merely a language that people use in the course of daily life for basic, routine communication. Often referred to as a native or mother tongue, it can have a defining significance for its speakers' sense of belonging to a national, regional, ethnic, or religious community. At the same time, a vernacular's esteem can vary, according to its use in different modes (speaking, performing, reading, writing) and contexts (for example, at home versus in school), by distinct categories of users (such as men versus women), and in relation to other languages. These might be the demotics of other peoples or languages of different stature, such as sacred languages, official state languages, or languages of high culture. All of these variables pertain to how Yiddish has been used and valued.

As a demotic, Yiddish is the language in which its native speakers have thought, even while engaging with other languages. These engagements are essential to its development, for Yiddish has never stood alone. Indeed, like other diaspora Jewish languages, it emerged from contact between different speech communities. Wherever Yiddish speakers have lived, they have always found themselves in multilingual environments. More precisely, these are multiglossic environments, in which not only are there several languages in use but they are each employed in distinct ways and toward distinct ends.

Yiddish is always positioned within a hierarchical relationship to the other languages in these various sociolinguistic configurations. Assigned a value regarding its scope, prestige, or other criteria vis-à-vis these languages, Yiddish seldom ranks at the top. This positioning of Yiddish reflects its association with the Jewish diaspora and with Jewish vernacularity.

Consequently, the varied esteem accorded to Yiddish corresponds to how both Jews and others conceptualize Jewish difference in diasporic settings and how the lives of *yidn fun a gants yor*—a Yiddish idiom meaning "ordinary Jews"—are understood in relation to elite populations, concepts, and mores, internal as well as external, traditional as well as modern. Over time, the relationship among Yiddish, its speakers, and their cultures has proved to be more unsettled, especially as Ashkenazim encounter modern ideas and practices that prompt new understandings of Jews as a people and how they might lead their lives, including their employment of language. These developments variously expand and contract Jews' use of Yiddish and alter their understanding of its significance.

The dynamics of Yiddish are manifold in their instability—if not more so than other languages, then widely perceived as such. This volatility is often regarded as a shortcoming, but it can be more useful to think of it as a defining feature. Therefore, rather than attempting to constrain the story of Yiddish within the rubric of a more conventional historical narrative, taking an unconventional approach to the topic, using the rubric of a biographical profile, enables the language's shifting complexities to be examined more on their own terms. Given the nature of Yiddish over the centuries, across continents, and among different, often divergent, speech communities, one needs to think nimbly and flexibly about what it has been and what it might yet be. Moreover, the story of Yiddish prompts larger questions about how a language is conceptualized, distinguished from other languages, and positioned in relation to them; how language continuity and integrity are constituted and debated; and how, apart from their ongoing use of a language to convey information, people can imbue it with potent symbolic value and wide-ranging definitional significance.

# 1
# Date and Place of Birth

Asking where and when Yiddish began its "life" evokes an especially vivid anthropomorphism. The suggestion of a language being "born" is inherently provocative, as are implicit notions of its "parentage" and the nature of its "conception." Though inquiring where and when it began may seem fundamental to learning about a language—and is, in fact, often addressed at the start of accounts of Yiddish—it is instructive to begin instead by interrogating the question itself. Doing so not only addresses the various models of the language's origins and resources that scholars have drawn upon to construct these explanations. This inquiry also reveals the intellectual and ideological motives that have prompted these theories of where and when Yiddish came to be.

However many years it has been in existence, probing the origins of Yiddish is a relatively recent phenomenon, as is the larger scientific interest in the history of individual languages and the development of human language generally. This inquiry emerged in the late eighteenth century, when scholars in western Europe paid new attention to vernacular languages, scrutinizing their distinct historical trajectories and foundational relationships with their respective speech communities. Philosopher Johann Gottfried Herder, a seminal figure in the modern study of language, argued that the formation of different languages by different peoples was a natural phenomenon, correlating to variations among human races and their physical environments. Moreover, he concluded, these differences engendered an inherent mistrust of other peoples, whose unfamiliar languages mark them as "barbarian."[1] Herder thus conceptualized the study of language as intrinsic to the study of different peoples, whose distinctions are organic. The ethnocentric assumption that the languages of others are barbaric—inferior as well as inscrutable—prompted notions of a gradation among languages and their native speakers, understood within an intractable hierarchy of race. These larger assumptions about the nature of language informed the first scholarly explanations of the beginnings of Yiddish.

Efforts to determine where and when Yiddish originated encounter multiple challenges. Because it has been a primarily oral language, the further back in time one looks, the less evidence exists of the Ashkenazic vernacular, and it is always refracted through the lens of written language. Yiddish is forged through contact between Jews and their neighbors, and its speakers have always known and used other languages. Therefore, the criteria for what might be considered manifestations of the beginnings of Yiddish as a discrete language are anything but straightforward. The use of non-linguistic sources to help determine its origins—including demographic data (for example, records of Ashkenazic settlement in Christian documents), material culture (such as the remains of medieval synagogues or tombstones), and the recent attention to genetic evidence—can raise questions on its own, both empirical and methodological.

Moreover, presuppositions about Yiddish that scholars bring to their analyses of its origins warrant scrutiny, beginning with how they conceptualize what it is. In addition to being classified as a language, Yiddish has also frequently been assigned a lower status as a dialect, creole, or patois. Some of its detractors have disparaged Yiddish as a jargon or dismissed it altogether as a "non-language." Contemporary linguists generally avoid such distinctions when studying a population's speech practices. Yet these terms are of historical and sociological significance, as they evince a hierarchy according to which the scope or quality of Yiddish has often been deemed less than a "full" or "proper" language. Similarly, the extensive discourse of Yiddish as something other than a "pure" language—usually characterized as a corruption of or deviation from German—impugns the integrity and legitimacy of Yiddish, with substantial implications for the esteem of its speakers as well. These discourses reflect larger inquiries regarding a language, its speakers, and their shared characteristics, as well as the relationship between language contact and interactions among different peoples, all of which inform the study of a language's origins.

Recorded attention among Christian speakers of German to the distinct character of the Ashkenazic vernacular dates as early as the fifteenth century. For example, in 1451 a German priest from Magdeburg described an acquaintance as someone who "looks like a Jew and speaks like one too,"[2] thereby linking notions of a recognizable Jewish appearance with detectible Jewish speech. Beginning in the sixteenth century, various Christian German speakers examined the vernacular language of their Ashkenazic neighbors, approaching it as a phenomenon of an alien culture while evaluating it in relation to their own language. Consequently, their notions of the origins of Yiddish assume the preexistence and preeminence of German, from which Yiddish deviated. These assumptions informed a Germanist perspective on Yiddish for centuries. Thus, author Johann Wolfgang von Goethe, who studied Yiddish as a young man in the late 1700s, characterized it as "*barockes Judendeutsch*"—baroque Jewish German—to indicate what he perceived as the "old-fashioned character" of the language when compared to his own speech.[3]

These early Germanist observers of Yiddish did not specifically address where or when the language began, though they often speculated on the cause of its divergence from German. Some implicitly linked the origins of Yiddish to the limited nature of Jews' contact with the German language, including their longstanding separate education and their ghettoization beginning in the fifteenth century. Others, however, maintained that Jews deliberately chose to "cultivate a special dialect of their own," whether motivated by a contempt for Christians or by the desire to develop a "secret language."[4]

Such approaches to understanding Yiddish continued to inform scholarship into the nineteenth century, including work by founders of Wissenschaft des Judentums (German: "scientific study of Judaism"). This movement, initiated in 1819 by Jewish scholars living in German states, employed modern Western methodologies to analyze the development of Jewish texts and practices since ancient times. By inventorying and historicizing the corpus of Jewish writings, these researchers aspired to supersede traditional rabbinic authority with modern scholarship and culture in order to support Jews' cultural and social integration into the European mainstream. These researchers, notes German studies scholar Jeffrey Grossman, regarded Yiddish as "the image of a culturally inhibiting anachronism" that became emblematic of "the entire process of casting off the constraints of the supposedly ghettoized world of traditional Jewish culture." Consequently, Wissenschaft des Judentums scholars were dismissive of Yiddish and, as a rule, considered texts written in the language to have little intellectual value. Like earlier Christian scholars, they characterized the origins of Yiddish as a deviation from German. Leopold Zunz, a founder of this movement, argued that in the sixteenth century "Jews also spoke the German of Christians," but the subsequent ghettoization of Jews in German towns "led to a degeneration of language."[5]

Other studies informed by this perspective attributed the origins of Yiddish to the migration of Ashkenazim into eastern Europe at the end of the Middle Ages, so that "the language then developed in isolation from its 'origin.'"[6] Implying that German lands are the homeland of Ashkenazim, with German as their native vernacular, this model affirms the rootedness of western Ashkenazim in German language and culture by associating the otherness of Yiddish with the exoticized character of eastern European Jewry.[7] More recently, in quite a different cultural context, the notion that Yiddish is a Jewish adulteration of German reappeared during the post–World War II period of Soviet scholarship on Yiddish, which asserted that it "is neither a Jewish language, nor a language at all, but a 'judaized jargon of German.'" Slavic studies scholar Wolf Moscovich argues that this characterization of Yiddish was politically motivated, intended to "prove that Jews do not constitute a separate nation" and that "Soviet Jews have nothing in common with the rest of the Jewish people." Here, too, Yiddish was configured as a signifier of the alien; "the mother tongue of Russian Jews," this Soviet scholarship insisted, "is Russian."[8]

• • •

Scholars who approach Yiddish as a language in its own right, rather than as a derivative of German, conceptualize its origins quite differently—not merely as to time and place but also with regard to the nature of how it came to be. In his *History of the Yiddish Language*, linguist Max Weinreich locates the beginnings of Yiddish in the ninth century, when Jews settled in towns along or near the Rhine River: Aachen, Mainz, Speier, and Worms. These Jews, he posits, migrated to the region from what is now northern France and northern Italy, where their vernacular was comprised of Jewish correlates of Old French and Old Italian. Weinreich refers to these languages collectively as Loez, a term from Biblical Hebrew that subsequently came to mean "foreign language." Upon arriving in the Rhine valley, these Jews encountered Christian speakers of local variants of Middle High German. This contact, Weinreich claims, engendered a new language, which is now called Yiddish. Solomon Birnbaum, a Yiddish cultural activist and pioneering scholar of the language, similarly argues that, from a sociological criterion, "when the Jews settled in Germany, with an intensive group life of their own, and adopted the German tongue, inside their society it was at once Jewish, and Yiddish came into being."[9] From this local point of origin, both scholars maintain, Yiddish speakers migrated eastward, starting in the thirteenth century, eventually developing an eastern Yiddish language and culture, which were to a significant extent distinct from their western counterparts. Yiddish speakers also moved southward into northern Italy and westward into the Netherlands, so that the language became a presence across northern Europe in the early modern period.

Weinreich not only provides the language with a significantly earlier beginning than the Germanist models do; he roots its origin in a German heartland, situating Yiddish as indigenous to the region, rather than an alien phenomenon. Both he and Birnbaum also position Yiddish within the long trajectory of diaspora Jewish languages, dating back to ancient times: "an uninterrupted development of speech and writing . . . , previous stages of which had crystalized into the language of the Bible, that of the Mishna [and] the Gemara."[10] This Yiddish-centered model presents the origins and development of the language in terms of continuity and growth. Moreover, Yiddish exemplifies diaspora Jewish cultural distinctiveness, adaptability, and tenacity—a phenomenon that Weinreich deems "among the highest achievements of the Jewish national genius."[11]

Though acknowledging the encounter of Jews with German speakers as essential to the beginnings of Yiddish, this model conceptualizes Yiddish as a discrete language from the start, distinguished by the established practice of diaspora Jews forging their own vernaculars through contact with their neighbors' languages. Rather than positioning Yiddish as diverging from medieval German, Birnbaum and Weinreich characterize these as two related languages developing alongside one another. Weinreich's dating the start of Yiddish to the ninth century situates it as more or less concomitant with the advent of other European vernaculars,[12] as well as with a shift in "the center of gravity of the Jewish people" from Asia and Africa to Europe.[13] Ashkenazim and their vernacular are thus positioned as part of Europe's emergence from the Dark Ages, rather than as adventitious or retrograde phenomena, and as vital to the establishment of Europe as the center of Jewish culture for a millennium.

This alternative to the Germanist conceptualization of the origins of Yiddish rests on a radically different understanding of diaspora Jewry. Weinreich characterizes the diaspora not as abject but as having long enabled Jews to maintain established beliefs and practices while living among an array of other peoples. The goal of Ashkenazim, he asserts, "was not isolation from the Christians but insulation from Christianity." Even as ongoing relations with Christian neighbors informed these Jews' folkways and customs, their culture, exemplified by Yiddish, was "specifically

Ashkenazic."[14] In contrast to Zionist characterizations of the diaspora as reducing Jews to a weakened, fallen state, their culture corrupted by contact with gentiles, Weinreich championed the diaspora as a defining virtue of Jewishness. He shared this conviction with political leaders who advocated for Jewish cultural autonomism in the first decades of the twentieth century, including historian Simon Dubnow, a founder of the Folkspartey (Folkists), and Vladimir Medem, a leader of the socialist Yidisher Arbeter Bund (Jewish Labor Bund).[15]

Weinreich's evidence for the origins of Yiddish is, by his own admission, scant. He marks the beginning of Ashkenaz as dating to 801, when, after centuries of there being no record of a Jewish presence in German lands since Roman times, "there emerges in Aachen . . . the name of a Jew Isaac," whom Weinreich deems "a kind of patriarch" inaugurating a "new and uninterrupted Jewish settlement in the area of the Middle Rhine."[16] The earliest linguistic evidence of Yiddish that Weinreich offers are distinctly Ashkenazic names of Jews mentioned in a late eleventh-century martyrology from the First Crusade and, from the same period, a small inventory of words described as "in the language of Ashkenaz" in commentaries on the Bible and the Talmud by the eleventh-century rabbinical scholar Rashi. It is not until the late thirteenth century that one finds a single dated Yiddish sentence, inscribed in the Worms *mahzor* (Hebrew: "holiday prayer book") of 1272, and a century later that there appears the oldest dated collection of Yiddish texts, known as the Cambridge Codex, from 1382. But rather than relying solely on "evidence that was preserved at random,"[17] Weinreich's thesis rests on a paradigm of diaspora Jewish language formation that precedes his start date for Yiddish by many centuries. From this approach, he and other linguists have generated a profile of proto-Yiddish—that is, a projection of the language at its earliest moment of formation—from historical sources in relation to the phonology of the modern language.[18]

Most subsequent work by Yiddish linguists accepts Weinreich's and Birnbaum's basic premise of how the language emerged, but some of this more recent scholarship locates the origin of Yiddish and of Ashkenazim in different times or places. Drawing on archeological evidence, Leo Fuchs argues that Jews' entry into the Rhine valley dates to Roman times and posits that the linguistic material Weinreich attributes to Loez as these Jews' prior vernacular indicates instead that they had previously spoken a Jewish correlate of Latin.[19] Other linguists situate the origins of Yiddish not in the Rhine valley but further east, close to the Danube, centered in the Bavarian towns of Regensburg, Nuremberg, and Rothenberg, when Jews arrived in the region from southern and eastern Europe beginning in the tenth century. These scholars base their model on analyses of phonological evidence in early Ashkenazic Hebrew and Yiddish texts compared to parallel sources of different dialects of Middle High German, arguing that the Jewish materials evince greater similarities to its Bavarian rather than its Rhenish variants.

In his theorization of the origins of Yiddish, Robert King also addresses the question of Jewish demography, arguing that available statistical evidence suggests "there were not enough Jews in western Europe to populate eastern Europe." The large number of Jews that eventually flourished there, he concludes, must have come, at least in part, from elsewhere. Moreover, "focusing narrowly on the linguistic evidence," King rejects the notion that Ashkenazic culture began in the Rhine valley, arguing that claims for "Romance lexical traces" (i.e., Loez) as evidence of Yiddish having a west German origin are "linguistically extravagant."[20] Dovid Katz posits that Jews in the Rhine valley once spoke a Germanic vernacular, but it disappeared, "though not without a trace—proper names and a few relic forms survive" in the language that developed further east, near the upper Danube, into Yiddish.[21]

Not all linguists are persuaded by the Bavarian model. Affirming the Rhine valley to be the locus of origin for Yiddish, David Gold critiques King's theory on demographic grounds as well as linguistic evidence.[22] Erika Timm asserts that "the Rhineland must remain the 'cradle' of Yiddish," as this is the source of the earliest written evidence of Ashkenazic Jewry. Timm also insists on the importance of the region's "relation to the pre-Yiddish area of Judaeo-Romance culture."[23]

Rather than arguing that the genesis of Yiddish occurs in a single time and place, Alexander Beider, among other scholars, offers a polygenetic model of its origins. He separates the origins of Western Yiddish and Eastern Yiddish, each having arisen in discrete locations, as opposed to the theory of a Yiddish continuum that follows a trajectory of Ashkenazic immigration from a single site of origin, moving primarily eastward. According to Beider, Western Yiddish began in the Rhineland and is mainly related to the East Franconian dialect of German, with a small Old French substratum, reflecting the Jewish vernacular previously used by the first speakers of Western Yiddish. Eastern Yiddish has a Bohemian German basis and is subsequently influenced by contact with the Silesian dialect of German spoken by colonists in medieval Poland. Beider considers the partial unity of Eastern and Western Yiddish to have arisen later, due to the circulation of printed texts across central and eastern Europe as well as to subsequent Jewish migrations. Based on "purely linguistic criteria," Beider argues against claiming the Germanic vernacular used by Jews before the fifteenth century to be a separate language. To be considered Yiddish, he maintains, the language spoken by Jews in a given region must be different from the Germanic dialect of Christians who live there. Parallel to his linguistic model, Beider concludes that Ashkenazim have "heterogeneous roots," as the descendants of a "merger" of three discrete medieval Jewish populations, which originated in the Rhine valley, in Czech lands, and further east in what is now Ukraine and Belarus.[24]

Other scholars locate the origin of Yiddish beyond the West Germanic language territory. Charles Nydorf argues that Yiddish is related to Gothic, an East Germanic language last spoken in the eighth century, with the exception of a variant that endured in Crimea through the late eighteenth century. Nydorf posits that "the eastern dialects of Yiddish formed as the result of three language contact events," beginning with "a form of Jewish Crimean and German [that] occurred along the trade routes between the German speaking lands and the Black Sea around 850."[25]

Paul Wexler argues against the prevailing assumption of Yiddish as a language of Germanic origin altogether. Rather, he characterizes Yiddish as resulting from a Germanic "relexification" of speech that was originally Slavic—initially among Jews who spoke the West Slavic language of Sorbian in Lusatia, a region of north central Europe located between the Elbe and Oder Rivers, at some time during the ninth to twelfth centuries. According to Wexler, the vocabulary of Yiddish became primarily Germanic as a result of contact with German-speaking immigrants in Sorbian and Polabian lands between the ninth and twelfth centuries. However, he maintains, the grammatical structures of Yiddish remained foundationally Slavic, and it should be considered a Slavic language. Wexler's model has provocative extralinguistic implications, as it posits that most Yiddish speakers did not descend from a continuous Jewish diaspora out of the ancient Middle East. Rather, he maintains, they originated elsewhere, especially among proselytes, as part of "rampant conversion to Judaism on all continents up to the beginning of the second millennium A.D.," including "the Judaized Turko-Iranian Khazar population that became Slavic-speaking after the collapse of the Khazar Empire in the late tenth century." Like some other linguists, Wexler considers Western Yiddish to be a separate phenomenon, a Germanic language that he terms "Rhineland Jewish," though he acknowledges that Western (Germanic) Yiddish and Eastern (Slavic) Yiddish were mutually influential.[26]

Both Nydorf and Wexler argue that genetic data on the origins of Ashkenazic Jewry should be taken into account in reconstructing the history of Yiddish. Nydorf cites genomic sequencing studies, published in 2013 and 2014, which suggest that contemporary Ashkenazim reflect an early, sizeable "admixture of a European and a Middle Eastern population," implying that "the majority of German Jews alive before 800 years ago did not contribute ancestors to the modern Ashkenazi population." This evidence, Nydorf argues, supports Weinreich's claim that the migration of Jewish scholars from Babylonia to Europe in the thirteenth century contributed to threshold changes in the development of Yiddish as well as in rabbinic law and scholarship.[27] Wexler offers a more recent theorization of the language's origins in a coauthored 2016 study of Ashkenazic and non-Ashkenazic Jewish genomes that posits Ashkenazim "originated from a Slavo-Iranian confederation, which the Jews call 'Ashkenazic' (i.e., 'Scythian')." Wexler asserts that this genetic model conforms to linguistic evidence demonstrating Yiddish as originally a Slavic language.[28] This article attracted considerable censure in both general and academic publications, and the journal in which it appeared published critical responses from scholars of genetics and of Yiddish.[29] Russian studies scholar Cherie Woodworth characterizes the strong reactions that Wexler's theories have elicited from other scholars of Yiddish as not simply due to intellectual dissent but as "deeply personal and a matter of identity itself,"[30] challenging fundamental assumptions about the origins and development of Ashkenazic Jewry.

• • •

All theories of the origins of Yiddish grapple with multiple difficulties: the limited amount of linguistic data prior to the early modern period, all of which is at some remove from spoken language; gaps in the historical record of Jewish settlements and migrations across Europe; incongruities in Ashkenazic demography, ranging from the nature of early encounters between Ashkenazim and Jews in Slavic lands to the eventual expansion of Ashkenazim, becoming the majority of world Jewry; the possibility of a language shift occurring among northern European Jewish populations—whether from Knaanic, the vernacular spoken by Jews in eastern Europe before their encounter with Ashkenazim from the west, or the adoption of Bavarian Yiddish by Ashkenazim located further west in the Rhine valley, or the Germanic relexification of a Slavic Jewish language in Lusatia—eventually resulting in a modern, pan-European Yiddish. Some recent theorists offer polygenetic models in order to accommodate linguistic data that is inconsistent and historical evidence of Jewish settlement across northern Europe that is scattered and discontinuous.

Given all these challenges, no theory of where and when Yiddish started and how it developed in the premodern period can be definitive. Rather, these models are of scholarly interest for the range of possibilities they offer for the language's trajectory and, moreover, for the implications of how they define the speakers of Yiddish, their history, and their culture. From the start, theorizations of where and when Yiddish originated are informed by preconceptions of the language and its speakers. These efforts have been bound up with polemical interests, whether validating Ashkenazim as constituting a nationality equal in longevity to their European neighbors or questioning this population's fundaments, age, or integrity. Approaches to the topic are also distinguished by epistemological choices, especially concerning the scope of relevant information. Whereas some scholars focus on "purely linguistic" data, others insist that "linguistic and social factors are closely interrelated in the development of language" and cannot be ignored.[31]

The question of where and when a language begins inevitably leads to other interests. In the case of Yiddish, the issue also addresses, if sometimes implicitly, the origins of Ashkenazic Jewry and its expansion to a population of unprecedented size in Jewish history. Did Ashkenazim begin among small communities in western Europe some eleven centuries ago, gradually migrating eastward until they spanned the continent? Were western European and eastern European Ashkenazim two (or more) distinct populations, though they shared certain religious practices and, eventually, the same traditional vernacular? Should Western Yiddish and Eastern Yiddish therefore be thought of as, at least originally, two separate languages? Were many, if not most, eastern European Yiddish speakers Jews of different origin—converts to Judaism among Sorbs or Khazars or migrants from the Middle East—who, at some point, encountered a small but influential population of Ashkenazim and gradually adopted (and adapted) their language and customs? These postulations integrate linguistic and extralinguistic evidence to support arguments with powerful implications for the present as much as for the past.

In addition to reflecting convictions regarding Jews, Germans, or Europeans generally, these models reveal varying assumptions about what does—and does not—constitute a discrete language and about the possibilities for understanding the nature of Jewish multiglossia or of contact among speech communities. To characterize Yiddish as a corruption of German is to deny the former language, in effect, a legitimate birth and to label it as misbegotten. Conversely, to claim Yiddish as a European language equal to those spoken and written by others on the continent may not correspond to how early Ashkenazim thought of their vernacular. To posit that Yiddish began in multiple, separate sites or among populations with no genetic ties either to one another or to other Jews disrupts widely held notions of Ashkenazic distinctiveness and of Jewish continuity. If the origins of Yiddish remain a mystery, the efforts to situate its date and place of birth constitute a subject of inquiry in its own right, though perhaps these endeavors sometimes reveal more about the assumptions and desires of those undertaking this quest than about the language itself.

# 2
# Family Background

Conceptualizing the relationship of Yiddish to languages that Jews knew previously and to the languages spoken by their neighbors is key to understanding the theories of its origin and discussions of its development across time and space. Yiddish can be situated among other modern European languages on a "family tree" that traces their emergence from earlier languages, branching out from a foundational Indo-European source. On this tree, Yiddish is a member of the family of Germanic languages as a descendant of West Germanic, along with Dutch, English, and German. This model of situating a language in relation to others is patently anthropomorphic, recalling genealogical charts that trace one's familial lineage over generations. Moreover, this approach scrutinizes the phonology, lexicon, morphology, syntax, and other formal elements of a language for traits shared with other languages, much as human DNA is probed to track a person's inherited characteristics. Given the nature of this analogy, attention to the family background of Yiddish readily extends beyond the language itself to an assessment of its speakers and their culture.

Notions of how Yiddish is related to its Germanic kin diverge in consequential ways. As discussed in the previous chapter, some theorists conceptualize Yiddish as a distinct language from the start, while others view Yiddish as an aberrant form of German. However this relationship is conceived, the anthropomorphic implications of contextualizing Yiddish within the Germanic family are telling not merely for the language but also for the stature of its speakers as Europeans. Either Yiddish is regarded as a rightful family member, having its own integrity as the language of a distinct ethnic or national group, or it is characterized as illegitimate, unwelcome alongside Faroese, Icelandic, and other members of this family and their speakers.

It is also possible to place Yiddish within a different rubric entirely, as a member of the family of diaspora Jewish languages. Though they are not situated together on the aforementioned language tree, linguists observe significant structural as well as functional similarities among these languages, of which there are more than a score, most of them very localized and some no longer spoken.[1] Diaspora Jewish languages reflect shared patterns of vernacular language formation and use as a consequence of centuries of Jews' settlement beyond the ancient Middle East, extending eastward into Asia, westward across North Africa, and throughout Europe. The primary component of each diaspora Jewish language develops from contact with the vernacular spoken by non-Jewish neighbors—for example, Judezmo vis-à-vis Spanish, Romaniote vis-à-vis Greek, Yiddish vis-à-vis German. In addition, diaspora Jewish languages all incorporate lexical and grammatical features of the Hebrew and Aramaic of traditional worship and devotional study, known as *leshon ha-kodesh* (Hebrew: "language of holiness," pronounced *loshn-koydesh* in Yiddish), and are typically written with the Jewish alphabet.

A diaspora Jewish language may also contain elements of prior Jewish vernaculars as well as features that enter the language later in its development. In some cases these elements reflect the speech community's history of migration. Thus, Old Spanish is the primary component of Judezmo, the vernacular of Sephardic Jews following their expulsion from Iberia in the fifteenth century, enhanced by other Iberian languages. In addition to the incorporation of terms from *leshon ha-kodesh*, later elements enter Judezmo (sometimes also called Ladino or Spaniol) from its speakers' contact with Ottoman Turkish, Arabic, Greek, Italian, and French, reflecting the post-exilic migrations of Sephardim.[2]

In contrast with the formal resemblances that identify related languages on the "tree" model, the similarities among members of the family of Jewish languages are structural. For example, a pattern shared by these languages is their use of the word for "school," in the respective non-Jewish language that forms their primary component, as a term for "synagogue." Thus, Yiddish *shul* (cf. German *Schule*) follows the paradigm of diaspora Jewish correlates to Greek (*skolé*), Latin (*scola*), Italian (*scuola*), French (*escole*), Provençal (*escola*), and Catalan (*scola*).[3]

The two different linguistic families in which Yiddish has been included—the Germanic and the Jewish—offer complementary anthropomorphic models of language development. Whereas the former resembles the genetic inheritance of common features via "nature," the latter centers on shared characteristics acquired through "nurture"—that is, by dint not of biology but of environment, learned behavior, and social engagement. As with probing the character of human beings, there is strong interest in the interrelation of these two competing models for understanding the constitution of Yiddish.

• • •

The two different rubrics for contextualizing Yiddish in relation to other languages can be synthesized by characterizing it as a fusion language, which is understood, whether by its speakers or by others, as integrating elements of two or more discrete languages. Although it deals with issues of lexicon, morphology, and syntax, the notion of a fusion language is perhaps best understood as a metalinguistic or extralinguistic issue. Many languages, after all, bear the traces of one or more precedent languages or admixtures of features from other languages acquired over time. In this instance, fusion is distinguished by a consciousness among those who use or study Yiddish that it is comprised of elements related to other languages, whose various sources remain apparent, and that these distinctions can be significant in their own right.

Though some of the earliest efforts to characterize the language manifest an awareness of its different components, identifying fusion as a defining feature of Yiddish is a hallmark of modern analyses, including the work of Shiye-Mordkhe Lifshits, a pioneer of modern Yiddish lexicography, in the 1860s, and philologist Matthias Mieses in the first decade of the twentieth century. Subsequently, Max Weinreich, a leading theorist of Yiddish fusion, deemed it both the foundational "act of creation" for the language and a process that is "continuous and cumulative."[4] Claiming fusion as a defining feature of the language may be, as some have suggested, "more ideological than linguistic."[5] Indeed, its speakers have variously regarded the conglomerate nature of Yiddish to be an attribute for good or for ill. Among the latter were *maskilim*, advocates of the intellectual movement known as the Haskalah (conventionally translated as the "Jewish Enlightenment"), whose agenda for Jews' integration into the mainstream of western European culture and society included developing proficiency in the languages of high culture.[6] Beginning in the late eighteenth century, *maskilim* called for abandoning Yiddish, which they derogated as an impure mixture of languages. By contrast, a group of early twentieth-century avant-garde American Yiddish writers known as the Inzikhistn (Introspectivists) embraced the language's hybridity as being well suited to addressing the "kaleidoscopic" nature of modern life, the "awesome labyrinth" of the individual psyche, and the "enormous variety" of the metropolis. Far from considering it to be less than a proper language, these writers described Yiddish as "independent enough to enrich its vocabulary from the treasures of her sister languages."[7]

Weinreich characterized fusion as a purposeful "systemization" of selection: "stock languages" are the "raw material" from which certain elements, classified as "determinants," become "potentially capable" of entering Yiddish; of these, elements that do become part of the language are termed "components."[8] The primary stock languages of Yiddish are Germanic (variants of Middle High German), Semitic (*loshn-koydesh*), Romance (Loez), and Slavic (including Czech, Polish, Ukrainian, Belorussian, and Russian). The last two components testify to the history of Ashkenaz. According to Weinreich, among others, the Jews who became the first Ashkenazim maintained a select number of words from Loez, which they had spoken before migrating to German lands, as they developed Yiddish. Some of these words, such as *antshpoyzn* ("to betroth"), *orn* ("to pray"), *dertornen* ("to repeat"), or *piltsl* ("girl"), have become archaic or obsolete, especially with the decline of Western Yiddish in the modern period. Among words from the Romance component still used in Yiddish are *bentshn* ("to bless, to recite a blessing"), *tsholnt* ("Sabbath stew"), *leyenen* ("to read"), *milgroym* ("pomegranate"), *sarver* ("waiter"), *stirdes* ("defiance"), and *plankhenen* ("to weep"). (Some linguists oppose recognizing Romance languages as comprising a component of Yiddish, arguing that there is limited evidence, if any, of their impact on its structure.)[9] The much more extensive Slavic component of Yiddish developed, most scholars maintain, as Ashkenazim migrated eastward and encountered speakers of Slavic languages, beginning in the thirteenth century. The development of this component is generally recognized as the salient linguistic distinction between Western Yiddish and Eastern Yiddish. The Semitic component of Yiddish, though a fundamental element of this and other diaspora Jewish languages, became the focus of ideological debates in the early twentieth century on the value of Yiddish and its future development. Secular Yiddishists variously hailed the Semitic component as the essence of the language or called for its dehebraization.[10]

Though the different components of Yiddish are most readily apparent in its lexicon, fusion entails more than simply integrating words from different components. In numerous instances, Yiddish words have a different form or meaning compared to their correlates in the stock languages. For example, the Hebrew noun *talit* ("prayer shawl") is feminine, and its plural is *talitot*, whereas *tales*, the Yiddish cognate, is masculine, and its plural is *taleysim*. In German, *schmecken* means "to taste"; in Yiddish, *shmekn* means "to smell" (though Yiddish also has *geshmak*, an adjective meaning "tasty" and an adverb meaning "heartily"). Synonyms from different components can acquire more restricted meanings in Yiddish than their equivalent terms in the stock languages. Thus, in Hebrew the word *sefer* means a book of any kind, as does *Buch* in German and *kniha* in Belorussian, whereas Yiddish distinguishes *seyfer* ("holy book," such as the Bible, prayer book, Talmud) from *bukh*, which refers to a non-sacred book, and Yiddish-speaking butchers use the term *knihe* for a cow's third stomach, the shape of which resembles a codex. Yiddish sometimes restricts the meaning of synonyms from different components to distinguish between Jewish and non-Jewish phenomena—for example, *beys-oylem* (Semitic component) refers to a Jewish cemetery, versus *tsvinter* (Slavic component) to a non-Jewish cemetery. At other times Yiddish expands or alters the meanings of terms, when compared to their correlates. Thus, in Yiddish *reynkeyt* is "purity, cleanliness" (cf. German *Reinheit*), while *reynikeyt* is a term for a Torah scroll. Unlike German *Jahrzeit* ("season [of year]"), the Yiddish cognate *yortsayt* means "anniversary of a person's death," while "season" is *tsayt fun yor, sezon*, or *tkufe*.

Yiddish manifests extensive fusion within individual words, including compound nouns that conjoin elements from different components:

Romance and Germanic: *tsholnt-|bretl* ("board for closing the oven in which Sabbath dishes are kept warm")
Semitic and Slavic: *khasene-|vetshere* ("wedding feast")
Slavic and Germanic: *vesne|tsayt* ("springtime")

A more pervasive form of fusion involves grammatical modifiers from one component joined with nouns or verbal stems from another. For example, the paradigm for conjugating verbs originates with the Germanic component, including verbs whose stems come from other components:

Germanic component stem: *shraybn* ("to write"):

| Present tense | |
|---|---|
| *ikh shrayb* | I write* |
| *du shraybst* | you write (singular informal) |
| *er/zi/es shraybt* | he/she/it writes |
| *mir shraybn* | we write |
| *ir shraybt* | you write (plural or singular formal) |
| *zey shraybn* | they write |

* *Ikh shrayb* can also be translated as "I am writing" or "I have been writing."

Past tense

| | |
|---|---|
| *ikh hob geshribn* | I wrote |
| *du host geshribn* | you wrote (singular informal) |
| *er/zi/es hot geshribn* | he/she/it wrote |
| *mir hobn geshribn* | we wrote |
| *ir hot geshribn* | you wrote (plural or singular formal) |
| *zey hobn geshribn* | they wrote |

Future tense

| | |
|---|---|
| *ikh vel shraybn* | I will write |
| *du vest shraybn* | you will write (singular informal) |
| *er/zi/es vet shraybn* | he/she/it will write |
| *mir veln shraybn* | we will write |
| *ir vet shraybn* | you will write (plural or singular formal) |
| *zey veln shraybn* | they will write |

Romance component stem: *leyenen* ("to read")

Present tense: *ikh leyen, du leyenst, er/zi/es leyent, mir leyenen . . .*
Past tense: *ikh hob geleyent . . .*
Future tense: *ikh vel leyenen . . .*

Semitic component stem: *kholemen* ("to dream"):

Present tense: *ikh kholem, du kholemst, er/zi/es kholemt, mir kholemen . . .*
Past tense: *ikh hob gekholemt . . .*
Future tense: *ikh vel kholemen . . .*

Slavic component stem: *dzhvign* ("to haul")

Present tense: *ikh dzhvige, du dzhvigest, er/zi/es dzhviget, mir dzhvign . . .*
Past tense: *ikh hob gedzhviget . . .*
Future tense: *ikh vel dzhvign . . .*

Yiddish has many periphrastic verbs, which consist of a conjugated auxiliary verb and a fixed infinitive. These verbs often combine Semitic infinitives with one of several Germanic auxiliary verbs (*hobn*, "to have"; *zayn*, "to be"; *vern*, "to become"):

*hanoe hobn* ("to enjoy")

Present tense: *ikh hob hanoe, du host hanoe, er/zi/es hot hanoe, mir hobn hanoe, ir hot hanoe, zey hobn hanoe*

Past tense: *ikh hob hanoe gehat, du host hanoe gehat, er/zi/es hot hanoe gehat . . .*

Future tense: *ikh vel hanoe hobn, du vest hanoe hobn, er/zi/es vet hanoe hobn . . .*

*mekane zayn* ("to envy")

Present tense: *ikh bin mekane, du bist mekane, er/zi/es iz mekane, mir zaynen mekane, ir zayt mekane, zey zaynen mekane*

Past tense: *ikh hob mekane geven, du host mekane geven, er/zi/es hot mekane geven, . . .*

Future tense: *ikh vel mekane zayn, du vest mekane zayn, er/zi/es vet mekane zayn . . .*

*nelm vern* ("to vanish")

Present tense: *ikh ver nelm, du verst nelm, er/zi/es vert nelm, mir vern nelm, ir vert nelm, zey vern nelm . . .*

Past tense: *ikh bin nelm gevorn, du bist nelm gevorn, er/zi/es iz nelm gevorn . . .*

Future tense: *ikh vel nelm vern, du vest nelm vern, er/zi/es vet nelm vern . . .*

Fusion also appears in verbs with prefixes or infixes:

Germanic prefix with Semitic stem: *iber|khazern* ("to repeat")
Germanic stem with Slavic infix: *hersh|eve|n* ("to tyrannize")
Germanic prefix with Romance stem: *fir|leyenen* ("to read aloud")

Some verb forms fuse grammatical structures from across stock languages. Forms of verbal aspect from the Slavic component, such as distinctions between an ongoing or repeated action versus a single or completed action, appear in some verb constructions that are composed entirely of words from the Germanic component:

Punctual aspect: *Zi tut a kuk* ("She takes a look," i.e., "she peeks").

Enduring aspect: *Zi halt in eyn kukn* ("She keeps on looking," i.e., "she stares").

The Slavic particle *zhe* can intensify verbs from other components in the imperative: *Kum aher!* ("Come here!") ~ *Kum-zhe aher!* ("COME HERE!"). Parallel to an emphatic form of verbal repetition found in Biblical Hebrew is a Yiddish construction that is sometimes employed as a means of emphasis or clarification. This, too, can be constructed entirely from words in the Germanic component. For example, *Arbetn arbet ikh in Manhetn, nor voynen voyn ikh in Bruklin* ("[As for] working, I work in Manhattan, but [as for] living, I live in Brooklyn").

Noun endings can entail all manner of fusion among different components:

Semitic noun with Germanic plural ending: *yam|en* ("seas")
Germanic noun with Semitic plural ending: *poyer|im* ("peasants")
Germanic noun with Romance plural ending: *lerer|s* ("teachers")
Slavic noun with Romance plural ending: *zhmenye|s* ("handfuls")
Romance noun with Germanic noun ending and diminutive suffix: *bentsh|er|l* ("booklet with the text of blessings recited after meals")
Slavic noun with Germanic diminutive suffix: *katshke|le* ("duckling")
Semitic noun with Slavic personal suffix: *kadish|nik* ("mourner during the year following a close relative's death")
Semitic noun with Germanic abstract suffix: *khaver|shaft* ("comradeship")
Germanic noun with Slavic endearment suffix: *Got|enyu* ("Dear God")

Epitomizing Yiddish fusion are individual words that integrate elements from three different components: for example, *balebat|eve|n* ("to domineer") combines a Semitic verb stem with a Slavic infix and a Germanic ending; *shlim|mazl|nik* ("ne'er-do-well") unites a Germanic adjectival prefix, a Semitic noun, and a Slavic personal suffix. In this word, the prefix *shlim-* (cf. German *schlimm*, "bad") figures in the language differently than it does in German. In Yiddish, *shlim-* is generally used as a prefix in constructions with *mazl* ("luck, fortune"), rather than as an adjective in its own right; instead, a more common Yiddish term for "bad" is *shlekht*, another word from the Germanic component (cf. German *schlecht*). This selectivity exemplifies a much wider development of the Germanic component in Yiddish in ways that diverge from German, which extends to morphology (for example, differences in their respective case systems), grammar (such as the lack of the preterit in modern Yiddish), and syntax (including a more flexible sentence structure in Yiddish with regard to the placement of past participles).[11]

• • •

Explanations of Yiddish to readers unfamiliar with the language often foreground its fusion character in general terms. A typical example appears in a short entry in the 1966 *Encyclopedia of the Jewish Religion*: "Judeo-German dialect . . . [that] contains a large admixture of Hebrew words (particularly the religious vocabulary) as well as of some Slavic, but the basic stratum of the language derives from medieval German."[12] Occasionally, books presenting Yiddish literature or culture to this readership provide detailed information on Yiddish as a fusion language. For example, a bilingual (English-Yiddish) edition of Morris Rosenfeld's *Songs from the Ghetto*, published in 1900, includes a glossary identifying the component of each Yiddish word that appears in these poems.[13] Leo Rosten's 1968 book *The Joys of Yiddish* similarly offers etymologies for the words in this popular compendium of humorous Jewish anecdotes connected to a lexicon of selected terms. These and similar works pay close attention to the origins of individual words as an enhancement of one's appreciation of Yiddish literature and lore and as a subject of interest in itself. Indeed, when the origin of a word is obscure, it can inspire much speculation. Such is the case with *davenen* ("to pray," used specifically to refer to Jewish worship), over which much ink has been spilt, though without any satisfactory resolution.[14]

Yiddish speakers demonstrate an awareness of the language's fusion character, if sometimes implicitly, in a variety of oral and written practices, especially with regard to *loshn-koydesh*, both as a component of Yiddish and as a referent. The Semitic component of Yiddish is traditionally spelled according to an orthographic system different from that used for the rest of the language. Variations in pronunciation can signal the distinction between Yiddish terms from the Semitic component (referred to as Merged Hebrew) and citations of Biblical or Rabbinic Hebrew within Yiddish speech (referred to as Whole Hebrew). For example, when the word בעל־הבית ("head of the house") is uttered in a Hebrew blessing recited after a meal, it will be pronounced *baal-habayis*, whereas the same word is pronounced *balebos* or *balbus* when addressing the head of the house in Yiddish.[15] Yiddish Bible translations of the early modern period avoid rendering Hebrew words with Semitic component cognates that would be familiar to Yiddish speakers and instead translate these words with terms from the Germanic stock language, even if they are less commonly used in vernacular Yiddish—for example, translating the Hebrew word *yerushah* ("inheritance") as *arb* (cf. German *Erbe*) rather than the more familiar Yiddish word *yerushe*.[16]

Attention to the different components of Yiddish is especially adroit in puns and other forms of language play. The proverb *Di beste kashe af der velt iz kashe mit yoykh* ("The best question in the world is cooked buckwheat with chicken soup") plays on two Yiddish words pronounced *kashe*, which are derived from different components and spelled differently in the traditional orthography: קשיא, a term in the Semitic component (from rabbinic Aramaic, meaning "difficult," therefore often used in Yiddish to refer to an intellectually challenging question) and קאַשע, its homier Slavic homonym.[17] The bathos in this shift, from the erudite to the quotidian, relies in part on values often associated with the Semitic versus Slavic components of Yiddish as elevated and earthy, respectively.

Jewish humor is replete with jokes that play on a miscomprehension or misuse of different stock languages, including anecdotes told by urban Jews in eastern Europe that mock the purportedly limited literacy of rural Jews, such as the following:

> While reading the *haggadah*, the village Jew bursts into tears at the Hebrew verse *tam ma hu omer*. [The simple one (*tam*), what does he say?]
>
> "Why are you crying?" asks his wife.
>
> "How can I not cry when I am mentioned? What will they ask *there*?" [In Russian, *tam* means "there." The rural Jew substituted the Russian meaning for the Hebrew word and assumed that the phrase referred to his being questioned "there"—that is, in heaven.]

Conversely, rural Jews lampooned other Jews' ignorance of their non-Jewish neighbors' languages. For example, "A yeshiva student . . . asked a village Jew how to say *tsibele* (onion) in Polish. The village Jew replied: *cebula* (pronounced *tsebule*). Then the talmudic student was sure he knew how to speak Polish: if *tsibele* was *tsebule*, then *benkl* (bench) is *benkule, shtivl* (boots) is *shtivule, hitl* (cap) is *hitule*, and so on."[18]

Yiddish speakers sometimes regard the language's different components as having their own distinct registers of meaning. For example, author and translator Maurice Samuel characterized the Slavic component of Yiddish as having a "peculiar pungency" and asserted that "wherever there are synonyms, or closely related words, of both Germanic and Slavic origin, it is the latter that seem closer to the folk."[19] Yet, as linguist Neil Jacobs notes, there is no ready correlation between a component of Yiddish and a particular "semantic domain."[20] Jacobs, among others, points out that, despite impressions to the contrary, the Semitic component of Yiddish is not always employed for terms pertaining to Jewish piety (for example: *akhsanye*, "inn"; *khilefn*, "to barter"; *mesugl*, "capable [of]"). Conversely, elements in the Germanic component are frequently used in specifically Jewish idioms. For example, *esn teg* (literally, "eating days") refers to the practice of providing meals, typically on the same day each week, to poor yeshiva students by more well-off Jewish families in order to support these students' devotional scholarship; *opgisn negl-vaser* (literally, "to pour fingernail water") means "to perform ritual handwashing upon waking in the morning." Similarly, the Slavic component includes the terms *meyre* ("piece of dough prepared for baking matzah"), *praven* ("to celebrate a religious holiday"), and *treybern* ("to remove veins and fat from meat to render it kosher"). Nor does the Semitic component of Yiddish necessarily convey a more scholarly or elevated register, as is sometimes assumed. Indeed, the reverse can be the case, as in the contrast of Germanic *hent* ("hands"), *hunt* ("dog"), and *esn* ("to eat") with Semitic synonyms, all of which connote coarseness: *yodayim* ("mitts"), *kelev* ("cur"), and *akhlen* ("to guzzle"). Along the spectrum of Yiddish terms for "to die," Semitic component verbs are variously cruder (*peygern*, "to croak") or loftier (*nifter vern*, "to pass away") than the neutral Germanic verb *shtarbn*.

• • •

At the turn of the twentieth century, the scope of Yiddish usage expanded both geographically and semantically, and its lexicon grew rapidly. Many of these additions are internationalisms, related to new technologies, ideologies, and fields of inquiry, such as *kino* ("cinema"), *anarkhizm* ("anarchism"), and *khemye* ("chemistry"). As Yiddish speakers immigrated beyond Europe to the Americas, South Africa, Palestine/Israel, and Australasia, contact with new languages—English, Israeli Hebrew, Portuguese, and Spanish, among others—introduced new lexical and grammatical features to the Yiddish used in these various locations. Yiddish spoken by American immigrants at the turn of the century included such neologisms as *olraytnik* ("parvenu," cf. English "all right"), *peyde* ("paycheck," cf. English "pay day"), and *oysgrinen zikh* ("to stop acting like a greenhorn [i.e., a newly arrived immigrant]"). This phenomenon attracted the attention of American journalist H. L. Mencken, among other observers of the impact of English on recent immigrants' speech. Mencken characterized Yiddish as "a lady of easy virtue among the languages," due to the ready integration into its Germanic base of terms from Slavic languages in eastern Europe and, more recently, Anglicisms among recent arrivals in the United States. The latter development was so extensive, he asserted, that Yiddish "is now nearly unintelligible, as spoken in the big cities of the East, to recent arrivals from Russia and Poland."[21] Some of these Anglicisms became more than regionalisms and were taken up in European Yiddish, exemplified by a humorous periodical published in Warsaw, beginning in 1926, called *Der blofer* (The bluffer).

Concurrently, the Yiddish spoken by Ashkenazim in Palestine reflected their considerable contact with speakers of Arabic and, to a lesser extent, Turkish and Judezmo. In addition to words related to local culture, such as foods (for example, *kadames*, "roasted chickpeas"), Palestinian Yiddish included terms for administration, commerce, and social standing (such as *beladi*, "native-born person"). These Yiddish speakers not only adopted individual Arabic words or expressions (for instance, *Kif khalak*, "How are you?"); their speech also integrated Arabic elements into established patterns of Yiddish fusion, such as the verb *azaren*, "to reprove" (thus, "*Er hot im azaret*," "He reproved him") and the noun *zbalnik* ("street cleaner").[22]

Contact with different languages informs the Yiddish currently spoken by Israeli *haredim* (Hebrew: "God-fearing people")—that is, those Jews who are most stringently observant of traditional practices and most resistant to mainstream culture—incorporating vocabulary and grammatical features from Israeli Hebrew, as well as a smaller number of terms from Arabic and English. Though some Anglicisms have entered *haredi* Yiddish in Israel via Modern Hebrew, linguist Miriam Isaacs notes that they are also encountered through extensive contact between Israeli *haredim* and those who live in Anglophone countries.[23]

Attention to Yiddish as a fusion language also entails notions, often highly variable and at times contentious, of what is *not* Yiddish—that is, which elements (usually lexical) found in oral or written usage are deemed inadmissible, though they may come from stock languages. This issue is especially charged with regard to modern German, for, as Weinreich notes, "German fusion material" is omnipresent in Yiddish. The concern to differentiate Yiddish from its closest relative in the Germanic family is not simply due to the Germanic component of Yiddish being "so vast and so variegated."[24] Rather, ideologies regarding this relationship diverged when the status and use of Yiddish received unprecedented internal scrutiny as a consequence of the Haskalah. In the nineteenth century, some advocates of efforts to elevate Yiddish as a *kultursprakh* ("language of [high] culture"), as the modern notion of *kultur* was itself coalescing among its speakers, encouraged integrating vocabulary from contemporary German into Yiddish, as well as imitating German orthography. Others argued that, rather than emulating German as a model of linguistic and cultural sophistication by copying it, Yiddish speakers should respond to this exemplar by making the language *vos vayter fun daytsh* ("all the further from German"),[25] while striving to be its equal in scope and stature. In either case, the Germanic component was the focus of attention, as both approaches sought to reshape Yiddish in order to "answer the needs of the modern world." Yiddish thereby confronted a challenge faced by other languages of national minorities as they augmented their lexicons, either by "borrow[ing] foreign words," which could be perceived as "patriotically demeaning," or by "inventing words from the existing semantic raw material," which ran the risk of seeming "pedantic and contrived."[26]

As part of their larger efforts to establish Standard Yiddish—a modern, uniform register of language for use in education, publishing, and cultural institutions—Yiddish linguists sought to distinguish the language from German. They argued, sometimes heatedly, over words often used by Yiddish speakers or writers that some scholars judged to be overly or improperly close to modern German. Given the preponderance of the Germanic component in Yiddish, as well as its ongoing practice of fusion and need for neologisms, questions arose as to what criteria could be formulated to distinguish an acceptable Yiddish word of Germanic origin from *daytshmerish*, a term denoting the overuse in Yiddish of loanwords from modern German. During the 1930s the issue was debated among linguists at the YIVO Institute for Jewish Research, as part of its commitment to promoting Standard Yiddish. This debate included an exchange between Weinreich and Noah Prylucki, a scholar of Yiddish and a cofounder of the Folkspartey. Whereas Prylucki called for contemporary popular usage as a guide, Weinreich advocated for the authority of scholars, who would research the history of terms in question to determine whether or not their entry into Yiddish has a legitimate precedent.[27] Words deemed unacceptable, he argued, should be replaced with neologisms crafted by informed linguists. The debate over *daytshmerish* was renewed among Yiddish linguists in the United States during the 1990s, with Dovid Katz and Mordkhe Schaechter taking up positions similar to Prylucki and Weinreich, respectively.[28]

• • •

Literature scholar Benjamin Harshav argues that Yiddish is a "uniquely open language," by virtue of its speakers' extensive contact with stock languages and a "radical" disposition to integrating elements from them. Doing so does not "endanger the nature of Yiddish," Harshav asserts, "since its basic grammatical framework, the patterns of fusion and of absorbing new words, [are] well established." In addition to enriching the linguistic resources of belletrists and scholars, everyday Yiddish speakers have also "enjoyed this propensity," as almost all not only are in some way multilingual but also do "not make much of the fashionable theories of an insulated 'national language.' Their modern culture [is] cosmopolitan, even when the thematics and ideology [are] 'Jewish.'" At the same time, Harshav maintains that there is a need to create a "pure, standard language," especially for the purpose of teaching Yiddish in modern settings.[29]

Valuing Yiddish as permeable and cosmopolitan or as standardized and nationalist reflects notions of its historical trajectory, both on its own and in relation to other languages. This is not simply a matter of considering to which family Yiddish might belong but how it is conceived as a language among others: as kindred, separate but equal? as eccentric, limited but distinctive? as an interloper of suspect parentage? Is Yiddish a staunch chauvinist advocating carefully guarded borders, a liberal internationalist who supports open frontiers, or a promiscuous wanton who mingles indiscriminately with others? In each case, the anthropomorphic implications of conceptualizing the language and its lineage are telling. For while discussions of the family background of Yiddish center on matters of vocabulary or grammar, what is at stake ultimately, if often tacitly, are extralinguistic concerns about cultural legitimacy, demographic integrity, social and political status, and the construction of a Jewish authenticity.

# 3
# Residence

Yiddish is a phenomenon of Jewish life in diaspora, a term that indicates displacement from a locus of rootedness. Therefore, notions of where the language "resides" are anything but straightforward. Efforts to locate Yiddish geographically can challenge conventional concepts of how a speech community, or a language itself, inhabits a place. Competing theories on the origins of Yiddish, as discussed in the first chapter, situate its formation in different locales. From its beginnings, wherever that may have taken place, Yiddish speakers migrated across northern Europe. By the seventeenth century, Ashkenazim had established communities, both large and small, as far west as the Netherlands, as far south as northern Italy, and extending throughout eastern Europe from the Baltic lands in the north to Ukraine in the south. In addition, some Ashkenazim had migrated to Jerusalem as early as the fourteenth century.

The settlement of Yiddish speakers in Europe was geographically distinctive from that of their neighbors.[1] Jews resided more in towns and cities than in the countryside, unlike Christians, the majority of whom were peasants living on farmlands or in rural villages. In some locations, notably Venice and Amsterdam, Ashkenazim lived alongside other diaspora Jewish communities. But for the most part, Ashkenazim were remote from other Jews, especially in eastern Europe. Beginning in the sixteenth century the number of Yiddish speakers expanded in the Polish-Lithuanian Commonwealth, eventually surpassing the Jewish population of German lands, where most scholars situate the beginnings of Yiddish. Over time, Jews became the largest local ethnic group in many of the hundreds of provincial eastern European towns in which they settled and at times comprised a town's majority of residents. In some instances, the growing numbers of Jews helped transform small towns into cities.[2]

Eastern European Yiddish speakers voiced a sense of local belonging through their own names for streets and other landmarks in the places where they lived, as well as for towns and cities themselves. Examples in interwar Poland include Apt (Polish: Opatów), Brisk (Brześć nad Bugiem), Ger (Góra

Kalwaria), Kuzmir (Kazimierz Dolny), Libivne (Luboml), Shekev (Osjaków), Tiktin (Tykocin). When authorities in the Habsburg and Romanov Empires enacted laws requiring all subjects to acquire family names, at some time between the late eighteenth and early nineteenth century, many Jews chose surnames that invoked their home towns or regions, for example: Avrich, Brody, Danziger, Golub, Krakauer, Litvak, Miropol, Ostrov, Pinski, Rovner, Starobin, Tomashevski, Vinograd, Zitomer.[3]

The mandate to adopt surnames was a consequence of the partitions of the Polish-Lithuanian Commonwealth in the final decades of the eighteenth century, when the territories that comprised this vast polity were annexed by its more powerful neighbors. The Yiddish-speaking population burgeoned in what became the westernmost provinces of the Russian Empire (an expanse known as the Jewish Pale of Settlement), Congress Poland (which was under Russian domination), and the northeast region of the Austrian Empire (called Galicia). At the same time, the use of Yiddish began to decline in German states, as Jews there shifted to German as their vernacular. This was a gradual transition, swifter among Jews who lived in cities, practiced Reform Judaism, and were wealthier than among those who were located in the provinces, were Orthodox in observance, and were less prosperous. During this period, attention to the differences between western and eastern European Jewry grew more pronounced in the realm of "high culture," reflecting these two populations' "divergent paths to modernity." However, historian Steven Lowenstein observes, such a distinction was more nuanced at the level of "folk culture," including language use, revealing that "the boundaries between East and West are quite varied and complex."[4]

From the 1880s to the 1930s, Jews' mass immigration out of eastern Europe brought large numbers of Yiddish speakers to major cities in western Europe—including Berlin, Brussels, London, Paris, and Vienna—as well as to the Americas and South Africa. Eastern European Jews' internal migration also extended the language's reach further east into Russia/the Soviet Union. Solomon Birnbaum notes that these decades ushered in "a new era in the geography of Yiddish," during which recent immigrant communities quickly came to constitute about one-third of the world's Yiddish speakers.[5] Indeed, by 1900, New York boasted the largest Jewish population of any city in the world, comprised mostly of recently arrived eastern European immigrants. New York swiftly emerged as a major center of Yiddish culture, in part because greater political freedoms and economic opportunities enabled publishing, theater, and political activism to flourish more readily in the

United States than they could in much of Europe. After World War II, the language's intercontinental distribution shifted radically once more. While some Yiddish-speaking Holocaust survivors returned to their prewar homes, notably in the western republics of the Soviet Union, most sought new places to live in Europe or left the continent altogether to settle in the Americas, Palestine/Israel, and Australasia.

Throughout this history, Yiddish has been the language of a minority in all these lands, even in regions where its speakers were most concentrated. In many places there has been no official recognition of Yiddish or documentation of the extent of its speech community. Yet the geographic presence of Yiddish can be reckoned by other means, especially in the modern era: evidence of Yiddish speakers found in correspondence, communal records, or cemeteries; the locations of publishers of Yiddish books and periodicals, as well as their subscription lists; the presence of schools, theaters, political parties, and other organizations that operated in Yiddish; and, by the turn of the twentieth century, the number of speakers reported in some censuses. On the eve of World War II, the estimated total of Yiddish speakers in Europe was over seven million—comparable to contemporaneous numbers for Czech or Greek in their respective countries—and worldwide approached eleven million (out of a total Jewish population of some seventeen million).[6] It was therefore possible to conceive of Yiddish as having the scale of a European national language, with substantial immigrant outposts beyond the continent, by dint of demography as well as the quantity and scope of the publications; the religious, educational, and cultural institutions; and the social and political organizations that functioned in Yiddish.[7]

Given the distinctive history of Ashkenazic settlement and language use, conceptualizing a residence for Yiddish entails grappling with contradictions. As a population concentrated in urban environments, Yiddish speakers could be a sizeable and at times predominant presence locally—for example, in a small town or a district of a large city—while at the same time constituting a minority within a municipality, a province of an empire, or a nation-state as a whole. At the local level of quotidian experience, it has been possible for Jews in some places to function largely in Yiddish—including, at times, when communicating with non-Jews. The public presence of Yiddish was manifest in certain locations by signage on stores and cultural institutions or by the appearance of Yiddish periodicals at newsstands and posters on walls. And on occasion Yiddish received official recognition as one of several languages in a multicultural state. For example, Yiddish appeared, together with Polish and Ukrainian, on currency issued by the short-lived Ukrainian National Republic in 1917, and was included alongside Belorussian, Polish, and Russian on the state emblem of the Belorussian Soviet Socialist Republic. On a more local level, Yiddish was one of four languages to appear on municipal postage stamps used in the town of Luboml at the end of World War I. Such acknowledgments of Yiddish have, however, been the exception rather than the rule and do not always correlate to the size of speech communities. Thus, Yiddish was officially recognized as a minority language in Sweden in 1999, where the number of speakers a decade later was estimated as being, at most, 1,500;[8] in Israel, where at least one hundred times as many Jews speak Yiddish, if not more, comprising about 2 percent of the population, the language has no official status.[9]

Though Yiddish lacked a territory "of its own" in a conventional geopolitical sense, by the turn of the twentieth century it thrived in a network of millions of speakers living in towns and urban neighborhoods on multiple continents. In each of these places Yiddish was used in homes, schools, workplaces, synagogues, and on the street as a shared vernacular and, especially

One of a set of five of postage stamps used for local mail delivery in the town of Luboml (now Liuboml, Ukraine), issued during the final year of World War I. On the stamps' borders the inscription "Luboml Municipal Postage" appears in four languages: German, Polish, Ukrainian, and Yiddish, reflecting the town's multiethnic population. This stamp depicts Luboml's main synagogue, built in the early sixteenth century.

in major population centers, in print matter, public performances, and educational, cultural, religious, social, and political institutions. These sites were connected with one another through the international circulation of mass media in Yiddish—including periodicals, books, sound recordings, and films—in addition to a robust private correspondence among relatives and other acquaintances. Further contact involved an array of travelers who moved throughout the Yiddish-speaking world: researchers, journalists, musicians, and theatrical troupes, as well as emissaries of philanthropies, religious institutions, cultural organizations, and political parties.[10] Beyond their instrumental role of linking Yiddish speakers throughout an expansive diaspora, these language practices had a symbolic value, creating a sense of at-homeness for Yiddish speakers despite their physical dispersal and the widespread notion of Jews as a "people without a land."

During the early twentieth century some activists challenged this notion by employing geopolitical idioms to advocate for Yiddishism, a movement committed to the language's potential to facilitate Jewish cultural autonomy and sustain a sense of nationhood in lieu of a sovereign state. For example, Chaim Zhitlowsky, a leading proponent of secular Yiddishism, grew up in the Vitebsk province of the Russian Empire (a region now in Belarus). He later described the milieu of his childhood, in which the use of Yiddish was predominant, as having "so little sense of exile" during the 1870s that it seemed to him as though Jews "did not live in exile among the Russians, but perhaps quite the opposite—that the Russians with whom we interacted lived in exile among us."[11]

Zhitlowsky's characterization of a place defined by the use of Yiddish has sometimes been referred to as *yidishland* ("Yiddishland").[12] This term does not merely identify a place of residence for Yiddish, whether actual or virtual, but ascribes territoriality, with its implications of rootedness and even sovereignty, to a language and its speakers widely thought of as placeless. *Yidishland* thereby both invokes and subverts the model of nationhood, then prevalent in Europe, as a claim on geographical turf, its scope delineated by the presence of speakers of what historian Benedict Anderson terms their "private-property" language.[13]

The word *yidishland* has come into frequent use over the course of the past century, whether as shorthand for the region of eastern Europe where Yiddish speakers lived before World War II or to refer to Yiddish speech communities of the present. *Yidishland* has been depicted in maps and other visual works and conjured in literary creations, especially Yiddish poetry.

For example, A. Almi's 1930 poem "Yiddish" uses elaborate geographical imagery to conjure a place for the language, conceived as a "scattered empire," to flourish on "blossoming islands, rivers, gulfs, streams," enumerated in a gazetteer of the Yiddish-speaking diaspora, starting in eastern Europe and extending outward to the Americas, Africa, and Asia, as Yiddish "makes the rockiest soil bear fruit."[14] This and similar works exemplify literature scholar Sidra Ezrahi's observations about the value invested in creating "imaginative space" in modern Jewish letters. She argues that, as a foundational project of modern Yiddish literature, "writing the exile" was "more than a response to displacement," becoming "in itself a form of repatriation, of alternative sovereignty."[15] Likewise, critic J. Hoberman describes the flourishing of Yiddish film in the 1930s as "not just a national cinema without a nation-state, but a national cinema that, with every presentation, created its own ephemeral nation-state."[16]

Some modern Jewish political movements that embraced the diaspora rather than repudiating it championed the power of Yiddish to realize a virtual homeland for its speakers on a grand scale. Through the principle of *doikeyt* ("hereness"), diaspora nationalist parties such as the Jewish Labor Bund and the Folkspartey asserted the right and the value of Jews to live "here"—that is, wherever they found themselves—as citizens of their respective countries and as Jews.[17] In its very articulation, *doikeyt* implies *yidishland*. By proclaiming a speaker's location as a site where Yiddish can flourish, *doikeyt* renders any place, however provisionally, as part of *yidishland*. In this respect, *yidishland* is a performative phenomenon, a locus summoned into existence by speech, suggesting that the place Yiddish and its speakers inhabit is both highly adaptable and highly mutable.

• • •

Complementing this notion of *yidishland* as a virtual home—in which Yiddish "resides" in an intercontinental network of scattered communities, large and small, linked by their use of the language in written and oral form—are efforts to root Yiddish speakers in a physical territory. In interwar Poland, Jews' interest in local history and geography was popularized and institutionalized through the *landkentenish* ("land knowledge") movement. The Yidishe gezelshaft far landkentenish / Żydowskie towarzystwo krajoznawcze (Jewish Society for Knowing the Land), founded in Warsaw in 1926, promoted learning about local environs through hiking, sports, lectures, reading, and photography as a fixture of modern Polish Jewish culture. *Landkentenish* was both inspired by and a response to the equivalent Polish *krajoznawstwo* movement, which often neglected or disparaged Jewish landmarks as sites of national interest. Through excursions, talks, and publications about Jews' longstanding presence in Poland, *landkentenish* employed Yiddish as a polemical instrument, demonstrating through the language as well as its subject that "Jews were 'settled inhabitants' in Poland and not 'aliens or guests,' as some right-wing Polish nationalists and Zionists contended."[18] The movement's bilingual publications in Polish and Yiddish symbolically placed both languages, as well as their speakers and their regional heritage, on equal footing.

Other efforts to situate Yiddish speakers in a territory of their own looked beyond established places of Jewish residence. At the turn of the twentieth century, Jewish philanthropies funded agricultural colonies in Argentina, Canada, and the United States for immigrant Jews from eastern Europe, seeking to relieve overcrowded Jewish neighborhoods in major cities and diversify Jews' social and economic circumstances. In the 1920s and 1930s, the Soviet Union resettled Ashkenazic Jews on collective farms in Ukraine and Crimea, in order to root this "landless" population in a place where they could engage in "productive" labor.[19]

The most elaborate effort to create a Yiddish-speaking polity took place in 1934, when the Soviet Union designated the oblast of Birobidzhan, located in far eastern Russia on its border with Manchuria, as a Jewish Autonomous Region, following its establishment as a Jewish agricultural settlement in 1928. In its heyday, Birobidzhan boasted a Yiddish theater, library, school system, and teachers' college; the region published its own Yiddish newspaper, and official documents were printed in both Russian and Yiddish.[20] Though Birobidzhan achieved only limited success as a Yiddish-speaking territory—its Jewish population briefly peaked at thirty thousand in the years immediately after World War II—it endures as a curiosity of Jewish history. In the post-Soviet era, Birobidzhan has become a destination for intrepid Yiddish enthusiasts, who seek out its landmarks of erstwhile Yiddish officialdom in the form of signs on streets and buildings.[21]

The Territorialist movement, which advocated creating a large-scale Jewish settlement in an unpopulated site somewhere in the diaspora, as opposed to the political Zionist agenda to create a Jewish state in Palestine, had been active since the early twentieth century. This effort intensified with the founding of the Frayland-lige (Freeland League) in 1935, which sought a place of refuge for eastern European Jews that would both afford them protection from political oppression and enable their cultural independence, including the use of Yiddish. During the next two decades the Frayland-lige pursued, without success, the possibility of establishing a Jewish territory in the Kimberley (a region of northwestern Australia) and in British, Dutch, and French Guiana. In the ensuing years the focus of the Frayland-lige shifted from territorialist advocacy to promoting Yiddish culture, and in 1979 the organization changed its name to the Yidish-lige (League for Yiddish). This shift is telling; whereas the Frayland-lige prioritized securing a physical place of residence for Yiddish speakers, the Yidish-lige promotes the use of Yiddish language and culture irrespective of its practitioners' geographic location.

• • •

The mass destruction and displacement of Yiddish culture during the middle of the twentieth century has inspired new efforts to situate the language in a home of some kind, whether striving to document its prewar rootedness and flourishing in Europe or to conjure a place for Yiddish through the imaginary. Among documentary undertakings are mapping projects, which depict the presence of Yiddish on either a local or a continental scale. The former appear most extensively in hundreds of *yizker-bikher* ("memorial books") that commemorate destroyed eastern European Jewish communities in municipalities large and small. For several decades after the war's end, former residents of these communities contributed personal memories of local history and lore to these volumes. Many *yizker-bikher* feature a map, usually drawn from memory, that depicts the topography of the town as it was once experienced by Jews. Often these maps identify streets and other landmarks with the Yiddish names used by the towns' Jews.[22]

Complementing these renderings of Yiddish speakers' local places of residence in prewar Europe are scholarly studies of variations in the language across the continent. Noah Prylucki, one of the first individuals to analyze Yiddish dialects systematically, published a seminal article in 1912 on regional differences in the gender of Yiddish nouns. Prylucki expanded on this work in book-length studies issued in 1917 and 1921, in which he "provided a simple and elegant solution to the problem of distinguishing Yiddish dialects based upon the pronunciation of a single diphthong [variously as *a*, *ay*, or *ey*], which remains, despite later refinements and additions, the foundation

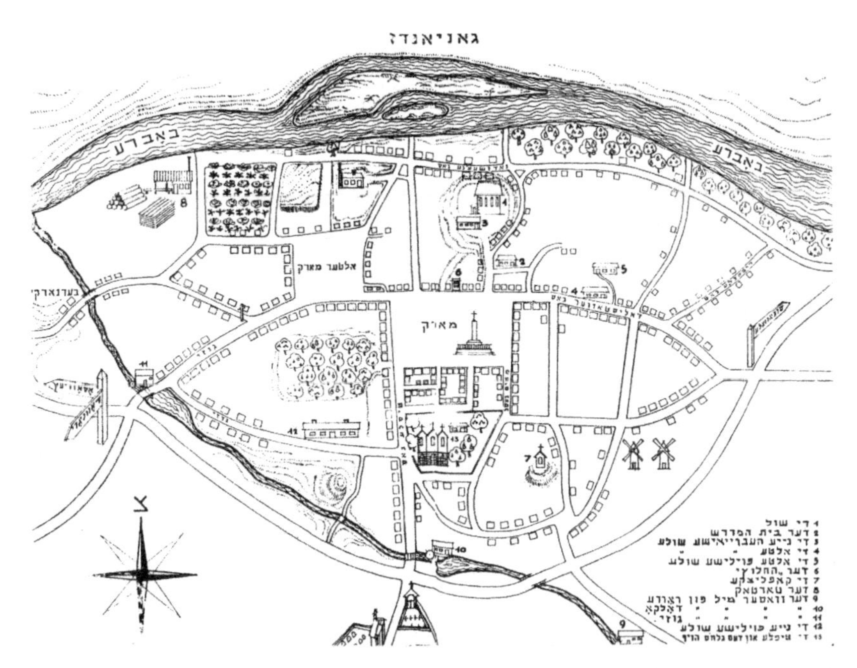


Map from the memorial book for the town of Goniądz, Poland, published in Tel Aviv in 1960. The map indicates street names and other landmarks according to their Yiddish names.

of the contemporary division of Yiddish dialects by scholars."[23] During the 1920s linguists in the Jewish Department of the Institute for Belorussian Culture Research analyzed Yiddish dialects in the western territories of the Soviet Union. This undertaking included an appeal to the public to assist in documenting local language use.[24]

The largest such endeavor, the Language and Culture Atlas of Ashkenazic Jewry (LCAAJ), maps regional configurations of Yiddish dialects across northern Europe, documenting phonological, lexical, and grammatical differences as well as related variations in traditional folkways, such as methods of preparing *farfl* ("egg barley") or customs to mark the end of Passover.[25] This elaborate research project, initiated by linguist Uriel Weinreich (the son of Max Weinreich) at Columbia University in the late 1950s, gathered responses to an extensive questionnaire, containing over three thousand individual questions, from more than five hundred native speakers of Yiddish. Unlike prewar studies of Yiddish dialects conducted in situ, the informants for the LCAAJ were all immigrants, most of whom were interviewed in the New York area or Israel.[26] Each informant represents a different site in Europe; these locations, which range from small villages to major cities, were selected to reflect the demographic distribution of Yiddish speakers across the continent before World War II. In the LCAAJ, the territoriality of Yiddish appears not as a bounded space, as national languages are conventionally rendered on maps, but as a constellation of representative individual speech sites.

The data collected from the project's many interviewees enabled Weinreich and his colleagues to inscribe onto the landscape of Europe a set of isoglosses that delineate different regional variants of Yiddish. Following earlier models, the LCAAJ identifies the major dialects of Yiddish as Western, Central, Northeastern, and Southeastern Yiddish, their boundaries drawn by mapping informants' pronunciation of the Yiddish phrase meaning "to buy meat."[27] Pronounced *koyfn fleysh* in Standard Yiddish—as reflected in its spelling, irrespective of dialect: קויפֿן פֿלייש —the vowel sounds generally differ according to region, as follows:

Western Yiddish: *kafn flash*
Central Yiddish: *koyfn flaysh*
Northeastern Yiddish: *keyfn fleysh*
Southeastern Yiddish: *koyfn fleysh*

These regional differences correspond to a considerable extent with other phonological variations:

"good" גוט (Standard Yiddish: *gut*)
Western Yiddish: *gut*
Central Yiddish: *git*
Northeastern Yiddish: *gut*
Southeastern Yiddish: *git*

"city" שטאָט (Standard Yiddish: *shtot*)
Western Yiddish: *shtot*
Central Yiddish: *shtut*
Northeastern Yiddish: *shtot*
Southeastern Yiddish: *shtut*

"today" הײַנט (Standard Yiddish: *haynt*)
Western Yiddish: *haynt*

Central Yiddish: *hant*
Northeastern Yiddish: *haynt*
Southeastern Yiddish: *hant*

Other phonological variations either reinforce these isoglosses or define dialect sub-regions. For example, the phenomenon called *sabesdiker losn* ("Sabbath language"), found among some Yiddish speakers in the Northeastern region, confuses or conflates hushing (*sh*) and hissing (*s*) sounds—thus, saying *losn* instead of *loshn,* or making no distinction between

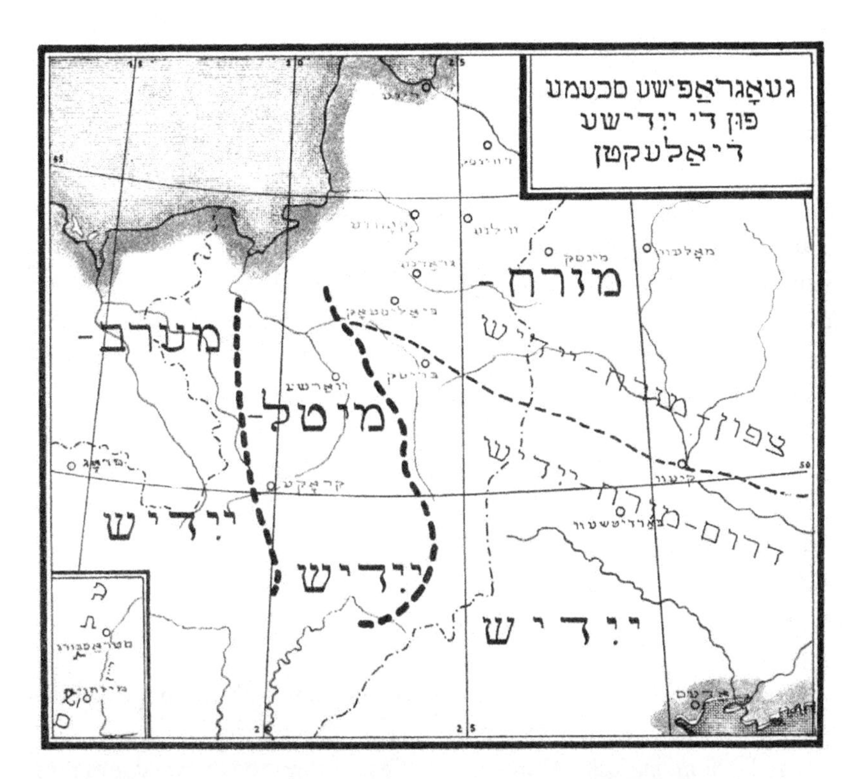


"Geographic Schema of Yiddish Dialects," a map accompanying Max Weinreich's article on Yiddish in the *Algemeyne entsiklopedye* (General encyclopedia), published in Paris in 1940. The heaviest dashed lines delineate (from left to right) Western Yiddish, Central Yiddish, and Eastern Yiddish. Eastern Yiddish is divided by a lighter dashed line into Northeastern and Southeastern Yiddish. Cities indicated on the map range from Riga to the north, Prague to the west, and Odessa to the southeast. An inset in the lower left corner extends the reach of Western Yiddish to include Alsace.

*visn* ("to know") and *vishn* ("to wipe").[28] Some Yiddish speakers in what is now northeastern Poland and northwestern Belarus pronounced the letter *lamed* (*l*) in some words with the sound of *w* in the English word "water"—for example, *gewebt* instead of *gelebt* ("lived"). This practice, known as *wamed woshn*, likely reflects contact with speakers of Polish, in which the letter *ł* is pronounced *w*.[29] Shifting the stressed vowel *a* to *o* in some words, heard among Yiddish speakers in southern Ukraine and Romania, is known as *tote-mome loshn* (thus, *tote* instead of *tate*, "father").[30]

Dialects are also distinguished by lexical and morphological elements. For example, among more than a half-dozen Yiddish terms for "floor," *dil* is found in Northeastern Yiddish, *podloge* in Central Yiddish, and *brik* primarily in Southeastern Yiddish.[31] Various plural forms of *noz* ("nose")—*neyz, neyzer, nezer*—tend to cluster in the Southeastern, Central, and Northeastern dialects, respectively.[32]

Grammatical variations among Yiddish dialects are most notable in Northeastern Yiddish, which departs from the three-gender system for nouns (masculine, feminine, neuter) used in the other dialects as well as in Standard Yiddish. In addition, the past tense of all verbs in Northeastern Yiddish is conjugated with the auxiliary verb *hobn*, whereas in the other dialects and in Standard Yiddish the past tense of several intransitive verbs is conjugated with the auxiliary verb *zayn*.

| | **Standard Yiddish** | **Northeastern Yiddish** |
|---|---|---|
| "I was" | *ikh bin geven* | *ikh hob geven* |
| "you [singular] went" | *du bist gegangen* | *du host gegangen* |
| "she ate" | *zi hot gegesn* | *zi hot gegesn* |
| "we smiled" | *mir hobn geshmeykhlt* | *mir hobn geshmeykhlt* |

Awareness of dialect differences was common among Yiddish speakers before World War II, evident in popular names of such variations as *sabeskider losn* and *tote-mome loshn*. Humor also reflects a common knowledge of these variants in jokes that rely on dialect confusion and comical characters who speak in dialect in Yiddish plays, such as the stock figure of the Lithuanian Jew who speaks *sabesdiker losn*.[33] The expression *Vu freyt ir zikh?* ("Where do you rejoice?") is an idiomatic play on *Vu voynt ir?* ("Where do you live?"), used by speakers of Northeastern Yiddish to avoid the unhappy confusion occasioned by their pronouncing *voynen* ("to live [i.e., to reside]") the same as *veynen* ("to weep").[34]

Yiddish speakers typically identified major dialects according to familiar geopolitical regions—for example, *galitsyaner* ("Galician"), *voliner* ("Wolynian"), *litvish* ("Lithuanian"), *poylish* ("Polish")—although these geographic designations did not completely conform to actual dialect distinctions. For example, Jews in easternmost Galicia spoke Southeastern Yiddish, whereas the rest of the Jews in the region spoke Central Yiddish. Unlike these conventional terms for mapping Yiddish speech, the dialect regions of the LCAAJ delineate a Yiddish geography distinct from political borders, past or present. Rather, in this mapping of *yidishland*, isoglosses articulate the idiomatic equivalent of provincial boundaries within a nation. At the same time, the primary focus on dialect differences produces a set of borders distinct from other descriptions of Ashkenazic geography. Lowenstein notes that the isogloss between Western and Eastern Yiddish lies considerably to the east of the boundary between the local practices of *minhag Ashkenaz* (Hebrew: "the Jewish customs of German lands") and *minhag Polin* ("the Jewish customs of Poland"). These two frontiers, he argues, delineate a "transitional area" between eastern and western Ashkenazim.[35]

Beyond mapping the dialects of Yiddish spoken in Europe before World War II, the LCAAJ imbues the geography of the language with intellectual as well as ideological value. Weinreich, a leading scholar in the field of language contact generally, posited that the configuration of modern European Yiddish dialects reflects the dynamics of Ashkenazic settlement across the continent over several centuries, thereby positioning Yiddish dialectology at the nexus of diachronic and synchronic linguistics. By conjoining time and space, Yiddish dialectology demonstrates that the language has a geography of its own as well as a singular history and reveals their interdependence.[36]

The LCAAJ also makes an important symbolic statement about the erstwhile territoriality of Yiddish in Europe. In 1963 Weinreich noted that the project had been rejected for funding under the United States National Defense Education Act, because Yiddish is not the official language of any country. In response, he argued that it is precisely the "lack of a self-contained territory" that endowed the project "with exemplary value for a particularly crucial problem in social history: the effect of communication channels and barriers on the diffusion of cultural innovations." Yiddish and its European speakers exemplify on a grand scale how "the geographic fragmentation of a culture and a language . . . yields an opportunity to reconstruct the influences of neighboring localities upon one another." Moreover, Weinreich claimed, preliminary data demonstrated that linguistic and cultural variations follow "definite regional patterns," with implications for understanding the relationship between culture and territory not just for this particular subject, but for the social sciences in general. At the same time that the project endows Yiddish with an impressive geographic expanse across northern Europe—which Weinreich described as surpassed only by the scope of Russian—the LCAAJ situates the language's diasporic territoriality as strategic to understanding the interrelation of Ashkenazic society with its European neighbors across time and space.[37] Rather than linking languages to discrete geopolitical territories, the LCAAJ implicitly presents a different way to conceptualize linguistic geography by focusing on the sites of contact among languages.

Complementing notions of a place where Yiddish resides that are based on either local memories or linguistic data are phenomena of folklore and the imaginary. Occasionally these examples focus on a particular location. For example, through generations of repeated tellings in multiple languages, comic folktales about the so-called "wise men" of Chelm—a town in Poland that, by the mid-nineteenth century, had come to be known as the quintessential Jewish town of fools—fostered a popular image of Yiddish as the language of provincial folly.[38] Major works of modern Yiddish literature by Sholem Yankev Abramovitsh and Sholem Aleichem established archetypal sites of Jewish poverty with the fictional towns Kabtsansk and Kasrilevke (their names formed by adding Slavic suffixes to *loshn-koydesh* words for "pauper"). In the middle decades of the twentieth century, Jewish summer camps in upstate New York were named after Boiberik, the Ukrainian summer colony mentioned in Sholem Aleichem's Tevye stories, and Nitgedayget (meaning "no worries"), a collective farm in works by Soviet Yiddish writer Peretz Markish.[39] Other names of places, whether real or fictitious—Hotseplots, Lespets, Pipiduvke—became bywords in Yiddish for remote locales at the imagined limits of *yidishland*.[40]

More generally, the term *ghetto* has extensive associations with Yiddish, including the urban neighborhoods to which Jewish residence was restricted in western European cities starting at the end of the Middle Ages. (The word originates with the ghetto in Venice, established in 1516.) Emancipation from ghettos during the nineteenth century coincided with the abandonment of Yiddish by western Ashkenazim for the vernaculars of their Christian neighbors, both developments understood as a departure from a way of life that had isolated these Jews from European society and culture. In actuality this separation was less thorough than subsequently imagined and was often initiated from within Jewish communities rather than imposed from without.[41]

Nevertheless, the mythic image of the ghetto fostered the notion of Yiddish as the linguistic equivalent of these locales and their constraints. Well after Jews left these urban districts, *ghetto* continued to define neighborhoods where Yiddish speakers lived in cities, with enduring connotations of abjection.[42] At the turn of the twentieth century, the crowded, impoverished sectors of some major cities in which Yiddish speakers settled in the United States were referred to as ghettos, though not, as a rule, internally; local Jews were more likely to refer to their neighborhood as *di yidishe gas* ("the Jewish street") or *der yidisher kvartal* ("the Jewish quarter"). Eventually, *ghetto* became synonymous in America with *slum*, irrespective of its inhabitants' identities. During World War II *ghetto* was revived in Europe to define the zones in which Jews were forcibly confined within cities and towns throughout countries occupied by Nazi Germany.[43]

Even more widespread is the use of the term *shtetl* ("town") as a metonym for Yiddish-speaking Jewry. Beginning in the nineteenth century, authors of modern Jewish literature conceptualized the provincial towns of eastern Europe as epitomizing social environments of traditional Jewish life, defined in part by the use of Yiddish. The term *shtetl* embodied these authors' ambivalent feelings about this cultural milieu, disparaged as a parochial backwater yet also celebrated as a "hub of true Jewish intimacy and spiritual self-sufficiency."[44] After the Holocaust, *shtetl* entered other languages, specifically referencing provincial Jewish communities in prewar eastern Europe, as opposed to the word's meaning in Yiddish simply as "town"—any town, anywhere, at any time, inhabited by anyone. With this more constrained definition, *shtetl* acquired added significance as the emblem of prewar Europe's Yiddish-speaking milieus, a "lost" or "vanished world," reimagined in works of literature, theater, film, and other cultural forms as well as in other languages.[45]

The world-wide reconfiguration of Jewish population centers in the wake of the Holocaust created new places of residence for Yiddish. *Haredim* use the language in neighborhoods of Antwerp, Brooklyn, Jerusalem, London, Melbourne, and Montreal, among other cities, as well as in towns (Kiryas Joel, Monsey, and New Square, all in New York State; Kiryas Tosh, in the suburb of Boisbriand, Quebec) where Hasidim have established a significant presence. Yiddishist summer camps and retreats, as well as intensive programs of instruction in Yiddish at universities and cultural institutions in North America, Europe, and Israel, have created temporary environments in which use of the language calls each of these sites into existence as a *yidishland.* The differences among these postwar locations exemplify divergent contemporary relationships with Yiddish: on one hand, as a vernacular used to reinforce a sense of community and stringent piety among *haredim,* distinguished from other Jews as well as from non-Jews; on the other hand, as a language taken up voluntarily by any interested parties, including some who are not Jews, often as an end in itself.

These relationships with the language converge in a remarkable recent exercise in Yiddish territorialism: Yiddish Farm, established in 2011 in Goshen, New York, which strives to "expand the role of the Yiddish language, serve as a bridge between Yiddish speakers of various backgrounds, and promote environmental stewardship through organic farming."[46] The farm invites guests and students for periods ranging from a day to several weeks to observe or participate in its commitments to sustainable farming and to creating a diverse Yiddish-speaking community, which includes visiting members of nearby Hasidic groups. Though recalling Jewish agricultural collectives of previous generations, Yiddish Farm is very much a product of contemporary projects that seek to bolster the Jewish identity of young American Jews (including other projects involving Yiddish).[47] The conjoining of Yiddish with farming integrates two ostensibly unrelated practices in a mutually reinforcing effort to nurture a local community: whereas the use of Yiddish marks agriculture as a Jewish undertaking, the farming implicitly marks Yiddish as rooted and organic.

In contrast to efforts to provide Yiddish with its own turf, the internet appears to offer the most expansive approach to establishing a place of residence for Yiddish. Online Yiddish periodicals, radio programs, blogs, podcasts, and videos circulate internationally, enabling the distribution of mass media and personal writing in the language with unprecedented facility. The internet facilitates learning Yiddish with dictionaries and other resources, including instructional media and interactive online classes. Social media platforms foster virtual communion among disparate individual Yiddish speakers. Linguist Tsvi Sadan writes that the internet "has a greater potential for diaspora languages like Yiddish than for non-diaspora languages for forming virtual communities, as the former have few non-virtual communities, while the latter already have communities outside the internet."[48]

It remains to be seen how the internet transforms the diasporic nature of Yiddish. At the same time that this medium seems to let Yiddish be anywhere, the internet sometimes does so by undoing the language's connections to actual people in particular locations, a longstanding basis for identifying a language's residence. As with every other location, physical or virtual, real or imaginary, in which a place for Yiddish has been sought or conjured, whether by its speakers or by others, the effort does not yield simple or stable results. This is not merely due to the migrations of Yiddish speakers or the various contingencies in which it has been used; this also reflects the limitations of conceptualizing something as evanescent and mutable as a language as residing, like a person, in a place of its own.

# 4
# Name

Naming Yiddish exemplifies both the attractions and the challenges of likening a language to a human being. Whereas people are usually named close to the time of their birth, languages can be spoken and even written for generations before being given names. And yet a language, like a person, can have more than one name. The terms used to refer to what is thought of as "the same language" can change with time, and it can be identified with multiple names concurrently by different users of the language as well as by speakers of other languages. Each name that people give to a language embodies their understanding of how it is used and what its value is.

The range of names that a language acquires over time reflects changes in the attention paid to it. New names may arise from a perceived need to distinguish the language from others or to examine the interrelation of the language and its speakers. In the case of the language now generally called Yiddish, both concerns are key to understanding the long, varied history of its naming. Indeed, widespread use of the term *yidish* in the language itself and of "Yiddish" (spelled Jiddisch, yídish, jidysz, идиш, etc.) in other languages is a relatively recent phenomenon. Therefore, literature scholar Jerold Frakes notes, it is "almost *de rigueur*" that a book on the language's history "devote a section or chapter to the names of Yiddish."[1]

As Yiddish was initially used primarily for oral communication, it is very difficult, if not impossible, to know how early speakers of the language might have referred to it. What may be the oldest references to Yiddish appear in an eleventh-century text written in Hebrew, a language that Jews had long since ceased to use as a vernacular but maintained for worship and devotional scholarship. Rashi's commentaries on the Bible and Talmud render a small number of obscure, ancient Hebrew and Aramaic words *bilshon Ashkenaz* ("in the language of Ashkenaz"), in keeping with a longstanding practice of studying Scripture by translating it into the vernacular. For example, Rashi offers *raytvogn* ("chariot") to gloss *risfak* (Aramaic: "sedan chair") and *vindlshteyn* for *lulim* (Hebrew: "winding stairs").[2]

At the time, Ashkenaz was the term local Jews used to identify what would come to be referred to as German lands—that is, a region of northwestern and central Europe where speakers of different variants of medieval German resided. The name Ashkenaz appears in the Bible, first mentioned among the descendants of Noah (Genesis 10:3).[3] Using this name to identify German lands exemplifies a wider diaspora Jewish practice of assigning ancient Hebrew names to territories in which Jews settled, including Sefarad for Iberia, Tsarfat for France, and Knaan for eastern Europe. This practice acknowledged the distinctiveness of both the regions' local non-Jewish populations and, later, the Jewish communities established in these places. The terminology is idiomatic; mapping the diaspora with names from Hebrew Scripture locates these territories in a panhistoric landscape of the Jewish imaginary.

Subsequently, the meaning of Ashkenaz changed, designating a distinct Jewish diaspora community within the region. The plural noun *Ashkenazim* referred to Jews of this locale, not their Christian neighbors. By the late Middle Ages, the Hebrew term *minhag ashkenaz* ("the customs of Ashkenaz") identified this Jewish population's particular practices of worship and ritual. Eventually, this term referenced the distinctive customs of Ashkenazim who settled beyond German lands.

Ashkenazim were also distinguished from other diaspora Jewish populations by their vernacular language. However, Rashi's term *bilshon ashkenaz* does not necessarily identify Yiddish as a language different from the German spoken by neighboring Christians. Rather, the term references a local vernacular that was intelligible to Rashi and his Jewish readership, for whom the modern distinction between Yiddish and German may not have been applicable. But by the early modern period, the meaning of *Ashkenaz* had come to identify this diaspora Jewish population with its own vernacular. Thus, the title page of *Mirkeves ha-mishne* (The second chariot)—the earliest extant Yiddish printed book, issued in Cracow in 1534—explains, in Hebrew, that this Bible concordance renders the original biblical text "into the language of Ashkenaz that is customary among us Ashkenazim."[4]

The ambiguity inherent in "the language of Askhenaz" also pertains to a term frequently used in the early modern period to refer, possibly, to Yiddish: *taytsh*. Related to the modern German word *Deutsch* (which was sometimes spelled *Teutsch*), a term derived from Old German *diutisk* and Latin *theodiscus*,[5] *taytsh* is mentioned frequently in works of what has come to be identified as early Yiddish literature. At times, *taytsh* appears to refer unambiguously to the vernacular of Ashkenazic Jews. For example, when discussing the customary practice of weekly readings of the Torah, Yiddish renderings of the Hebrew book of morals *Sefer ha-yirah* (Book of awe), published in the mid-1500s, advise that one should read the biblical text twice in Hebrew and once in translation; if one doesn't read the traditional *targem* ("translation of the Bible into Aramaic"), then it should be read in *taytsh*.[6] But in other instances, *taytsh* might refer to German—that is, the language, or at least the literature, of the Christian neighbors of Ashkenazim. Thus, the introduction to a Yiddish translation of the Torah published in Constance in 1544 touts the book as providing a virtuous alternative for Jewish women and girls who know how to read *taytsh* and therefore "spend their time with foolish books"—specifically, German epics about legendary medieval heroes such as "*Dietrich von Bern, Hildebrant*, and the like"—that were also published in the *alef-beys* (Yiddish: "Jewish alphabet").[7]

Compared to modern notions of what differentiates Yiddish from German, this ambiguity is telling. During the early modern period, it appears that Ashkenazim did not consistently regard their internal demotic as discrete from the language spoken and written by their Christian neighbors. To the extent that Jews did perceive this difference, they regarded the boundary between Christian and Jewish vernacular language as permeable. Thus, in his 1660 quadrilingual glossary of words in Hebrew, Italian, Latin, and Yiddish, Nathan Note Hannover explains, in Hebrew, "I have selected the *loshn ashkenaz* from the easy language current among us, and very little from the *loshn ashkenaz* of the Gentiles that is not found in our language."[8] The meaning of *loshn ashkenaz* or *taytsh* was fluid; these terms reflected Ashkenazic Jews' contingent understanding of vernacular language, whether in oral, written, or printed form, and whether among Ashkenazim or their neighbors. At the same time, Hannover's explanation distinguishes between Jewish and Christian usage of the "same" language.

*Taytsh* is not the only term used to reference the Ashkenazic vernacular in this ambiguous manner. The publication of *Dietrich von Bern* in the *alef-beys* (Cracow, 1597) is described as "taken from *galkhes* [Yiddish: 'the Latin alphabet'] and rendered into Yiddish." As Max Weinreich notes, the word *yidish* (which can mean either "Jewish" or "Yiddish") here may reference a difference in alphabet, rather than language.[9] An early eighteenth-century text, described as taken "from *galkhes* into our language,"[10] similarly distinguishes between alien (i.e., Christian) writing and a familiar idiom. Context is key; the term *yidish* marks the first text in question as somehow especially for Jewish readers, though what distinguishes the text may not be a separate language as this is understood today. Rather, the distinction appears to be a particularly Jewish practice of engaging the text, which renders its language, per the second example, as "ours." Conversely, referring to Yiddish with the term *loshenenu* (Hebrew: "our language") or, in modern times, *mame-loshn* (Yiddish: "mother tongue") implies a closeness between speaker (or writer) and the language. However, these terms do not reference Yiddish specifically, but could be used to identify a bond between any population and its language.

The contingent, ambiguous nature of defining the vernacular of Ashkenaz before the modern period is borne out by Yiddish terms that reflect an earlier understanding of *taytsh* as signifying neither a Jewish nor a gentile language per se, but rather a demotic used by Jews in relation to *loshn-koydesh*. *Ivre-taytsh* refers to a form of Yiddish used to facilitate *ivre*—reading the Hebrew of the Bible and other sacred texts, such as the prayer book—by rendering it in the Ashkenazic vernacular. In his Yiddish thesaurus, lexicographer Nahum Stutchkoff lists *tkhine-taytsh* and *Tsene-rene-taytsh* as terms for a similar kind of Yiddish, referring specifically to core sacred texts encountered in the language: *tkhines*, supplicatory prayers written for women, and *Tsene-rene* (Go forth and see), the most widely read Yiddish rendering of the Bible.[11]

Though no longer serving as a term for Yiddish (or the German language, which in Yiddish now is *daytsh*), *taytsh* is glossed as "meaning, sense." It figures as the stem in several verbs—*oystaytshn* ("to analyze"), *arayntaytshn* ("to interpret, to read into"), *(far)taytshn* ("to translate")—and in the idiom *Staytsh*?, a contraction of *Vos taytsh?* ("What does it mean? How come?"). In these various forms, *taytsh* remains a signifier of semantic accessibility, though not necessarily in Yiddish, German, or any other language.

• • •

The terms by which non-Jews have referred to Yiddish reflect their varied recognition that Ashkenazim have a distinct vernacular. Here, too, identifying Yiddish, compared to how it is understood today, could be ambiguous. For example, without further modification, the Russian adjective *evreiskii* can mean "Jewish," "Hebrew," or "Yiddish." Thus, the sentence *On evreiskii pisatel'* could be translated as "He is a Jewish author," "He is a Hebrew author," or "He is a Yiddish author." To disambiguate the term, Russian has sometimes distinguished Hebrew as the ancient (*drevne-evreiskii*) and Yiddish as the new (*novoevreiskii*) or colloquial (*raziovorno-evreiskii*) Jewish language; in the Soviet era, the term *idish* also appears.[12]

German speakers' efforts to name the Ashkenazic vernacular proved especially consequential for their Jewish neighbors. In pioneering scholarly efforts to study the language, published in the eighteenth century, German authors variously refer to it as *die jüdischteutsche Sprache* ("the Judeo-German language"), *Jüdisch-Teutsch* ("Judeo-German"), or *die Judensprache* ("the Jews' language").[13] These terms are ambivalent, perhaps deliberately, as to whether they identify a language in its own right or a Jewish variant of the language in which these terms are situated. Weinreich argued that calling Yiddish Judeo-German and other diaspora Jewish languages Judeo-Arabic, Judeo-Greek, Judeo-Spanish, and the like not only minimizes their integrity as independent languages; these terms also constrain how these languages might be studied, implying that they should be analyzed in relation to their non-Jewish counterpart rather than in their own right.[14]

As this scholarly scrutiny of Yiddish was under way, Jews in German states gradually forsook it for German as their language of daily life. The transition did not go unnoticed by some of their Christian neighbors, who detected in these efforts at linguistic assimilation the remnants of something ineluctably Jewish. (Of course, this shift, even if executed flawlessly, was itself a Jewish endeavor.) These Christian observers insisted that if German Jews no longer spoke Yiddish, they nevertheless spoke German "like Jews"—that is, with traces of Yiddish idioms or intonation—and named this practice *jüdeln* or *mauscheln*. The latter word, a derogative for displaying recognizably Jewish behavior, is generally explained as derived from *Moshe*—that is, Moses.[15] (Similarly, Poles disparaged the way Jews spoke Polish, inflected by their native Yiddish, as *żydłaczć*.) Though not terms for Yiddish per se, they named an Ashkenazic way of speaking understood as tainted by Yiddish.

Such disparagement notwithstanding, the transition from Yiddish to German figured prominently in the efforts by *maskilim* in German states to embrace modern Western culture and thereby forge a new way of being Jewish. The effects of the Haskalah would eventually be felt by all Ashkenazim, even those who opposed it. As *maskilim* generally considered Yiddish emblematic of its speakers' failure to integrate into the Western cultural mainstream, abandoning—and, moreover, repudiating—the language was a central tenet of the Haskalah.[16] Yet at first some *maskilim* continued to speak and write the language, even while they disparaged it. Indeed, their derogation of Yiddish engendered its own Yiddish vocabulary for naming the object of their contempt: *hiltserne taytsh* ("flawed [literally, 'wooden'] German"), *kugl-loshn* ("pudding language"), *shulhoyf-loshn* ("the language of the synagogue courtyard").[17] These last two terms deride Yiddish by its association with mores (traditional food, the commotion made by Jews congregating outside a synagogue) emblematic of the Ashkenazic culture that *maskilim* wished to leave behind. The most enduring maskilic term of opprobrium for Yiddish was *zhargon* ("jargon"). Derived from an Old French word for the jabbering of birds, the term has come to mean either the inscrutable language of a closed group or a debased, uncivilized form of speech—in either case, something less than a full, proper language.

When eastern European Jews first encountered the Haskalah at the turn of the nineteenth century, its call for abandoning Yiddish did not meet with the same widespread compliance as had been the case among Ashkenazim further west. The perpetuation of Yiddish—and, moreover, its expansion—in eastern Europe reflects the very different sociolinguistic circumstances of the Ashkenazim living there compared to Jews in German states. This difference exemplifies a larger distinction between the culture of western and eastern Ashkenazim, which linguist Dovid Katz characterizes as an inward turn by the latter group, developing an "increasingly compact and intensive Jewish life," in contrast to the integrationist turn of the former.[18]

Despite this difference, the linguistic self-consciousness emblematic of the Haskalah had a profound impact on the intellectual culture of eastern European Jews. This new way of thinking about language use as definitional for modern Jewish life eventually informed divergent language ideologies, which had in common their rejection of Yiddish. On one hand, *maskilim* developed a modern Hebrew that refashioned the language, traditionally used for sacred practices, into a secular vehicle for writing and, later, speaking. On the other hand, the Haskalah advocated mastering local languages of high culture and state power: German in the Habsburg Empire, Russian in the Romanov Empire. However, the great majority of eastern European Jews did not follow this maskilic agenda and maintained the use of Yiddish as their vernacular.

Moreover, toward the end of the nineteenth century a countermovement among eastern European Jewish intellectuals revalued Yiddish, championing it as a Jewish national language to be cultivated rather than condemned. This movement, known as Yiddishism, positioned what was then the vernacular of the great majority of eastern European Jewry at the center of a new, largely secular culture. Yiddishists argued that the language could support a Jewish national consciousness in the diaspora, thereby imbuing Yiddish with symbolic value beyond its longstanding use as a demotic. As a consequence of promoting the language for modern education, high culture, and political organizing, calling the language *yidish*—implying a tautological relationship among Jewish language, Jewish people (*yidn*), and Jewish mores (*yidishkeyt*)—became more widespread and ultimately prevailed over other names.

Nevertheless, *zhargon* endured as a familiar term for Yiddish, notwithstanding its pejorative implications, among those who spoke and wrote the language as well as among others. By the turn of the twentieth century, the use of *zhargon* ranged considerably in connotation, having become for some Jews, in effect, the name of the Ashkenazic vernacular. The term appears in titles of Yiddish textbooks (for example, *Zhargon-lerer*, [Jargon/Yiddish teacher], Warsaw, 1886) and dictionaries (*Zhargonishes fremd-verter-bukh* [Dictionary of foreign terms in Jargon/Yiddish], Vilna, 1907). The *zhargon komitetn* ("jargon/Yiddish committees") established in the mid-1890s by Jewish revolutionaries in the Russian Empire translated works of fiction and nonfiction into Yiddish for the Jewish proletariat.[19] Some nineteenth- and early twentieth-century Hebrew publications use *zhargon*, in parentheses, as a gloss for other terms referring to Yiddish: *ha-safah ha-meduberet* ("the spoken language") or *ha-lashon ha-medubar benenu* ("the language spoken among us").[20] Hebrew dictionaries of the early twentieth century also rendered Yiddish as *zargoni* or *yahadut* ("Jewishness"), reflecting other efforts to separate Modern Hebrew (and its attendant culture) from what then was, for many of its advocates, their native language.[21]

As modern Yiddish literature coalesced in the latter half of the nineteenth century, the term *zhargon* figured in writers' assessments of this phenomenon's merits. In his 1888 anthology *Di yidishe folksbiblyotek* (The Jewish people's library), a landmark work of advocacy for the artistic value of Yiddish literature, author Sholem Aleichem (né Sholem Rabinovitsh) refers to Yiddish writers, literature, and orthography as *zhargonishe shrayber, literatur*, and *oysleygen*, distinct from his use of the adjective *yidish*, meaning "Jewish."[22] By contrast, poet Shimen Frug disparaged the literary value of Yiddish as limited, compared to other languages, in his essay "Lider fun dem yidishn zhargon" (Poems in the Jewish jargon), written at the turn of the twentieth century.[23] A generation later, historian Simon Dubnow traced the development of modern Yiddish letters in his 1929 collection of essays *Fun zhargon tsu yidish* (From jargon to Yiddish). Dubnow juxtaposed these two terms as emblematic of the rapid advancement of this literature from the mid-nineteenth century, when *zhargon* was "considered the stepchild of culture," to the 1920s, in which Yiddish "had become the language of literature, journalism, and scholarship," rivaling "Hebrew and even the more sophisticated languages" in its achievements.[24] Though Yiddish is both the subject of discussion and the language in which these three texts were written, each author's juxtaposition of the terms *yidish* and *zhargon* reveals a different understanding of the use of Yiddish in relation to its symbolic value.

As a consequence of growth in publishing and other activities in the language, the name *yidish* became more widespread during the nineteenth century, both among its speakers and in other languages, and ultimately prevailed in the next century. The establishment of this term reflects new valuations of Yiddish: its capacity to unite millions of Jews throughout eastern Europe and an international network of immigrant centers through a rapidly expanding print culture, and the increasing importance of Yiddish in facilitating new visions of Jewish political and cultural life. The consolidation of *yidish* as the language's name did not, however, preclude other terms from arising in new engagements with the language.

Yiddishists' assertion of the language's defining role in realizing a secular Jewish culture and a national Jewish consciousness prompted their greater attention to the quality of Yiddish usage. As a result of this new kind of scrutiny, Yiddishists coined terms of opprobrium for what they deemed substandard forms of their language, reminiscent of how *maskilim* had previously mocked Yiddish as debased German. Once again, differentiating these two languages proved especially fraught. In eastern Europe the perceived overuse of terms from modern German for which there were more idiomatic equivalents in Yiddish was derided as *daytshmerish* or *dizn-dazn-loshn*, the latter term mocking the use of the German pronoun *diese* and article *das*. In America, Yiddishists sometimes ridiculed immigrant speech riddled with what they considered excessive Anglicisms as "potato-chicken-kitchen language."[25] Like the maskilic term *kugl-loshn*, the use of common food terms to signify vulgarity implicitly disparaged this form of the language through associations with the traditional work of women, reflecting a more pervasive gendering of Yiddish that denigrated the language as feminine.

Weinreich argues that establishing *Yiddish* as the name of the language in English at the turn of the twentieth century influenced speakers of other languages to adopt similar terms that transliterate *yidish* and thereby distinguish the language from *Jewish* as a more general term.[26] However, many native speakers of Yiddish have often referred to the language, when speaking in English, as *Jewish*, preferring to translate, rather than transliterate, its name and thereby also maintain its tautological relationship with Jewish people and their culture. Anthropologist Jonathan Boyarin characterizes this usage as evincing the ambivalent nature of immigrant culture, an "attempt to display attachment and competence in an ancestral idiom on the one hand, while demonstrating an educated, responsible awareness of the new idiom on the other."[27]

Conversely, the term *Yiddish* has been used in English as an adjective to describe something pertaining to eastern European Jews or to Jews generally, without its necessarily having any connection to the language. This practice includes external applications, such as "Yiddish jokes" that are anti-Semitic jests in English, sometimes referencing Yiddish through derisive dialect humor (and that certainly do not have Yiddish sources).[28] Among examples internal to Jewish culture is the term "Yiddish dance," used to refer to traditional eastern European Jewish folk dance, in which the Yiddish language plays a nominal role.[29] English-speaking Jews' fluctuating use of *Yiddish* and *Jewish* disrupts the traditional tautological relationship equating the Yiddish language with its speakers and their culture. At the same time, the undoing of this tautology prompted the need to distinguish references in Yiddish to the language as opposed to Jewish people, literature, or other phenomena, resulting in a nuanced grammatical differentiation. Thus, *yidishe limudim* can mean either "Jewish studies" or "Yiddish studies"; to resolve this ambiguity, the latter is sometimes rendered *yidish-limudim* (in which *yidish* is not an adjective but a noun and therefore is not declined).[30]

Changes in the use and significance of Yiddish after World War II engendered more new terms related to the language. Leo Rosten's *The Joys of Yiddish* popularized the term *Yinglish* to identify Yiddish words that had become widely used in American English (for example, bagel, mish-mash). Rosten designates as *Ameridish* neologisms coined by Yiddish speakers in the United States, such as *boychik* ("boy, fellow") and *nextdoorekeh* ("female next-door neighbor").[31] In his 1995 book *Frumspeak*, Chaim Weiser offers the term *Yeshivish* to name the speech of Orthodox yeshivas in communities of American *haredim*. Weiser argues that Yeshivish—which integrates elements of English, Yiddish, Israeli Hebrew, and *loshn-koydesh*—has since become an established vernacular among *haredi* men and boys beyond the confines of the classroom. To demonstrate its linguistic possibilities he offers playful translations of a variety of texts into Yeshivish, including the

American Pledge of Allegiance: "I am meshabed myself, bli neder, to hold shtark to the simen of the United States of America and to the medina which is gufa its takhlis; one festa chevra, be-ezras Hashem, echad ve'yuchid, with simcha and erlichkeit for the gantza oilam."[32] More recently, Chaim Dalfin published a glossary of what he terms *LubavitchSpeak*—that is, "words, sayings, and colloquialisms" in Yiddish and *loshn-koydesh* used by contemporary Lubavitcher Hasidim in the course of devotional scholarship and worship as well as in their quotidian "street language," exemplifying this community's "lifestyle and its holiness."[33] Yinglish, Ameridish, Yeshivish, and LubavitchSpeak all name linguistic phenomena perceived as indebted to Yiddish yet substantively different.

• • •

What does this inventory of more than a dozen terms for what has been (or might be considered) Yiddish reveal? In addition to evincing the contingency of naming the language, responsive to time, place, population, and ideology, these terms evince shifts in conceptualizations of the language. They range from a demotic shared to some degree with local Christians to a defining signifier of the essence of Jewishness; from a vehicle for rendering sacred texts intelligible to a degrading gibberish; from a complete, integral language to a fragment of one, which can be merged with other languages; from the epitome of Jewish disability to the foundation of a modern national Jewish culture. Indeed, it may be more useful to think of these names not as identifying "the same language" but as signs of the dynamics of Ashkenazic vernacularity, which entail varying notions of its speech community, scope of usage, distinctiveness, and symbolic worth.

In his landmark survey of the names of Yiddish, Weinreich asserts that "sociolinguistic and purely linguistic factors combine and force the conclusion that since the name *Yiddish* is accepted today that it be valid for all times since the beginning of the language." This is common practice in modern scholarship and applies to this book as well. Yet terming the extensive dynamic of Ashkenazic vernacular language *Yiddish* both encapsulates and obscures shifting and, at times, incompatible notions of this phenomenon. Weinreich also acknowledges that, in general, "names of languages are fixed retrospectively," thereby arguing, if tacitly, for thinking of Yiddish as having the same length, breadth, and depth as other languages readily recognized by a single, venerable name—especially those identified with modern national cultures and sovereign states.[34] Therefore, to speak of the foundational Ashkenazic vernacular as Yiddish is not merely exigent but polemical—as is calling it *taytsh, Jüdisch-Deutsch, zhargon, mame-loshn*, or Jewish. Each of its names embodies a partial truth about language use among Ashkenazim, simultaneously consolidating and constraining its protean character. The complex slippage among the signifiers and signifieds of its naming epitomizes the challenges, as well as the rewards, inherent in probing the story of the language now called Yiddish, behind which extends a long and at times contentious chronicle of efforts to give this phenomenon of Jewish language use a name.

# 5
# Gender

Gender has a multivalent presence in the "life" of a language. As an epistemic system that differentiates among categories of phenomena, gender not only is expressed through language but also structures its form and meaning, as do noun cases, verb tenses, word order, and other grammatical systems. The gendering of speakers can inform their language use, as when there are different linguistic registers, text practices, or even languages spoken or written by men versus women within the same population. In addition, a language can be thought of as having a gender, whether as a means of distinguishing it from other languages or in order to characterize what is perceived as its essence, independent of what is articulated in the language or by whom. Yiddish exemplifies this complex of anthropomorphisms, as a language that has been imagined as having a gendered body, whose "actions" have been understood as gendered, and in which gender defines one of the internal systems that enable the body to function.

The concept of gender is realized through elements of language that signify, and thereby effect, different categories of phenomena—most conventionally, distinguishing male and female beings: for example, Yiddish *hon* ~ *hun* ("rooster" ~ "hen"), *yingl* ~ *meydl* ("boy" ~ "girl"). As in many other European languages, Yiddish generally differentiates between males and females in the same role with the base form of the noun understood as implicitly male (or as unmarked) and the addition of a suffix to specify that the noun denotes a female. Yiddish implements this distinction with a variety of suffixes: *lerer* ~ *lererin* ("male teacher" ~ "female teacher"), *advokat* ~ *advokatke* ("male lawyer" ~ "female lawyer"), *dokter* ~ *doktershe* ("male doctor" ~ "female doctor"), *khaver* ~ *khaverte* ("male friend" ~ "female friend"). In the case of *lesbyanke* ("lesbian") and *matke* ("madam," i.e., procuress), an apparent feminine suffix signifies the femaleness of a noun's signified when the noun has no masculine base form. Feminine endings can also indicate a woman's status in relation to her husband—for example, *kremerke* can mean either a female shopkeeper or a shopkeeper's wife—or can mark different roles for male and female, particularly in religious life. Thus, *zoger* is a male preacher, whereas *zogerin* or *zogerke* defines a woman who reads prayers aloud in the women's section of the synagogue during congregational worship, as a guide to other women. These meanings can evolve with time. The term *khaznte* originally meant only "wife of a cantor" (*khazn*), traditionally a role held exclusively by men. But with the advent of women who performed cantorial music in the first decades of the twentieth century, *khaznte* also came to designate what was then known in English as a "lady cantor."

Beyond correlating to conventional biological concepts of gender, linguistic gendering can extend much further to embrace all nouns, as is the case in Yiddish, and to a gender system that is more than binary. Standard Yiddish as well as most dialects have three genders of nouns: masculine, feminine, and neuter. In Yiddish, the gender of a noun is not always readily apparent on its own but is signified in context by the noun's definite article (in the nominative case: masculine *der*, feminine *di*, neuter *dos*) and the endings of modifying adjectives. The gendering of nouns in Yiddish is therefore integrated with the language's case system, which articulates a noun's role in a sentence—as its subject (nominative), direct object (accusative), indirect object or object of a preposition (dative)—through the inflection of modifiers in the noun phrase.

The gendering of nouns can be semantic in some cases and formal in others. Among the first group, nouns denoting male roles—for example, *almen* ("widower"), *eydem* ("son-in-law")—are masculine, and female roles—*rebetsin* ("rabbi's wife"), *heybam* ("midwife")—are feminine, as a rule. In Standard Yiddish, certain categories of nouns are assigned the same gender (for example, names of months, holidays, and nationalities are masculine; names of countries, cities, and colors are neuter). With regard to form, nouns with certain endings have a uniform gender, irrespective of meaning. For example, all nouns with the suffixes -*ung*, -*keyt*, -*ents*, and -*shaft* are feminine, thus: *di tsaytung* ("newspaper"), *di narishkeyt* ("foolishness"), *di konferents* ("conference"), *di manshaft* ("sports team"). The diminutive forms of all nouns are neuter, irrespective of the gender of their base: *der shteyn* ~ *dos shteyndl* ("the stone" ~ "the pebble"), *di kats* ~ *dos ketsl* ("the cat" ~ "the kitten"), *dos bukh* ~ *dos bikhl* ("the book" ~ "the booklet"). Gender can distinguish among homonyms—*di zun* ("the sun") ~ *der zun* ("the son")—or can mark different meanings of a noun: *di bekeray* ("the bake shop") ~ *dos bekeray* ("the art of baking").[1]

Sometimes the gender of Yiddish nouns can seem arbitrary. They do not always match the gender of their cognates in the modern forms of their component languages: for example, Yiddish *di shif* ("the ship") ~ German *das Schiff*; Yiddish *shabes* (plural: *shabosim*) "Sabbath" is masculine ~ Hebrew *shabbat* (plural: *shabbatot*) is feminine. Variant forms of the same noun can have different genders, such as *der banan* ~ *di banane* ("the banana"). The gender of some nouns can even appear to be heterologous in relation to their semantic value. Thus, in Standard Yiddish *vayb* ("wife, woman") is neuter, *bord* ("beard") is feminine, and *eyershtok* ("ovary") is masculine.

Deviations from this standard are widespread in actual use, especially in spoken Yiddish. The gendering of nouns varies considerably among Yiddish dialects—most notably, the apparent presence of only two genders in Northeastern Yiddish compared to three genders in other dialects. On closer inspection, however, Uriel Weinreich observed that the declension of nouns in Northeastern Yiddish entails no fewer than seven genders (including distinct patterns for mass nouns and animate nouns), even though they all take either *der* or *di* as their definite article in the nominative case.[2] There are also numerous individual examples of nouns to which speakers variously assign more than one gender, as attested to by modern Yiddish dictionaries. Indeed, because of this variability, lexicographer Alexander Harkavy abandoned his attempt to indicate the gender of nouns in his 1928 Yiddish-English-Hebrew dictionary after its first two pages.[3]

In some cases, migrations of Yiddish speakers beyond Europe have prompted shifts in the grammar of gender. For example, linguist Steffen Krogh observes that the Yiddish spoken by Satmar Hasidim in the United States and other places where they settled after World War II exhibits an "extensive loss of gender and case distinctions."[4] By contrast, the Yiddish *Forward*, an online daily newspaper published in New York, follows the Standard Yiddish gendering of nouns, including differentiating between male and female professionals, even as that practice is increasingly abandoned in contemporary American English.[5] Maintaining or abandoning rules for the gender of nouns can therefore distinguish the nature of different speech communities' valuations of Yiddish in relation to other languages and in its own right.

Variations in the gendering of nouns, whether systematic or idiomatic, reflect the diffuse nature of Yiddish, distributed over a sprawling, shifting geographic, ideological, and linguistic landscape and having limited opportunities for—or commitment to—standardization. In this respect, the gender system exemplifies the nature of Yiddish generally: rooted in extensive and varied vernacular practices, shaped by dynamic contingencies, and open to alternatives.

• • •

Because Yiddish is usually spoken and written in multiglossic contexts, its use can be gendered, as can the language itself. Perhaps it is more appropriate to say "herself," for the notion that Yiddish has a gender typically identifies it as female. Not only is Yiddish often referred to as a mother tongue, a common metaphor for one's first language generally; the term *mame-loshn* is sometimes used as a name for the language itself. The long history of associating Yiddish with women dates at least to the advent of printed books in the language during the sixteenth century. This new technology produced Yiddish works that complemented canonical Jewish liturgy, Scripture, and rabbinic scholarship. Written in *loshn-koydesh*, this canon was read primarily, and in some cases, exclusively, by an all-male learned elite, in keeping with the traditional gendering of Jewish devotional scholarship. Rabbinic Judaism commands men to engage as much as possible in studying these works, following established learning practices. This obligation reflects the longstanding principle that Jews maintain their covenant with God, which had been observed before the destruction of the Temple in ancient Jerusalem through sacrificial offerings, by studying the laws of sacrifice and, by extension, Jewish law generally. Conversely, a precept of traditional rabbinic Judaism forbids women from studying the Talmud or other works within the all-male purview of authoritative devotional scholarship.

Yiddish publications translated or elaborated on this canon for a general audience, which included many, if not most, Ashkenazic men. Nevertheless, women came to be identified as the emblematic readers of these early works of Yiddish. Max Weinreich characterized the gendering of early modern Yiddish literature in general as "a kind of legal fiction." Women—whose access to texts in Hebrew and Aramaic was restricted and who were assumed, moreover, not to be able to read these languages sufficiently (though some of them could)—covered for the large number of men illiterate in *loshn-koydesh*. In effect, Weinreich asserts, "The woman provided a kind of permission for Yiddish in writing."[6]

Moreover, women emerged as a special audience for Yiddish books. Literature scholar Israel Zinberg proclaimed the advent of print among Ashkenazim as constituting an "enormous revolution . . . in the life of the

Jewish woman," in which she "became a national cultural factor in the life of the people."[7] Similarly, Weinreich argued that this new attention to a Jewish female readership "was the innovation of Ashkenaz," manifest in works of ritual and instruction that address issues of particular concern for women.[8] These books include guides to *mitsves noshim*—the commandments that Jewish women are traditionally charged with observing (kindling Sabbath and holiday lights, baking bread for ritual purposes, and maintaining taboos associated with menstruation)—and collections of *tkhines*, a devotional literature composed specifically for women.

Literature scholar Jean Baumgarten notes that women not only were readers of this literature but also "took part in all stages of the production, dissemination and transmission of Yiddish books. We find references to women who copy or commission copies of texts, who write, print, [and] sell books."[9] So important had reading become as a new practice for Ashkenazic women that this early literature includes texts explaining the proper way to read Yiddish, instruction regarded as essential to reinforcing women's piety and ensuring that their devotional practices would be carried out properly. These guidelines discuss recommended times for reading, the value of rereading and of hearing texts read aloud, whether alone or in groups, and the importance of attentive comprehension.

The graphic appearance of early Yiddish publications signaled the emblematic gendering of their readership forthrightly. The special fonts widely used for Yiddish during the first centuries of printing in the language were sometimes referred to as *vaybertaytsh* ("women's Yiddish"), thereby signifying a gendered reader through these works' visual presentation. However, the title pages of only a minority of the earliest Yiddish books indicate that they are intended especially for women; more often, these works are addressed to "men and women" or to "men and women, boys and girls." The inclusion of women and children indicates the desired comprehensive reach of these books to an audience sometimes described as "common people," as opposed to an elite readership of adult males.[10] Still other early Yiddish works characterize their readers as "women and men who are like women, that is, that they are not educated,"[11] implying a tripartite gendering of Ashkenazim, defined by both biology and literacy.

The emblematic role of the woman reader is ensconced in the reputation of the most frequently reprinted Yiddish work: *Tsene-rene*, a Yiddish rendering of the liturgical Hebrew Bible (that is, the Pentateuch plus selections of the Prophets and Writings read during public worship on the Sabbath and holidays) imbricated with narrative expansions and commentaries from a range of rabbinic sources. First published in the early seventeenth century, *Tsene-rene* came to be known as the "women's Bible" and is often characterized as a fixture of pious Jewish matrons' reading, such as the following late twentieth-century description of the book: "It evoked images in my mind of a wizened *bubba* [grandmother], sitting and reading, the flickering *Shabbos* [Sabbath] candles the only source of illumination."[12] The name by which the book is known references the opening of Song of Songs 3:11—"Go forth and see, daughters of Zion"—understood as implying a female readership. However, the title page of the earliest extant edition indicates that *Tsene-rene* was intended for men and women, and it was widely read by both.

The gendering of Ashkenazic language use has included ritual practice and worship. For example, a manuscript from eighteenth-century Alsace describes the local practice for a *pidyon ha-ben*, the rite of symbolically redeeming a firstborn son from priestly service, as had been done in ancient Jerusalem. In the prescribed dialogue between the newborn boy's parents and the *kohen* (Hebrew: "descendant of the priestly line"), he addresses the mother in Hebrew and she responds in Yiddish.[13] A more widespread use of Yiddish to provide women with a distinctive voice in Jewish ritual life are *tkhines*. These supplicatory prayers, written not only for but also, in some cases, by women, began to appear in the seventeenth century and continued to be composed into the twentieth century.

The earliest *tkhines* were Yiddish versions of mystically imbued prayers, originally composed in Hebrew and translated to make this new kind of liturgy accessible to a wider readership. Over time, Yiddish *tkhines* evolved as a distinct genre of prayer in its own right, centered on the traditional ritual duties of Jewish women, marking seasonal and life-cycle celebrations, as well as women's ongoing roles as wives and mothers. While some *tkhines* are addressed to God, others beseech the biblical matriarchs—Sarah, Rebecca, Leah, and Rachel—to intercede on behalf of women praying for, say, the safety of their husbands while traveling or for their own well-being upon giving birth. Anthropologist Chava Weissler characterizes *tkhines* as voicing an "alternative rhythm" within Ashkenazic practice, reflecting the extent to which women "participated in another religious world, with its own set of concerns,"[14] marked as such by this liturgy's use of Yiddish.

Advocates of the Haskalah generally scorned *tkhine-loshn*, the distinctive style of Yiddish used for these prayers, as part of the movement's more extensively gendered disparagement of Yiddish and the traditional Ashkenazic mores that the language exemplified. *Maskilim* regularly devalued texts written in Yiddish as suitable only for women and uneducated men, recalling the gendered formulation of the readership of early modern Yiddish works, though in order to deride rather than cultivate this audience.[15] And yet female readers proved to be strategic for promoting the Haskalah in eastern Europe, similar to their role as the emblematic audience for those earlier Yiddish publications.

As a consequence of the traditional obligation incumbent upon Jewish men to engage as fully as possible in devotional scholarship, anything else that they might read, especially texts that challenged rabbinic authority, could be denounced as *treyf-posl* ("heretical literature"). By contrast, women were free to read widely, including texts men were warned against. Maskilic authors writing in Yiddish in the middle decades of the nineteenth century availed themselves of this gendered configuration of traditional Jewish literacy by sometimes addressing works to their *tayere lezerins* ("dear female readers"). This strategy situated these texts at a cultural periphery that afforded both authors and readers greater latitude. Consequently, literature scholar Iris Parush argues, women served as "both a pretext and a conduit" for maskilic writing in Yiddish, "through which the range of literary kinds could be expanded, habits of reading artistic fiction nurtured, and the cloaked maskilic ideas it contained, propagated."[16] Neither this nominally designated female audience nor rabbinic prohibitions against maskilic publications prevented men from reading this *treyf-posl*, though they might have had to look on the sly at what women could read openly. Indeed, these works proved to be among the books most widely read by eastern European Jews in the mid-nineteenth century.

• • •

Even as some male writers embraced Yiddish as a modern literary language during the second half of the nineteenth century, they occasionally voiced anxiety about this decision in relation to the longstanding "myth of Yiddish 'femininity,' usually negatively valenced." Literature scholar Naomi Seidman characterizes the gendered discussion of Yiddish among some of its leading writers at this time—in a discourse that occasionally bristles with fears of debasement and emasculation—as constituting a "sexual exorcism" of scorned, feminized Yiddish.[17] Typically, these writers turned to Yiddish after earlier literary efforts in Hebrew or Russian—established languages of prestige for a modern Jewish belletrist in eastern Europe—which reached only a limited audience. Authors' apologias for writing in Yiddish sometimes referenced its gendered readership or inherent feminineness. Thus, in a reflection on his literary career, Sholem Yankev Abramovitsh explained his turn from Hebrew to Yiddish by comparing the latter language to a "foreign" seductress whom the author found irresistible, despite—or because of—the illicit nature of her allure.[18] Abramovitsh characterized the attraction as both erotic and exotic, conjuring his Yiddish femme fatale not as a familiar figure but, within the milieu of modern literature, as an alien.

Sholem Rabinovitsh described the adoption of his famous pseudonym as a device for avoiding the gendered shame associated with being a Yiddish writer: "How can one bring oneself to write in a language . . . in which they print women's prayer books? It was then that the pen name Sholem Aleichem was invented."[19] The author repeated this feminized image of Yiddish as humble and antiquated on his tombstone, which bears an epitaph of his own composing that coyly describes the author as "*a yid a posheter / geshribn yidish-taytsh far vayber*" ("a simple Jew / who wrote in old-fashioned Yiddish for women"). In fact, Sholem Aleichem's fiction regularly probed modernity's troubling of traditional Jewish gender roles, most famously in his series *Tevye der milkhiker* (literally, "Tevye the milky man," generally translated as *Tevye the Dairyman*). Tevye's "milky" attribute associates him with the feminine, and he repeatedly asserts in his monologues that "*Tevye iz nit keyn yidene*" ("Tevye is no mere woman"), as he is proved a hapless and helpless patriarch by his daughters, each of whom tests the possibilities of modern romance with calamitous results.

These and other authors' sexualized anxieties about writing in Yiddish were shaped considerably by the language's juxtaposition against Hebrew as a modern literary language. The *shprakhnkamf* ("language war") that polarized Yiddishists and Hebraists in the first decades of the twentieth century was often waged in gendered images of the two languages. The configuration of this metaphor was not consistent. Though Hebraists often championed their language as masculine, its alleged virility superior to the female weakness of Yiddish, both languages were sometimes depicted as different kinds of women: Hebrew as a nubile maiden compared to Yiddish as an old crone; Hebrew as a respectable bourgeois lady versus Yiddish as a humble servant.[20] These comparisons appeared, among other places, in cartoons in the American Yiddish press, which often subverted the analogies' implications by asserting the appeal of Yiddish despite its inferior status in the eyes of Hebraists.[21] When not juxtaposed with Hebrew, Yiddish was regularly depicted by the same cartoonists as female, sometimes dressed like a contemporary matron and other times as an allegorical figure in classical flowing robes.[22] This last representation is also evoked in texts praising a personified Yiddish, such as one that literary critic Joseph Judah Lerner composed in 1889: "On the green hill where all the muses stand before the throne of glory, the Yiddish muse has an honored place and has been graced with an equal measure of loveliness and beauty."[23] This use of archetypal female figures derived from Western culture bespeaks a larger tension in modern Jewish life regarding gender, as traditional Jewish notions of both womanhood and manhood were challenged by Western ideals of femininity and masculinity.[24]

• • •

Though women were widely recognized as key readers of Yiddish books, they had less often been writers of these texts. Exceptions include a small number of extant poems composed by women between the sixteenth and eighteenth centuries,[25] the female authors of some *tkhines*, and, most notably, a singular work of early modern Yiddish literature: the memoirs of Glikl bas Leyb, a prosperous Jewish merchant and mother of twelve, whose account of her life in German lands in the late seventeenth to early eighteenth century is an unparalleled personal document for its time and place, let alone being written by a woman or in Yiddish.[26] The relative dearth of works in the language by women changed abruptly in the first half of the twentieth century, as many dozens of female authors on both sides of the Atlantic began to publish in Yiddish. Indeed, the embrace of women writers during this period as exemplars of literary modernism prompted some male authors to publish works under female pseudonyms. Among these was Jacob Glatstein, who submitted some of his early poetry to the *Freie Arbeiter Stimme* (Free voice of labor) under the penname Klara Blum, after efforts to see his work accepted by the newspaper proved unsuccessful. Not only were his poems then published, but the paper's editor, Shaul Yanovski, also praised Blum's talent in print.[27]

However, the efflorescence of women Yiddish writers at this time was not free of gendered constraints. Leadership positions in this literary world—editors, publishers, critics, presidents of writers' associations—were, with rare exception, taken by men. As a case in point, the 1928 anthology *Yidishe dikhterins* (Yiddish women poets), which includes over three hundred poems by seventy women, was edited by Ezra Korman.[28] This volume also reflects a view then prevalent among Yiddish literati, as literature scholar Anita Norich notes, that women were inherently more suited to writing poetry rather than prose, especially novels—a notion that endured into the second half of the twentieth century, despite the considerable number of female authors of Yiddish narrative fiction.[29] Pious women's writing in Yiddish also flourished during the century's first decades, if less extensively. In literary works published in Poland by the Bais Yaakov schools for traditionally observant Jewish girls, Yiddish signified a resistance against secularism and cultural assimilation. Here, too, men played a guiding role in fostering this literature. Praising Bais Yaakov's eponymous magazine in 1932, journalist Heszel Klepfisz asserted that its mission should include "the task of attracting women to literary work. It should awaken women's slumbering artistic possibilities. Women, take up your pens!"[30] At the same time, women could also be castigated for abandoning Yiddish. Champions of the language in interwar Poland accused arriviste middle-class Jewish women of *shmendrikizm*—that is, "being embarrassed to speak Yiddish in public and preferring Polish," in an effort to integrate into the mainstream culture.[31]

Yiddish culture after World War II entails notable changes in the gendering of the language's use as well as new associations of Yiddish and gender. Among contemporary Hasidim, Yiddish is employed differently by men and women, reflecting the extensive gender distinctions within Hasidic culture. Anthropologist Ayala Fader notes that although Yiddish is taught in contemporary Hasidic girls' schools in Brooklyn, young women often speak the language less as they mature, marry, and have children, primarily talking among themselves in English. By contrast, Hasidic boys and men use Yiddish in their education, even though for them the language is not curricularized as a subject itself, as it is for girls. As a result, male Hasidim use Yiddish more extensively in general conversation as well.

Fader posits that this disparity can be attributed in part to women's role as the primary mediators between their families and the non-Hasidic world in the course of daily activities. The gendering of contemporary Hasidic Yiddish also reflects the history of language use among the Hasidim who settled in the United States after World War II. At first, most American Hasidic communities did not establish their own schools for girls, who instead attended Orthodox Jewish schools in which the language of instruction was English. As a consequence, transmission of the language between generations of

Hasidic women was impeded; hence, many American Hasidic girls now emulate their mothers' more extensive use of English.[32] Among these Hasidim, the longstanding association of Yiddish with women has shifted. As Fader notes, now "Yiddish is definitive of Hasidic masculinity."[33]

Conversely, the traditional linking of Yiddish and women has attracted new interest among Jewish feminists. Beginning in the final decades of the twentieth century they have both embraced and transvalued this longstanding association, exploring forgotten or marginalized examples of Yiddish culture by women in order to create original works of liturgy (including feminist *tkhines*) and to translate and perform works by modernist women Yiddish writers of the past.[34] Beginning in the mid-1970s, anthologies of women's Yiddish writing in translation have appeared, bringing new attention to this overlooked body of work, its authors, and its significance for understanding the gendering of Yiddish literature and culture.[35]

Forging connections between second-wave feminism and Yiddish culture, whether centuries-old pious works or early twentieth-century avant-garde writings, was not inevitable. Rather, it emerged from some women's desires to integrate what had been experienced as two discrete, if not inimical, cultural milieus.[36] Among these women are literature scholar Evelyn Torton Beck, musician and educator Adrienne Cooper, and poets Irena Klepfisz and Adrienne Rich, all of whom were members of Di Vilde Chayes (The wild beasts), a political Jewish feminist group founded in New York in 1980. Each also addressed feminist concerns through her work with Yiddish in performance, research, writing, or translation. For example, in her bilingual Yiddish/English poems, Klepfisz employs the movement between the languages both to call attention to the disjuncture in literacies and sensibilities that these languages represent and to suggest new possibilities for Yiddish as a feminist resource.[37] Among more recent undertakings that connect Yiddish and feminism is the podcast series *Vaybertaytsh*, inaugurated in 2016. Locating the term's origin in conjunction with "Yiddish commentaries on the Torah that were written in Yiddish by men for women," the podcasts' creators explain, "We're flipping the concept of 'vaybertaytsh' on its head, explaining and commenting on our own terms."[38]

Some of Klepfisz's essays and poetry written in the 1980s also heralded the emergence at the turn of the twenty-first century of Queer Yiddishkeit.[39] Creators of these works of music, film, journalism, poetry, and performance art juxtapose LGBT and Yiddish cultures to challenge their respective parameters. For some practitioners, the conjoining of queer culture and Yiddish culture unites parallel systems of alterity. Journalist Alisa Solomon describes this development as a "postmodern marriage" that provocatively asserts an inherent "affinity between queerness and Yiddishkeit," which she characterizes as their common diasporism; rootless cosmopolitanism; a penchant for transgression, border crossing, and being proudly, defiantly different; and standing as a challenge to broader societies' sense of "certitude and power."[40] Conversely, some works of Queer Yiddishkeit juxtapose these two cultures not to wed them but to use each to problematize the other, disrupting both the widespread heteronormativity of Yiddish culture and frequent assumptions of the incompatibility of queerness with ethnic communion or religious spirituality.[41] Like Yiddish books published centuries earlier for "women and men who are like women," works of Queer Yiddishkeit employ the language to complicate common assumptions about gender and thereby expand possibilities for engaging Jewishness. Sometimes this effort prompts innovations in the language itself, exemplified by the creation of such neologisms as *min-flisik* ("gender-fluid"), *tsis-normativ* ("cis-normative"), and *transfobish* ("transphobic").[42]

Over time and at different levels of language use, the interrelation of Yiddish and gender has been inconsistent, fluid, at times provocative—anything but straightforward. The language has been described as having a gendered voice and a gendered ear and has been dressed in gendered garb. Yiddish has also given voice to gender, variously affirming or troubling Jewish notions of maleness and femaleness. As gender suggests new possibilities for categorizing Yiddish speech as well as its speakers, the parameters of gender are tested—and all the while, it operates as one of the systems that animate the language.

# 6
# Appearance

Though the primary use of Yiddish has long been oral, there is an ample record of Yiddish as a written language dating back to the sixteenth century, with more limited evidence from earlier centuries. The appearance of these texts—the spelling of words, and even the form of letters—itself offers revealing evidence of the language's history. As a vernacular that has always existed alongside other languages, used over an intercontinental expanse, flourishing largely beyond official oversight, and imbued with a range of ideological values, the appearance of Yiddish reflects diverse visions of its place in Jewish life over the centuries.

A hallmark of most Jewish languages is that they are written in their own alphabet, called the *alef-bet* in Modern Hebrew and *alef-beys* in Yiddish. This alphabet has semiotic value in its own right. Its use to record a text conventionally marks it a priori as being for a Jewish readership— even when the text is entirely in an ostensibly "non-Jewish" language. Examples of this practice range from Moses Mendelssohn's translation of selections from the Hebrew Bible into German, printed in the Jewish alphabet in 1783, to signage on Jewish shops in New York's Lower East Side during the first half of the twentieth century that render English phonetically in the *alef-beys*: בארבּער שאפּ ("Barber Shop"), טשיקען מארקעט ("Chicken Market").[1] Therefore, though scholars have debated whether the language of early Ashkenazic manuscripts—notably the fourteenth-century verse epic *Dukus Horant* (Duke Horant), which appears in the Cambridge Codex—is German or Yiddish, its appearance in the *alef-beys* clearly marks it as intended particularly for Jewish readers.[2]

The Jewish alphabet, as developed many centuries ago to record Hebrew, uses twenty-two basic consonants primarily to indicate syllables. Some consonants can also be used to indicate vowel sounds; in other instances, vocalization is either implicit or can be indicated by the addition of *nekudot* (Hebrew: "vowel signs"; Yiddish: *nekudes*), marks that are written above, below, or within consonants. For example: *emunah* אמונה ~ אֱמוּנָה ("faith"). Using this alphabet to record a non-Semitic language—not only Yiddish but also Judezmo, Romaniote, and Jewish correlates of Italian, Persian, and Turkish, among others—necessitates some orthographic innovations that correlate to the alphabet of its primary component. Hence, the traditional spelling of Yiddish accommodates two different orthographic systems. First, it largely maintains the conventional Hebrew and Aramaic spelling of terms in the Semitic component; second, Yiddish spells words from the other components of the language in a system that generally emulates the Roman alphabet by using each letter (or cluster of letters) of the *alef-beys* to signify the sound of a consonant, vowel, or diphthong rather than a syllable. The primary distinction of the latter system, which to some extent follows the orthographies of earlier diaspora Jewish languages, concerns the indication of vowel sounds. This system evolved over centuries; in modern writing, the vowels and diphthongs in Yiddish are rendered as follows, per YIVO Standard orthography, which is now the most widely used system in secular and academic publications:

| Letter | Name | Sound | | Example | |
|---|---|---|---|---|---|
| אַ | *pasekh-alef* | a (as in *far*) | וואַנט | *vant* | "wall" |
| ע | *ayen* | e (as in *bed*) | שפּעט | *shpet* | "late" |
| י | *yud** | i (as in *igloo*) | מיד | *mid* | "tired" |
| אָ | *komets-alef* | o (as in *for*) | אָפֿט | *oft* | "often" |
| ו | *vov*** | u (as in *put*) | קוקן | *kukn* | "to look" |
| יי | *tsvey yudn* | ey (as in *hey*) | צוויי | *tsvey* | "two" |
| ײַ | *pasekh tsvey yudn* | ay (as in *bayou*) | קרײַד | *krayd* | "chalk" |
| וי | *vov-yud* | oy (as in *toy*) | בלוי | *bloy* | "blue" |

When a non-*loshn-koydesh* word starts with a vowel sound other than *e, a*, or *o*, Yiddish follows the precedent of Hebrew orthography and begins the word with a *shtumer* ("silent") *alef*. As the name suggests, this letter does not signify a sound of its own but indicates, in this position, that an initial vowel written with *vov* or *yud* follows:

* *Yud* serves as both a consonant (like the letter *y* in *yes*) and a vowel. In some dialects of Yiddish, vocalic *yud* is variously pronounced as a short vowel (like the letter *i* in *big*) or a long vowel (like *ee* in *seem*). For example, in these dialects, בין is pronounced like the English word *bin* when it means "[I] am" and like the English word *bean* when it means "bee."

** When doubled, this letter is a consonant (וו), called *tsvey vovn*, with the sound *v* as in *very*.

| | | |
|---|---|---|
| אומעטום | *umetum* | "everywhere" |
| אויסמײַדן | *oysmaydn* | "to avoid" |
| איצט | *itst* | "now" |
| אייניקל | *eynikl* | "grandchild" |
| אײַזנבאַן | *ayznban* | "railroad" |

*Shtumer alef* has also been used to disambiguate the use of *yud* and *vov* as consonants versus as vowels or diphthongs when the letters would otherwise appear adjacent to one another:

| | | |
|---|---|---|
| פּרואוואונג | *pruvung* | "ordeal" |
| שנייאיק | *shneyik* | "snowy" |

YIVO Standard orthography distinguishes these different uses of *vov* and *yud* by adding *nekudes* to these letters when used as vowels adjacent to their use as consonants or in diphthongs:

| Letter | Name | Example | |
|---|---|---|---|
| וּ | *melupm-vov* | פּרוּוונג | *pruvung* |
| יִ | *khirek-yud* | שנייִק | *shneyik* |

Additional Yiddish orthographic innovations include consonant clusters, signifying sounds not present in *loshn-koydesh*:

| Letter | Name | Sound | Example | | |
|---|---|---|---|---|---|
| טש | *tes-shin* | tsh (like *ch* in *chair*) | טשערעפּאַכע | *tsherepakhe* | "turtle" |
| זש | *zayen-shin* | zh (like *z* in *azure*) | זשאַלעווען | *zhaleven* | "to begrudge" |
| דזש | *dalet-zayen-shin* | dzh (like *j* in *joy*) | דזשימדזשיק | *dzhimdzhik* | "gadget" |

There are four pairs and one triad of consonants that are homophonic in both Ashkenazic Hebrew and Yiddish. In modern Yiddish orthography, only one letter in each group is used for these sounds, except for words from the Hebrew and Aramaic components, when maintaining their traditional spelling:

| Sound | Consonant used for all non-*loshn-koydesh* words | Example | Consonant used only in *loshn-koydesh* words | Example |
|---|---|---|---|---|
| v | וו<br>*tsvey vovn* | ווער<br>*ver* ("who") | בֿ***<br>*veys* | עבֿירה<br>*aveyre* ("sin") |
| kh | כ<br>*khof* | כאַפּן<br>*khapn* ("to catch") | ח<br>*khes* | חלום<br>*kholem* ("dream") |
| t | ט<br>*tes* | טאָפּ<br>*top* ("pot") | תּ<br>*tov* | תּמיד<br>*tomed* ("always") |
| k | ק<br>*kuf* | קומען<br>*kumen* ("to come") | כּ<br>*kof* | כּלה<br>*kale* ("bride") |
| s | ס<br>*samekh* | סלוי<br>*sloy* ("jar") | שׂ<br>*sin*<br>ת***<br>*sof* | שׂימחה<br>*simkhe* ("joy")<br>אַחריות<br>*akhrayes* ("responsibility") |

Words that fuse Semitic components with other components, such as adjectival or verbal affixes, likewise integrate the two spelling systems:

| | | |
|---|---|---|
| מורא | *moyre* | "fear" |
| מוראדיק | *moyredik* | "fearful" |
| גנבֿ | *ganev* | "robber" |
| געגנבֿעט | *geganvet* | "robbed" |
| חזיר | *khazer* | "pig" |
| חזירלעך | *khazerlekh* | "piglets" |

As is typical of writing in other vernacular languages that lack a widely accepted standard orthography for most of their history, Yiddish texts have manifested considerable differences in spelling in both manuscript and printed form. At the same time, certain norms appear regularly among this

*** Following Hebrew orthography, these letters never appear at the beginning of a word.

diversity of spelling systems. Thus, the earliest Yiddish manuscripts reflect some of the conventions of Hebrew orthography, rather than strictly imitating the spellings of Middle High German dialects—for example, the aforementioned use of the *shtumer alef* at the beginning of words with certain initial vowel sounds and the distinctive final forms of five consonants: *khof / langer khof* (כ/ך), *mem / shlos mem* (מ/ם), *nun / langer nun* (נ/ן), *fey / langer fey* (פֿ/ף), *tsadek / langer tsadek* (צ/ץ). The orthographic norms of these early works continued with relatively little variation for centuries and informed the spelling systems of the first Yiddish publications.[3]

• • •

Both written and printed works of early Yiddish manifest a distinct visual presence compared to Ashkenazic texts in Hebrew and Aramaic of the same period. Because differences in handwriting in early Yiddish texts were more variable than contemporaneous writing in Hebrew, they provide more specific evidence of where and when they were written.[4] Early in the history of Yiddish print a special set of typefaces was widely used for the language, both in publications that were entirely in Yiddish and to distinguish Yiddish from Hebrew in bilingual works. Printing Yiddish with these special fonts continued into the early nineteenth century. These typefaces were referred to by a variety of names, including *mesheyt* or *mashket* and, later, *taytsh, ivretaytsh, kleyn-taytsh, vayberksav*, and *vaybertaytsh*.[5] As noted in the previous chapter, the last two terms reflect a gendered association of Yiddish literacy with women.

By the turn of the nineteenth century some Yiddish publications began to use *nikudes* to indicate all vowel sounds. The *nikudes* are often redundant markers of vowel sounds (for example, הָאבֶּען vs. Standard Yiddish האָבן [*hobn*]); other times, they indicate vowels that are represented by letters in Standard Yiddish orthography (דֶר vs. Standard Yiddish דער [*der*]). The presence of *nikudes* reflects a presumption of readers' familiarity with reading devotional Hebrew texts that use these vowel signs, such as a prayer book, and also implicitly relates Yiddish literacy to reading *loshn-koydesh*.

Changes in Yiddish orthography became more programmatic as a new self-consciousness about Yiddish and its place in modern Jewish life developed during the 1800s. Efforts to model norms for Yiddish spelling appear early in the century—for example, in the *maskil* Mendel Lefin's translation of Ecclesiastes into Yiddish.[6] A threshold development of modern Yiddish

שמות דברים באלפא ביתא
אלף

| German | Latin | Hebrew | Yiddish |
|---|---|---|---|
| Apfel | Pomum | תפוח | אפפיל |
| Adler | Aquila | נשר | אדלר |
| Antzlit | Facies | פנים | אנצליט |
| Aug | Oculus | עין | אויג |
| Acken | Ceruix | עורף | אק |
| Arm | Brachium | זרוע | ארם |
| Armbrust | Balista | בליסטר | ארם פרושט |
| Achsel | Humerus | כתף | אכשיל |
| Arsch | Anus | תחת | ארש |
| Acker | Ager | חלקה | אקר |
| Angster | Vitrũ angustũ | צנצנת | אנגשטר |
| Angel | Hamus | חכה | אנגיל |
| Tûrangel | Cardo | ציר | טור אנגיל |
| Aier | Oua | ביצים | אייער |
| Aimer | Vrna | דלי | איימור |
| Aiß | Glacies | קרח | אייז |
| Aisen | Ferrum | ברזל | אייזן |
| Aißen | Vlcus | מורסה | אייסן |
| Aiter | Tabes | ליחה | אייטר |

A 2

A page from Elijah Levita's *Shemot devarim* (Names of things), a lexicon glossing terms in German, Latin, Hebrew, and Yiddish, published in 1542. The Yiddish terms (listed in the right-hand column) are set in the distinctive font, sometimes called *meshket* or *vaybertaytsh*, that was used most often for Yiddish during the first centuries of Jewish book publishing.

orthography is the publication of Shiye-Mordkhe Lifshits's Russian-Yiddish and Yiddish-Russian dictionaries, first issued in 1869 and 1876, respectively. Lifshits introduced enduring principles of Yiddish spelling that reflect the language's phonology (other than vocabulary terms in the Semitic component, for which he maintained their traditional spelling).

In contrast with these efforts, many publications of modern Yiddish literature in the late nineteenth and early twentieth centuries adopted orthographies influenced by German spelling, including the use of redundant double consonants, added unstressed vowels, and the inclusion of *ayen* or *hey* to indicate long vowels. This spelling reflects a larger notion then prevalent that literary Yiddish should emulate German.

| **Pronunciation** | **Definition** | **Standard spelling** | **"Germanized" spelling** | **German correlate** |
|---|---|---|---|---|
| *yor* | "year" | יאָר | יאָהר | *Jahr* |
| *ale* | "all" (pronoun) | אַלע | אַללע | *alle* |
| *(d)ertseylung* | "story" | דערציילונג | ערצעהלונג | *Erzählung* |
| *vider* | "again" | ווידער | וויעדער | *wieder* |
| *farfirn* | "to seduce" | פֿאַרפֿירן | פערפיהרען | *verführen* |
| *sheyn* | "pretty, nice" | שיין | שעהן | *schön* |

The twentieth century witnessed multiple attempts by institutions to establish a standard Yiddish orthography. These efforts reflect not only the burgeoning demands of publishing in the language and the expanding dispersal of Yiddish speakers but also new ideological valuations of Yiddish in relation to other modern languages of high culture. Given the wide range of publishing and instruction in Yiddish at the time, as well as the general lack of centralized institutions in a position to enforce standards, they have been contested at least as much as they have been adopted. This lack of consensus indicates, in part, a greater desire among different groups (and sometimes individual authors) to distinguish their use of the language from others' than to support orthographic consistency among all Yiddish writers.

Exceptional are the Soviet Union's mandated radical reforms of Yiddish spelling in the 1920s, which included eliminating the use of those consonants found only in words of *loshn-koydesh* origin and requiring these words to be spelled phonetically, rather than traditionally. Soviet Yiddish orthography also eliminated the distinctive final forms of five consonants, though they were reinstated later.

| | | **Traditional spelling** | **Soviet spelling** |
|---|---|---|---|
| *emes* | "truth" | אמת | עמעס |
| *sholem* | "peace" | שלום | שאָלעם |
| *levone* | "moon" | לבֿנה | לעוואָנע |
| *kasril* | "pauper" | כּתריאל | קאסריל |
| *soyne* | "enemy" | שׂונא | סוינע |

These developments paralleled Soviet orthographic reforms of the Cyrillic alphabet, which similarly eliminated phonetically redundant letters. Soviet Yiddish spelling was also part of a larger effort to distance the language from Hebrew, derogated for its association with religion and Zionism.[7] However, no attempt was made to abandon the *alef-beys* altogether for another alphabet. Versions of Soviet orthography were also adopted by some left-wing Yiddish writers and publishers outside the Soviet Union, including books and periodicals used in American secular Yiddish schools affiliated with the Communist Party in the 1930s.

After years of development, the YIVO Institute codified its standard orthography in 1937.[8] At the same time that this system was implemented by secular Yiddish schools and publishers in interwar Poland, traditionally observant Yiddish speakers promoted an alternate system, created by Solomon Birnbaum.[9] Supporters of his orthography, which was adopted by Bais Yaakov schools in 1930, argued that it better reflected how Yiddish was spoken by the majority of eastern European Jews, as opposed to the YIVO Standard, which more closely resembled the speech of a Lithuanian-based minority of Yiddish speakers. Moreover, Birnbaum's standard, which he called "traditionalist" in contrast to YIVO's "nationalist" system, was hailed as closer to the pious origins of early Yiddish writing and therefore would serve as a bulwark against secularism.[10]

| | | **YIVO Standard orthography** | **Birnbaum's "traditionalist" orthography** |
|---|---|---|---|
| *perl* | "pearl" | פּערל | פּעֶרל |
| *bin* | "[I] am" | בין | בּיִן |
| *hoykh* | "high, loud" | הויך | הוֹיך |
| *ort* | "place" | אָרט | ארט |
| *gezunt* | "health" | געזונט | גיזונט |

Though the YIVO Standard is widely used today, efforts to see that secular Yiddish schools, newspapers, and publishers conform to this system continued to meet with opposition after World War II. For example, Yiddishists picketed the New York offices of the *Jewish Daily Forward* in 1970 to protest its resistance to adopting YIVO orthography (which the newspaper eventually did).[11] In the postwar era, Hasidic Yiddish publications manifest a variety of orthographic practices, reflecting the widely scattered geographic dispersion of Hasidim after the Holocaust as well as differences among Hasidic communities.[12] The advent of Yiddish language curricula in Hasidic schools has fostered efforts to standardize spelling within individual communities.

• • •

Even as the Jewish alphabet has been central to writing and publishing Yiddish throughout its history, the language has occasionally appeared in other systems, including sign language and shorthand.[13] In addition, distinctive gestural practices have signified the oral language visually. Observers of eastern European Jews frequently described Yiddish speakers' gesticulations, in both written accounts and illustrations. Anthropologist David Efron analyzed the gestures of "traditional" (as opposed to "assimilated") speakers of what he termed "ghetto-Yiddish" among immigrants in New York City and concluded that "the 'traditional' Eastern Jew very seldom displays physiographic or symbolic gestures," in contrast to neighboring immigrants from southern Italy. Rather, "the ghetto Jew is more likely to give a *gestural notation* of the process" of his thinking, constituting a "gestural description of the 'physiognomy' . . . of his discourse." For example, he may use his arm as "a pointer, to link one proposition to another, or to trace the itinerary of a logical journey."[14]

By far the most widespread alternative to the *alef-beys* for visualizing Yiddish is the Roman alphabet. Romanization occurs most often when Yiddish words or phrases are embedded in texts written in other languages or in reference systems, such as the United States Library of Congress, which catalogs Yiddish publications with a romanization system similar to the YIVO Standard. Romanized Yiddish is also widely used on the internet and for texting, especially outside of Israel.

Publishing entire Yiddish works in the Roman alphabet, however, is a relatively infrequent phenomenon, and a recent one, reflecting a variety of rationales for doing so. For example, the challenge of integrating Yiddish text into a notation system that runs in the opposite direction of the *alef-beys* emerged at the turn of the twentieth century with the publication of Yiddish songs in sheet music, which typically romanizes Yiddish lyrics.[15] Several books issued during the early decades of the twentieth century use the Roman alphabet to facilitate access to Yiddish texts for readers who do not know the *alef-beys* but for whom comprehension of the language or even access to the sound of these texts would be of some interest. These publications include the anthology appended to philologist Leo Wiener's *The History of Yiddish Literature in the Nineteenth Century* (with English translations facing the romanized Yiddish)[16] and two popular collections of Yiddish folklore for readers of German, compiled by folklorist Immanuel Olsvanger: *Rosinkess mit Mandlen* (Raisins and almonds, 1920) and *Rêjte Pomeranzen* (Red oranges, 1936).[17] These books offer the inverse of works in German published in the Jewish alphabet, such as Mendelssohn's Bible translation, though in both cases the alphabet of publication serves as a bridge between texts and readers that is at the same time a sign of the disparity in literacy between language communities.

Among the earliest efforts to modernize Yiddish orthography by using Latin letters was a system designed in the early 1880s by Ludovik Lazarus Zamenhof, the subsequent inventor of Esperanto.[18] During the first decades of the twentieth century, a notable number of Yiddishists, including Nathan Birnbaum (the father of Solomon Birnbaum) and Chaim Zhitlowsky, also proposed that Yiddish be written with the Roman alphabet. Their aim was both to standardize its orthography and to mark its transformation from a traditional vernacular to the official language of a European nationality.[19] Though none of these efforts met with success, a number of romanized Yiddish publications did appear in Europe in the years immediately following World War II, such as posters and newspapers printed in displaced persons' camps in Germany. Then, however, the motive was not ideological but exigent, as printers' type in the Jewish alphabet could not readily be found, having been destroyed during the war.

Romanization is especially common in ludic uses of Yiddish, such as isolated words or idioms that appear in mock dictionaries or on various collectibles, in which familiarity with Yiddish is assumed to be limited, and the interplay between Yiddish and another language is often central to their playfulness. Exemplifying this phenomenon is a premium that the Yiddish Book Center in Amherst, Massachusetts, gave to donors in the late 1990s: a wooden yoyo with OY OY printed on one side and אוי אוי on the other side.

Displaced persons camp poster, printed in Munich in 1949, announcing a dance on the holiday of Simchas Torah. The poster uses the Roman alphabet to spell the Yiddish text, likely due to the lack of type in the *alef-beys* in postwar Europe. (From the Archives of the YIVO Institute for Jewish Research.)

This T-shirt, available for purchase online in 2019, is one among a wide assortment of mass-produced items printed with Yiddish words. These objects typically romanize Yiddish and often integrate it into a phrase or sentence in another language, playfully transgressing conventional linguistic boundaries. The "kosher-style" lettering imitates the distinctive serifs of a traditional Jewish alphabet font.

Romanized Yiddish words inscribed on T-shirts, coffee mugs, and a variety of other objects sometimes appear in fonts that imitate the distinctively curved serifs of the *alef-beys* in its traditional block form. These are, in effect, "kosher-style" Roman alphabet fonts, having the semblance, if not the substance, of Jewish tradition.[20]

The visual appearance of Yiddish has anthropomorphic implications, which emerge when its orthography is compared with other semiotic systems signifying Jewish presence. The diversity of Yiddish orthographies parallels internal variations in dress worn by different Jewish communities—including head coverings, standards of modesty, and men's facial hair—which indicate these Jews' respective ideologies. Use of the *alef-beys* versus romanization, which marks texts as either closed or accessible to those who cannot read Yiddish, correlates to Jews' public visibility perceived as either different or assimilated. And the rendering of Yiddish in a "kosher-style" Roman alphabet flouts any such simple boundary, suggesting that the language and its speakers are distinctive yet readily approachable.

# 7
# Health

Much of the discussion of Yiddish, especially in the modern period, centers on its health—or, more often, its unhealthiness. The earliest external examinations of Yiddish regularly pathologized it; this notion was subsequently taken up by Ashkenazim who disdained the language and then rebutted by other Jews who championed it. This discourse of disability targeted not only the language itself, conceived as a living entity whose well-being was in question, but also the impact of Yiddish on its speech community—in effect, likening the language to a communicable disease and conflating Yiddish speakers' bodies with the anthropomorphized ailing language. Beginning in the late eighteenth century, the characterization of Yiddish as unhealthy influenced many Jews' abandonment of it for other vernaculars and contributed to the larger discourse of modern anti-Semitism. At the same time, the pathologizing of Yiddish informed the way that its advocates have both come to its defense and worked to reform the language.

The earliest descriptions of Yiddish as unhealthy appear in the work of Christian scholars, both clergy and early humanists, including some Jewish converts to Christianity. After beginning in the mid-1500s, this scholarship flourished in the following century and continued into the late 1700s. The authors were German speakers, writing first in Latin and then in German, a shift reflecting a larger turn to producing scholarly work in European vernaculars as their stature rose.[1] As noted earlier, these scholars assessed Yiddish in terms of its variance from German, rather than as a language in its own right. Their scholarship had an enduring impact on how future generations evaluated Yiddish as deviating from a presumed linguistic norm. This approach was not inevitable; it may have arisen from concomitant attention to German, especially its increasing scholarly prestige and its significance in defining Germans as a people with an inherent common character and an incipient national identity. Because German speakers then lived in a cluster of separate polities and their Christian majority was divided between Protestants and Catholics, language played a salient role in articulating a shared Germanness. In this milieu, Yiddish marked a non-Christian minority that incurred economic and political restrictions imposed by various governing authorities, repeated theological attacks by Christian clergy, and occasional violent assaults by Christian neighbors. From a Germanist perspective, Jews' linguistic deviance manifested their aberrant and abject nature. According to Jeffrey Grossman, many Germans came to perceive Yiddish and its speech community as "an anarchic element that undermines the image of a culturally homogeneous Germany."[2]

The discourse of Yiddish as unhealthy centered on concepts of purity and honesty, which, though focused on language, redounded to the nature of Ashkenazic Jews. When Germanist scholars compared the Germanic component of Yiddish to their own language, they perceived the differences as signs that Yiddish was either archaic or distorted. The language's imbrication of terms and grammatical features from its Semitic determinant made Yiddish seem mongrel and arcane. As Germanists sought to refine their own language in order to facilitate a unifying high culture for the German people, Yiddish exemplified the opposite. Its hybrid character bespoke a contaminated language and, moreover, a threatening Judaization of German. The perception of Yiddish as esoteric prompted concerns about its use to deceive or harm Christians in business dealings. Studies of *Rotwelsch* (German: "thieves' slang") highlighted the use of terms derived from the Semitic component of Yiddish in the argot of the German-speaking underworld. Christians also feared that the "secret language of the Jews" was used to propagate anti-Christian teachings.[3]

More than a formally adulterated language, historian Aya Elyada argues, Yiddish was perceived as an "antilanguage, . . . an extreme version of a nonstandard social dialect, deliberately created by socially inferior and marginalized groups antagonistic to the dominant society."[4] The trope of Jews' language as a perniciously obfuscating force persisted into the twentieth century and eventually informed the racialized anti-Semitism of National Socialists. Thus, Adolf Hitler wrote in his 1925 manifesto *Mein Kampf* (My struggle): "On this . . . lie, that the Jews are not a race but a religion, more and more lies are based in necessary consequence. Among them is the lie with regard to the language of the Jew. For him it is not a means for expressing his thoughts, but a means for concealing them. When he speaks French, he thinks Jewish, and while he turns out German verses, in his life he only expresses the nature of his nationality."[5]

The widely shared perception of Yiddish as tainted German spread by unhealthy Jews inspired multiple diagnoses of this disease's etiology. Some

This 1851 cartoon, published in the German humor magazine *Fliegende Blätter* (Flying leaves), depicts two Jewish speculators speaking in German and Yiddish, respectively: "Baron, the boy is stealing your handkerchief!" "Let him go, we also started out small." The slippage between the two languages, which would have been comprehensible to the magazine's readers, reinforces the portrayal of Jews as morally lax.

scholars posited that Ashkenazim had once spoken the same German as their Christian neighbors, but, by dint of cultural isolation or immigration, the German of these Jews either became atrophied or devolved into a corrupted variant. Thus, Herder "ascribes to Jews a process of decay produced by the changing cultures and geographies of diaspora existence," with deleterious impact on their language that, in turn, "signals a decline in national consciousness" as Jews.[6] Other scholars characterized Yiddish as evidence that Ashkenazim never mastered German properly in the first place but either "deliberately cultivated a language of their own" or "were simply not capable of speaking 'proper German.' "[7]

As noted earlier, Jews in German states began to shift their language of daily life from Yiddish to German during the eighteenth century, as part of a larger refashioning of Ashkenazic culture. This change took place in response not only to their Christian neighbors' contempt for Yiddish but also to these Jews' desires to integrate into a Germanic social and cultural mainstream. Both the initiative of Reform Judaism to reconceive Jewish life as a religion parallel in scope to Protestantism and the intellectual agenda of the Haskalah advocated for the abandonment of Yiddish as a salubrious advance.[8] Philosopher Moses Mendelssohn, who is generally recognized as the progenitor of these developments, argued that the traditional vernacular of Ashkenazim was an impure mixture of German and Hebrew that hindered effective communication and was even symptomatic of a moral corruption.[9]

The discourse of Yiddish as a disabled and disabling language did not end with these Jews' shift to German. On the contrary, during the nineteenth century their Christian neighbors extended the pathologizing of Yiddish to its perceived vestigial presence in the idioms and inflections of these Jews' German speech. As German language assumed a central role in defining a collective, normative Germanness, its defenders asserted that the efforts of Jews, as ineluctable aliens, to assimilate the language could never succeed. Rather, their impaired German would inevitably reveal their diseased Jewish selves, through the telltale symptom called *jüdeln* or *mauscheln*.

Some German-speaking Jews internalized the anti-Semitic ideology that Jews were intractably stigmatized by Yiddish, which infused their rhetoric—even when they spoke "perfect" German—and exposed their Jewishness. As a result, historian John Efron observes, "German-Jewish hostility to Yiddish was a sentiment made all the more neurotic because of the proximity of the two languages. Linguistic familiarity bred contempt."[10] Historian Sander Gilman argues that this pathologizing of Jewish language "served as the basis for self-hatred," in which Jews' efforts to enter mainstream German culture and "deal with their real fear of being treated as a Jew" compelled them to "accept the qualities ascribed by [Christian German speakers] to their own language" and "ingratiate [themselves] into European society through self-hatred."[11]

Remarkably, this self-hatred later engendered a radical revaluation by some German-speaking Jews of the symbolic worth of Yiddish and its eastern European speakers. During the final decades of the nineteenth century, certain intellectuals, including the philosopher Martin Buber, developed an interest in the Yiddish-speaking eastern European Jew as an object of contemplation, which they could use to redefine their own sense of Jewishness by taking "an older, anti-Semitic model of nonacceptable Jewish language . . . and transform[ing] it into a positive image." Eventually, German Jews identified eastern European Jewry as providing "an idealized image of the 'good Jew,' " in contrast to "the pathology of 'self-hatred,' an illness attributed to [western European] Jews."[12] Rather than characterizing Yiddish as diseased, its abandonment—and what this exemplified for German Jews as the loss of a forthright Jewish authenticity—became the illness. Thus, author Arnold Zweig, writing in German, characterized the eastern European Jew as having "a life that is lived to the fullest" and asserted that "Jewish ideas live in him and through him." However, Zweig feared that an encroaching modernity would compromise eastern European Jews, as had already happened among Ashkenazim to the west: "Will there still remain this Eastern Jewry in its ethnic richness and authenticity? For this is the last part of the Jewish people on earth which has created its own new songs and dances, rituals and myths, languages and forms of community."[13]

In fact, many *maskilim* in eastern Europe had followed the lead of German Jewry by repudiating Yiddish. However, they did so in a different milieu, shaped by its own constellation of languages and their uses. In addition, advocates for the Haskalah in this region grappled with a different set of external economic and social circumstances as well as the internal challenge posed by Hasidism. Benjamin Harshav characterizes the posture of eastern European *maskilim* toward Yiddish as "intimate and hated at the same time," their rejection of it constituting a recoil "from their parents' home in the *shtetl*, corroded by idleness and Jewish trading, and from the world of prayer, steeped in the scholastic and irrelevant study of Talmud, and the irrational and primitive behavior of the Hasidim."[14]

• • •

This "vituperative maskilic condemnation" of Yiddish, Efron notes, "runs like a red thread through all Jewish discourse concerning Hebrew from the eighteenth to the twentieth century."[15] What coalesced as a *shprakhnkamf* between Hebraists and Yiddishists at the turn of the twentieth century continued to rage for decades. Hebraists' anti-Yiddish sentiments perpetuated some of the pathologizing tropes that had originated generations earlier among Christian writers and were adopted by *maskilim*. As Hebraists embraced Zionism, they extended the attack on Yiddish by characterizing it as "a perverted language . . . reflecting the perversion of the soul of the Diaspora Jew."[16] Some Hebraists linked longstanding associations of Yiddish and women with the anti-Semitic pathologizing of Jewish men as feminine, and therefore weak. Consequently, many Zionists viewed Yiddish as either a cause or a symptom of Jewish emasculation and disempowerment.

The repudiation of Yiddish was especially consequential in Palestine, as Zionists struggled to establish Modern Hebrew as the sole language of Jewish settlers, many of them native Yiddish speakers who were often far from fluent in Hebrew.[17] In 1910, Labor Zionist leader and future prime minister of the State of Israel David Ben-Gurion (né David Grün) argued against the party issuing publications in Yiddish, insisting that they use only Hebrew in order to ensure "our future as a healthy nation."[18] Yiddish came under especially strong attack for its association with the diaspora as a locus of Jewish "subservience and decline" and for its evocation of "the degenerate commercial agent," still mired in "bitter exile," as opposed to the *haluts* (Hebrew: "pioneer"), the secular Zionist ideal of the healthy Jew.[19]

Even as eastern European Jews who immigrated to Palestine strove to adopt Modern Hebrew as their vernacular, the perceived threat of Yiddish contamination endured. In his efforts to correct the pronunciation of Hebrew among his followers, right-wing Zionist leader Vladimir Jabotinsky decried their "slovenly pronunciation, lacking any line or rule or taste" as evidence of having "jargonized [i.e., Yiddishized] our speech and defiled our language." Similar to the anti-Semitic mockery of Jews' Yiddish-inflected German as *mauscheln*, Jabotinsky also decried the singsong typical of traditional Yiddish speech as the "tune of the ghetto," describing it as not merely "ugly" but a "sick frenzy" that is "the result of the Diaspora" and "is nothing but an echo of this national disease."[20]

When Yiddish-speaking immigrants arrived in large numbers in the United States at the turn of the twentieth century, their language often met with apprehension and disdain. On New York's Lower East Side, home to the country's largest concentration of Yiddish speakers, the "jargon of the street" indexed a community associated with unsanitary and morally suspect conditions.[21] In addition to scorn from much of the Anglo-Saxon establishment, given its dim view of newly arrived immigrants generally, Yiddish was held in low regard by German-speaking Jews who had come to America from western Europe in the middle decades of the nineteenth century. Yiddish was mocked in vaudeville sketches, joke books, and early comic sound recordings, as part of the broad spectrum of American dialect humor in the popular culture of the period, and was also derided in observations on immigrant life by patrician writers from Henry Adams to Henry James.[22]

Efforts to Americanize immigrants centered on replacing their "Old World" languages with English. Public schools in New York City, home to the largest immigrant Jewish population in the United States, strove to suppress students' use of Yiddish. Historian Deborah Dash Moore reports that a German Jew who was superintendent of schools on the Lower East Side during the early 1900s was an "extremely zealous Americanizer" who "forbade children to speak Yiddish among themselves during recess or in the halls and bathrooms" and instructed teachers to "wash out with soap the mouths of those who relapsed." Moore also notes that the city's Board of Education "regularly penalized Jewish applicants for [teacher] certification if their speech was Yiddish accented."[23] A similar concern to remove the stigma associated with this sound inspired the Jewish Theological Seminary to hire an elocution instructor to teach immigrant rabbinical students how to speak English without a Yiddish intonation.[24] In light of this extensive pathologizing of Yiddish, Leo Wiener remarked at the turn of the twentieth century that "there is probably no other language in existence on which so much opprobrium has been heaped."[25]

• • •

Repeated assaults on the health of Yiddish galvanized the language's advocates to come to its aid. The discourse of Yiddish as a disabled language and a disabling presence in Jewish life prompted the language's defenders to make the case for its linguistic health and its beneficial value for Jews. This undertaking paralleled the concomitant *Muskeljudentum* (German: "muscle Jewry") movement, initiated by Zionists at the turn of the twentieth century for "the physical transformation of the Jew"[26] through participation in athletics, as a response to anti-Semitic critiques of Jewish bodies as habitually weak or racially inferior. By emulating the standards of Western culture, whether linguistic or gymnastic, Jews strove to demonstrate their fitness both to other Europeans and as Jews wished to perceive themselves, refracted through the prism of their neighbors' sensibility.

Yiddish literature played a salient role in defending the language, both as a subject of writing and in the deployment of literary activity as the foundation of modern Yiddish culture. During the late nineteenth century, some of the most prominent Yiddish writers saw their task as not only to compose and publish in the language but also to advocate for its value. Early in his career, Sholem Aleichem undertook unprecedented efforts to promote Yiddish literature by issuing two landmark anthologies in 1888 and 1889. In the first of these collections he addressed the importance of establishing principles for a proper literature of the Jewish people in their vernacular, with regard to form (including orthography) as well as content. Sholem Aleichem denounced escapist Yiddish fiction and championed literature that engaged the actualities of contemporary Jewish life in eastern Europe.

Sholem Aleichem's conceptualization of this literature was retrospective as well as prescriptive. He constructed a "great tradition" for Yiddish letters in the form of a genealogy, in which he positioned Sholem Yankev Abramovitsh as its grandfather and himself as Abramovitsh's grandson.[27] This implicitly biological schema imparted to Yiddish literature an image of organic continuity and growth. Naomi Seidman argues that Sholem Aleichem's patriarchal genealogy also refuted notions of Yiddish as feminine, with its connotations of weakness and intellectual inferiority, thereby making this literature "safe for men."[28]

Related to this dynastic vision of Yiddish letters is the embrace of Abramovitsh, Sholem Aleichem, and Isaac Leib Peretz as the literature's *klasiker* ("classic figures"). Their stature as founders of modern Yiddish literature was secured following their deaths in close succession: Peretz in 1915, Sholem Aleichem the following year, and Abramovitsh the year after that. Coinciding with the great upheavals of eastern European Jewish life during World War I, these authors' passings marked the end of a formative period in Yiddish letters and the beginning of another era. The *klasiker* figured prominently in the flourishing of interwar secular Yiddish culture on both sides of the Atlantic. The anniversaries of their births and deaths occasioned commemorative events, their collected works were published in multivolume editions, and selections were incorporated into the curricula of secular Yiddish schools. Some of these schools were named after the *klasiker*, and their portraits hung in classrooms, comparable to the display of political leaders' pictures in government-run schools. Hailing these writers as "classic" supported the high-culture status that Yiddishists sought for this literature, and the public display of these writers as iconic leaders implied that Yiddish literature constituted the voice of a thriving nationality.

Yiddish schools became an important proving ground for establishing a standard language, with a regulated phonology, orthography, and grammar. Beyond pedagogical concerns for teaching correct usage, secularists deemed a standard Yiddish essential for a language of high culture shared across a widely scattered speech community. Reflecting on this issue in the years immediately following World War II, linguist Roman Jakobson maintained that "under conditions of diaspora, a rigorously unified standard is even a much more vital premise for the being and development of a cultural language than

In this textbook illustration, a classroom in a secular Yiddish school is decorated with portraits of the three *klasiker* (*from left to right*): Abramovitsh, Sholem Aleichem, and Peretz. From David Bridger's primer *Der onheyber* (The beginner), first published in New York in 1941 by Farlag matones, for use in schools run by the Sholem Aleichem Folk Institute.

it is in a closely-knit speech community. There cannot be approximate knowledge of a literary language for its users. Full mastery or illiteracy—*tertium non datur*."[29]

In addition to legitimating Yiddish as a vehicle for high culture, standardization served as a hallmark of a thriving modern national language. A standard language not only facilitates comprehension across a nationality's regional, class, and other internal divisions. It also requires an authoritative body and a social system capable of establishing and implementing language regulations on a scale that exemplifies a cohesive nationality.[30] To forge this shared language, standardization imposes constraints on a speech community's actual usage, restricting existing options in spelling, vocabulary, and grammar. Deviations from the standard may be marked as regionalisms or colloquialisms, connoting a lesser stature, or they may be identified as foreign or otherwise inadmissible elements that fall outside the standard's boundaries. During the first decades of the twentieth century, Yiddishists committed to establishing a standard language embraced this task, despite a general lack of social and political resources for realizing language regulation as well as a geographically and ideologically disparate speech community that, on the whole, demonstrated little enthusiasm for conforming to a common version of Yiddish.

Efforts to promote a standard Yiddish have employed the discourse of language purity and health, especially with regard to Germanisms deemed inadmissible as *daytshmerish*. In a 1913 essay on the tasks of Yiddish language development, political and cultural activist Ber Borochov asserted that, "far from being corrupted German, it was Yiddish that was being corrupted *by* German."[31] Max Weinreich likened *daytshmerish* to *shatnez*—cloth made of an "impure" mix of linen and wool fibers and therefore unfit for use by traditionally observant Jews.[32] Both Borochov and Weinreich inverted the rubric of language purity that had been used to denigrate Yiddish as a contaminated merging of German and Hebrew to repudiate the mingling of modern Yiddish with modern German as the true adulteration. In place of Germanists' diagnosing the corruption of their language as due to Jewish obstinacy, backwardness, or laxity, Weinreich attributed the problem of *daytshmerish* to Jews' linguistic negligence and lack of regard for Yiddish. Mordkhe Schaechter invoked the biological model of language health when revisiting the issue of language standardization in 1969. Schaechter examined different arenas of contemporary Yiddish usage, especially the popular press, to assess the degrees to which the language was "susceptible" to the influence of modern German or was relatively "immune."[33]

Much of the foundational scholarship on Yiddish by its supporters strove to demonstrate its fitness as a language and a subject of study. In a landmark article published in 1863, Shiye-Mordkhe Lifshits defended Yiddish by analogizing its characteristics to major European languages, comparing its hybridity to that of English and likening the relationship between Yiddish and German to that of French and Latin.[34] In his 1907 essay "In Defense of the Yiddish Language," Matthias Mieses made similar arguments: "The tongues of Molière and Victor Hugo, of Cervantes and Lope de Vega, of Dante and Tasso, of Shakespeare and Byron are as much jargons as the language of Mendele and Morris Rosenfeld. . . . From a philological viewpoint, in its development our people's tongue is not below the Romance languages."[35] Subsequent scholarship on Yiddish often stressed the orderliness of the language, flouting its derogation as lacking in rules. Max Weinreich emphasized the systematic character of Yiddish as a fusion language both in its origins and in its development over centuries of expansion, negating views of the hybrid character of Yiddish as "haphazard, sloppy, uncouth, unsystematic."[36] Uriel Weinreich theorized the regional variations of Yiddish as a "structural dialectology" that not only reveals cohesion in dialect regions but also correlates these speech territories with the dynamics of Ashkenazic social and cultural history.[37]

More recent scholarship defends the vigor of Yiddish in the face of longstanding notions to the contrary. Dovid Katz's 2014 study of "Yiddish and power" challenges stereotypical associations of the language with diaspora Jewry's political weakness. Katz traces the history of Yiddish from its earliest manifestations to the present, highlighting the language's role as an empowering force in the lives of Ashkenazic Jews over the centuries. Thus, he hails the wealth of Yiddish cultural activities during the first decades of the twentieth century, undertaken almost entirely without external support, as "one of the most successful language-for-power movements in human history."[38]

Complicating the question of the fitness of Yiddish is a slippage that sometimes occurs between its instrumental and its symbolic value—analogous, perhaps, to disparities between a person's physical and mental health. There can be striking differences between Jews' use of Yiddish and the sentiments they attach to it. Just as *maskilim* could hold the language in contempt, even as they continued to speak and write Yiddish, it has been possible for others to proclaim their love of the language while having little or no command of it.

In the post-Holocaust era the discourse of Yiddish as unhealthy continues, but its significance has shifted. Seldom characterized as a diseased language or a disabling presence in Jewish life, the rhetoric has shifted to concerns for the viability of Yiddish. The language is often regarded as a "fabulous invalid"—ailing but enduring in the face of repeated threats to its existence.[39] Rather than a symptom of its corruption, the infirmity attributed to Yiddish has become emblematic of its tenacity. At the same time, this defiant discourse entails new concerns by raising the possibility of this long-suffering language's eventual demise.

# 8
# Religion

The connection of Yiddish to Jewish religiosity may seem self-evident and straightforward. Yet there is a remarkable range of interrelations between the language and Ashkenazic Jews' observances and tenets. So wide-ranging and mutable are these relationships that they not only challenge any simple connection between Yiddish and Judaism but also question the aptness of "religion" as a relevant concept for understanding Yiddish-speaking Jewry for much of its history. Indeed, *religye* is a distinctly modern word in Yiddish, compared to more venerable terms signifying Jewish devotional practice or conviction: *din, das, halokhe, khok* ("rabbinic law"); *mineg, regiles, shteyger* ("custom"); *frumkeyt, tsidkes, yires-shomayim* ("piety"); *emune, betokhn* ("faith").

As noted earlier, the oldest evidence of the language now called Yiddish concerns its role as a vernacular used in devotional scholarship to translate sacred texts. At least as far back as Rashi's eleventh-century glosses, the "language of Ashkenaz" has been used to render *loshn-koydesh* words comprehensible in familiar terms. Today the practice of studying sacred texts by translating them into Yiddish continues among some *haredim*, including in settings where it is no longer the language of daily life.[1] The movement between the language of sacred texts and the vernacular was bilateral. Thus, Aramaic terms of rabbinic discourse entered the general vocabulary of Yiddish speakers, such as the following: *agev* ("by the way"), *aderabe* ("to the contrary"), *avade* ("certainly, definitely"), *gufe* ("itself"), *dehayne* ("namely"), *dafke* ("deliberately, precisely"), *legabe* ("concerning"), *mistame* ("probably"), *nafke-mine* ("distinction"), *sugye* ("topic of discussion"), *kashe* ("question, problem"). These and other terms appear in the contemporary phenomenon called Yeshivish, which emerged after World War II as an exigent language for Talmudic study among immigrant Yiddish-speaking instructors teaching American-born Anglophone yeshiva students.

Yiddish has long been employed to comment on Ashkenazic ritual observance, as evinced by the earliest known recorded Yiddish sentence: *Gut tak im betage / se veyr dis makhazor in beys hakneses trage* ("A good day comes / to the one who carries this prayer book into the synagogue").[2] Found in the 1272 Worms *mahzor*, this rhymed couplet offers a vernacular recognition of the social practice of conveying this large, elaborately ornamented tome into the synagogue on special occasions.

Yiddish books describing local customs for holidays and life-cycle observances date as far back as the beginning of the sixteenth century.[3] In some Passover Haggadahs published at this time, the canonical Hebrew and Aramaic text is imbricated with Yiddish instructions on the seder's ceremonies; later editions of the Haggadah also sometimes include translation and commentaries in Yiddish.[4] Indeed, from their first appearance in the 1500s and for centuries thereafter, books published in their vernacular provided a general Ashkenazic readership with renderings and elaborations of sacred texts, literary adaptations of biblical narratives, guides to the observance of ritual obligations and customs, works of moral exhortation, and an expansion of liturgy for women. These books fostered new devotional practices for Ashkenazim outside the learned elite, which could be termed, albeit anachronistically, "popular religion."[5]

Translations of the Bible into Yiddish consolidate in book form the language's long-standing use to study this sacred text by glossing it into the vernacular. The format of these books evolved over time, beginning with *Mirkeves ha-mishne*, a Hebrew/Yiddish concordance issued in Cracow in 1534. The earliest printed Yiddish translations of the Bible, published in 1544 in Augsburg and Constance, emulate the syntax and morphology of Hebrew in word-for-word translations that imitate the traditional

The oldest known Yiddish sentence, inscribed in open spaces within the letters of the Hebrew word בדעתו, in the Worms *mahzor* of 1272. (From the National Library of Israel.)

pedagogical practice of rendering the Hebrew text into the form of Yiddish known as *ivre-taytsh*. Subsequent renderings integrate the biblical narrative with homilies and commentaries in a running Yiddish text.[6] Rather than simply serving as aids to deciphering the original Hebrew, these works could stand on their own, engendering new devotional reading practices in the vernacular.

The best-known Bible translation into Yiddish of this kind, and the most frequently reprinted work in the language, is *Tsene-rene*. Compiled by Rabbi Jacob ben Isaac Rabbino of Janova in the early seventeenth century, *Tsene-rene* soon became a mainstay of Ashkenazic piety. The earliest extant edition of this work was issued in Hanau in 1622; its title page references earlier printings issued in Cracow and Lublin. Many dozens of editions of *Tsene-rene* have since been published, eventually including translations into other languages.[7] The text of this popular work changed over time. Yiddish typefaces, orthography, and grammar were updated to reflect shifts in usage; additional commentaries were sometimes added to the text, as were illustrations.[8] Though its form has varied, *Tsene-rene* exemplifies the Bible's enduring place in the domestic devotional practices of Ashkenazim. Moreover, this book complements the male-centered recitation of Scripture during communal synagogue worship with the practice of private, domestic reading, often by women, parallel to the relationship between public, collective Hebrew prayer and the individual recitation of Yiddish *tkhines*.

During the early modern period, Yiddish translations of other Hebrew texts (prayer books, books of moral instruction), as well as original Yiddish works on Jewish customs and ethics appeared for the express purpose of making devotional and didactic materials more accessible to the Ashkenazic public. Some of these works integrate instruction with engaging narratives, such as the *Ku-bukh* (Book of cows, 1595), which combines edifying fables with earthy humor. Other texts elaborate biblical episodes in the form of epic poetry, including *Seyfer melokhim* (The book of kings, ca. 1515), *Shmuel-bukh* (The book of Samuel, 1544), and *Doniel-bukh* (The book of Daniel, 1557). These verse narratives not only were read but also were sung. (The texts of other early modern Yiddish epics mention that they were set to the melody of the *Shmuel-bukh*.)[9] In addition, Yiddish plays were staged on the festival of Purim as part of its carnivalesque observances. These folk dramas adapted the book of Esther or another biblical narrative ("The Selling of Joseph" being especially popular) and sometimes interpolated comic or parodic material, in keeping with the ludic spirit of celebrating

Purim.[10] Hebrew manuscripts and publications outnumber the inventory of extant Yiddish texts during this period. However, the latter corpus represents a wider engagement by Ashkenazim with sacred narratives and devotional practices, reaching men, women, and children in their vernacular.

• • •

Hasidic leaders began to promulgate a radically new approach to Jewish spirituality during the late eighteenth century, beginning in small towns in western Ukraine and soon spreading throughout much of eastern Europe. Yiddish was put to innovative use in realizing core principles of Hasidism. The language figured strategically in the movement's commitment to popularizing esoteric mystical teachings and practices. In addition, Yiddish helped empower the movement's charismatic leaders, variously called *rebeyim* ("masters") or *tsadikim* ("saintly men"), who served their followers as spiritual mentors and as mediators with God. Preaching and storytelling in Yiddish imbued the language with new significance as a demotic point of entry to transcendent exultation, along with other practices of daily life, such as singing, dancing, and feasting, that Hasidism invested with an elevated stature.

Not only were foundational Hasidic texts disseminated in Yiddish; it was the primary language of oral communication between the *tsadik* and his community, a practice widely maintained to this day. Innovative customs distinctive to Hasidism are marked by terminology that transforms common Yiddish words into the names of spiritually charged phenomena: each *tsadik* has a *hoyf* ("court"), where he ministers to his followers; there, a Hasid arranges to meet with the *tsadik* for guidance on personal matters by submitting a written request, called a *kvitl* ("note"). Hasidim gather with their *tsadik* on the Sabbath and holidays for a festive meal, known as a *tish* ("table"), at which he offers discourses on sacred texts appropriate to the occasion. While praying, a male Hasid wears a *gartl* ("sash") around his waist to symbolically separate the upper, more spiritual part of his body from the lower part.[11]

Hasidim were not the only Jews in eastern Europe to regard Yiddish with a newly deliberate awareness of its value in maintaining piety at this time. Moshe Sofer (known as the Hatam Sofer), a leading rabbinic authority in Moravia and Slovakia during the early decades of the nineteenth century, insisted that Jews should maintain Yiddish in opposition to the linguistic assimilation advocated by the Haskalah. Sofer rooted this conviction "in a

Talmudic source," notes historian Jacob Katz, the purpose of which was "to distance Jews from their non-Jewish surroundings."[12]

The advent of secular ideologies among Yiddish speakers at the turn of the twentieth century not only posed further challenges to east European Jewish piety but also inspired innovative practices involving the language among traditionally observant Jews. Political movements, Yiddish newspapers, schools, and theater instantiated new forms of Jewish culture that were ambivalent, if not hostile, toward Jewish piety. The widespread appeal of these developments soon prompted traditionally observant Jews to adapt these new practices to their own purposes. At the start of the twentieth century, they established political organizations—the non-Zionist Agudath Israel and the Zionist Mizrachi—which later employed Yiddish in interwar Poland to field candidates in elections, publish journals, and sponsor school systems and youth groups.[13] Like secular Yiddishists, these organizations fostered a continued commitment to Yiddish, in the face of Jews' increased adoption of state languages as vernaculars, while asserting the importance of Yiddish as a mainstay of Jewish piety.

After World War II the relationship of traditionally observant Ashkenazim with Yiddish changed both instrumentally and symbolically. As the language figured less in other Jews' religiosity, the use of Yiddish, whether as a language of daily life or a language of devotional study, came to distinguish *haredim* from other, less stringently observant Ashkenazim. Indeed, some *haredim*, especially Hasidim, use Yiddish both to maintain connections to east European traditions and to articulate the divide between themselves and other Jews, including those who speak the language. Thus, some Hasidim will refuse to speak Yiddish with less pious Jews.[14]

Contemporary Hasidim use Yiddish for internal communications through newspapers and magazines as well as with posters displayed on exterior walls in some Hasidic neighborhoods. These posters, which can include texts in Hebrew, Russian, and English as well as Yiddish, promote communal policies and agendas, announce events, and advertise goods and services. For Hasidim, information on these posters reinforces authoritative figures, institutions, and practices; for other people in these locales, the posters' presence denotes a Hasidic enclave, materializing the audial presence of Yiddish speakers and thereby, according to sociologist Samuel Heilman, constituting "an assertive . . . taking over [of] the public space."[15]

Contemporary Yiddish books for Hasidic adults include instruction on pious conduct and hagiographies of *tsadikim* as well as works of fiction that

Advertisement for a sale on *shtraymlekh*, fur-trimmed hats worn by married Hasidic men on holidays and special occasions, which was posted on the street in Boro Park, Brooklyn, in the 1990s. The Yiddish text interpolates some English-language terms in both the Roman alphabet and the *alef-beys*.

provide entertaining reading compatible with community values. Yiddish also appears in a wide assortment of products for Hasidic children—picture books, board games, puzzles, coloring books, stickers—that foster language learning in conjunction with reinforcing pious practices and beliefs. Thus, the preface to *Di yidishe shprakh, undzer tsirung* (The Yiddish language, our jewel) states that this workbook links "teaching children how to write Yiddish without mistakes" with "inculcating values of devotion to God and good conduct."[16] Recordings of Yiddish songs as part of what has been termed "Orthodox popular music" provide a similar melding of instruction with entertainment,[17] as do videos of Yiddish plays staged on Purim or during Succos. These recordings sometimes identify the performers as "*heymishe yunge layt*"—that is, young men who are members of Hasidic communities (whose protocols of modesty forbid women from performing in the presence of men). Here, the Yiddish word *heymish*—pronounced *haymish* by most Hasidim—is assigned a distinctive meaning. Whereas the word more generally means "homey, intimate, familiar, informal," Hasidim use *haymish* to signify that which is normative within their communities.[18] In addition to identifying performers or performances as *haymish*, the word has been used in advertising to signify as acceptable services by musicians and health-care providers, as well as a variety of products, including baked goods and even a brand of kosher imitation seafood.[19]

As extensive as their commitment is to Yiddish as a language of daily life, Hasidim also value the language for its circumscribed role within their complex multiglossia. This constellation of languages also includes *loshn-koydesh*, used in worship and devotional scholarship; Hungarian or Polish, which had been spoken in pre–World War II locales, now mostly used among older Hasidim; and current local languages: English in New York, London, and Melbourne; Flemish and French in Antwerp; French and English in Montreal; Israeli Hebrew in Jerusalem. How a Hasid employs these languages conforms to particular contexts of speaking, reading, or writing and is further differentiated by the Hasid's gender, generation, level of education, occupation, and particular community.[20]

Moreover, the languages used among Hasidim can seem fungible, not only to an outsider but also to members of their own community. American Hasidic women reported to Ayala Fader that neither their children nor they themselves are always sure what language they are speaking. What Fader distinguishes as Hasidic English is infused with Yiddish, as Hasidic Yiddish is with English (especially among women) and *loshn-koydesh* (especially among men).[21] Even as Hasidim attribute a defining value to using Yiddish, rather than their neighbors' vernaculars, hybridization of what are conventionally understood as discrete languages is extensive. Consider the text on a sticker, sold in a Hasidic Brooklyn neighborhood in the 1990s, given as a reward to children for doing well at reciting their prayers:

I Davened
געשמאקן![22]

What would be "I prayed with gusto!" in English or "איך האָב געדאַוונט געשמאַק! / *Ikh hob gedavnt geshmak!*" in Yiddish is rendered in two different alphabets and what are arguably three distinct languages: English,

Jewish English (in which "to daven" is conjugated like a regular English verb, hence the past tense "davened"), and Yiddish.[23] In addition, the sticker's text invokes yet more language: liturgical *loshn-koydesh*.

Given the fluid character of their multiglossia, Hasidim can find scrutiny of language use to be a fraught issue. Whereas some Hasidim make more conscious efforts to bolster the use of Yiddish, especially through its curricularization, others have worried that increased attention to standardizing Yiddish usage and expanding its lexicon smacks of Yiddishism. Beyond its association with secularism, the notion of Yiddishism raises concerns for Hasidim as an undue devotion to Yiddish for its own sake. Thus, explanations of Yiddish grammar and vocabulary featured in a Hasidic family magazine in the early twenty-first century inspired one reader to write in, complaining, "Who says that there has to be a Yiddish word for everything? Not all languages are equally rich."[24] Rather than weakening Yiddish, Hasidim regard constraints on the scope and use of the language as bolstering its power to signify their communities' distinct piety. As a linguistic gatekeeper, Hasidic Yiddish both limits its speakers' access to the larger world and separates them from other Jews.

At the same time, Yiddish has emerged as a language of nonconformist cultural creativity among some individuals who have left Hasidic communities and as a vehicle for dissent by others who choose to stay. Several former or marginalized Hasidim have participated in the creation of film and television dramas, spoken partly or entirely in Yiddish, that scrutinize Hasidic mores: *Mendy* (2003), *Romeo and Juliet in Yiddish* (2010), *Where Is Joel Baum?* (2012), *Félix and Meira* (2014), *Menashe* (2017), and *Unorthodox* (2020).[25] In defiance of their leaders' condemnation of the internet, growing numbers of dissident Hasidim, including those remaining in their communities, avail themselves of the anonymity afforded by this medium to air criticisms of communal corruption or voice doubts about theological tenets, using both Yiddish and English. Fader terms these covert writers a heretical "counterpublic" that has "challenged the authority of the ultra-Orthodox religious public sphere."[26]

• • •

The relationship of Yiddish with Jewish piety also includes its rejection by some speakers. Secular Yiddishism separates the authority of the rabbinate and the observance of rabbinic law from Jewishness and reconceptualizes it exclusively as an ethno-national identity. This phenomenon originated at the turn of the twentieth century among Jewish revolutionaries in the Russian empire, who sought to engage in international class struggle while maintaining a collective Jewishness through vernacular language. On this political foundation Yiddishists developed a secular culture centered on the written word—newspapers and other periodicals, as well as works of history, political theory, and belles-lettres—and engaged through an array of performances: lectures, rallies, community choruses, theatrical productions. Historian Barry Trachtenberg observes that for the founding generation of secular Yiddishists, the language "was more than a practical instrument through which to further their revolutionary nationalist aspirations. Rather, it was the highest expression of the Jewish people and contained the potential to transform their existence within the Russian empire."[27]

Secular Yiddishists have had a distinct relationship with religiosity that extends beyond its abandonment. They have replaced the definitional role of piety with their own authorities and ideals, realized in an alternate array of practices. Political leaders, authors, performers, public intellectuals, and cultural activists replace clergy and other traditional scholars, educators, and preachers as community authorities; the rational pursuit of humanistic knowledge replaces Jewish devotional study; political activism and expressive works of high culture replace worship and sacred texts. Originally embraced as the common language of the Jewish masses, Yiddish has assumed among these secularists the elevated stature, if not the sanctity, traditionally attributed to *loshn-koydesh.*

At its most programmatic, secular Yiddishism has nevertheless remained engaged with religiosity, even when it serves as a negative model. In the Soviet Union, state-approved Yiddish culture was not merely secular but forthrightly anti-religious, producing literary works and propaganda that repudiated rabbinic authority and ridiculed traditional Jewish practices such as circumcision and dietary rules. However, literature scholar Anna Shternshis notes, instead of either realizing the state's envisioned integration of Jews into a common Marxist ethos or simply resisting state efforts to eradicate Jewish traditions, Soviet Jews of the 1920s and 1930s evolved a self-styled, hybrid culture of old and new, official and unofficial, public and private—a way of being both "Soviet" and "kosher."[28]

At the same time, secular Yiddishism in the Americas developed beyond its radical origins. As the language came to play a central role in defining Jewishness, irrespective of a particular political ideology, Yiddishism became, in effect, a civil religion, providing foundational value to a Jewish collective with the same gravitas as a religious identity. Secular Yiddishists have reworked elements of traditional Jewish religious practice, exemplified by their transformed definition of the word *shul*. Originally meaning "synagogue," *shul* more recently came into use as a Yiddish term for a modern, non-religious school, along with other terms: *shkole* (cf. Polish *szkoła*, Russian *shkola*) and, in America, *skul*. Secular Yiddish primers published in the United States taught the word *shul* as meaning only "school," referring specifically to the secular Yiddish school and implicitly negating the older meaning of the term as "synagogue."[29]

Similarly, canonical Jewish texts and traditional observances have been transvalued as fundaments of secular Yiddish culture. The rendering of the entire Hebrew Bible into modern literary Yiddish by the poet Yehoash (né Solomon Blumgarten), first published in 1926, was hailed as "a refined work of modern art"—a cultural, rather than religious, achievement.[30] In the 1930s, American secular Yiddishists inaugurated the *driter seyder* ("third Passover seder"), which remade the centuries-old domestic ritual commemorating ancient Israelites' freedom from Egyptian slavery, traditionally understood as an act of divine redemption, into a communal gathering, at which the performance of Yiddish music and drama recalls the Exodus as a paradigm of an ongoing human struggle for freedom that extends beyond Jewish experience. For some secular Yiddishists, the history of Jews' persecution, from ancient times to the present, has inspired a commitment to the struggles of other oppressed peoples, both in the United States (for example, the Civil Rights movement) and abroad (the Spanish Civil War).[31]

• • •

As a language forged by Jews living amid Christian majority populations, Yiddish has been shaped by European Jewry's long, complicated relationship with Christianity. The language distinguishes between Christian and Jewish phenomena, sometimes with terms that are neutral in connotation, such as *yontef* ("Jewish holiday") ~ *khoge* ("non-Jewish holiday"), *davenen* ("to pray [as a Jew]") ~ *molyen zikh* ("to pray [as a Christian]"), *kloyz* ("Jewish chapel") ~ *kaplitse* ("Christian chapel"). Other terms for Christians or Christianity, however, are derogatory, such as *sheygets* ("Christian boy"), which can also mean "rascal," and *tifle* ("Christian house of worship"), which is related to a Biblical Hebrew word meaning "folly" or "immorality." These terms exemplify what is known as *lehavdl-loshn*—literally, "separation language"—vocabulary used to distinguish between Jewish and non-Jewish subjects. Moreover, inserting the term *lehavdl* between these two kinds of phenomena serves as a rhetorical marker signifying this divide.

Early works of Yiddish literature also articulate this distinction, whether by excising or emending Christian elements in German or Italian epics when they were rendered in Yiddish[32] or by including polemics against Christian theology in Yiddish literary expansions of biblical narratives. Such is the case with *Shire fun Yitskhok* (The song of Isaac) and *Akeydes Yitskhok* (The binding of Isaac). These sixteenth-century adaptations of Genesis 22:1–19 in prose and poetry, respectively, obliquely refute Christian readings of Abraham's near sacrifice of his son as prefiguring the death and resurrection of a messianic Jesus and assert instead this episode's significance for Jews' enduring covenant with God.[33] Zalman Zvi Aughausen's *Yidisher teryak* (Jewish antidote), published in 1615, offers a singularly forthright riposte in Yiddish against Christian anti-Jewish accusations.[34]

Historian Elisheva Carlebach observes that the culture of early modern Ashkenazim "had built in strategies of internal resistance to the religious narrative of Christian society, trenchant polemic in the guise of folklore."[35] This practice is exemplified by a sizeable corpus of folkways concerning Christmas—including names, lore, and observances for the holiday—that constitute a counter-practice in which familiarity with Christianity inspires Jewish ripostes. There are more than a dozen different terms for Christmas among Yiddish dialects, in addition to *nitl*, the most common word. Some of these terms are bilingual puns, such as *veynakht* ("woe night"), a play on German *Weihnachten* ("Christmas eve").[36] This ludic term epitomizes the eastern European Jewish response to Christmas, both acknowledging and flouting this source of anxiety. This pattern is also manifest in Yiddish terms for Jesus, which either observe a taboo against uttering his name—instead referring to Jesus obliquely as *oyse ish* ("that man") or *der tole* ("the one who was suspended")—or deride the notion of his divinity. Thus, calling Jesus "Yosl Pondrik" or "Yoshke Pondre" references *Toledot Yeshu* (History of Jesus), a medieval Hebrew work, later translated into Yiddish, which debunks claims that Jesus is the Messiah and asserts instead that he was the illegitimate son of a Jewish woman and a man named Pandera.[37]

Prominent among Christians' varied interests in Yiddish during the early modern era was the desire to use the Jews' vernacular to understand their heretical beliefs and thereby provide a point of entry to their conversion. Missionaries issued multiple translations of the New Testament into Yiddish—dating as early as 1540, making this publication of Christian Scriptures in "*vesta Judaica*" among the first printed books of any kind in the language.[38] Efforts to instruct Christians in Yiddish for the purpose of evangelizing among Ashkenazim include Johann Christoff Wagenseil's 1699 *Belehrung der Jüdisch-Teutschen Red- und Schreibart* (Instruction in speaking and writing Judeo-German) and courses in the language offered at the University of Halle in the 1700s, the first institution of higher education anywhere to do so.[39] Among the most dedicated Christians to this undertaking was the eighteenth-century Lutheran theologian Wilhelm Christian Justus Chrysander, who "offered Yiddish courses and published a Yiddish textbook as well as a theological tractate on the importance of learning Yiddish—all in the name of the missionary cause."[40] Protestant missionizing to Jews in Yiddish continued well into the twentieth century. In the United States, "evangelical institutions of higher learning, such as the Moody Bible Institute, established programs to train professional evangelists to the Jews," including the study of Yiddish. It is remarkable, notes religion scholar Yaakov Ariel, that in America "conservative Christian schools of higher learning offered courses in Yiddish decades before secular . . . or Jewish institutions of higher learning did."[41]

As part of this work, American evangelicals published new Yiddish translations of the New Testament, as recently as Henry Einspruch's 1941 rendering of *Der bris khadoshe*. In his review of the translation, Yiddish writer Melech Ravitch encouraged Jews to read the book, praising the quality of the rendering and insisting on its value in the Yiddish literary canon as a work that no "intelligent Jew" could "afford to ignore."[42] Yet shortly before Ravitch subverted the significance of this translation, recasting its intended challenge to Jewish belief as a validation of the cosmopolitan capacity of secular Yiddish literature, the Yiddish literary world had been roiled by Sholem Asch's 1939 novel *Der man fun Natseres* (published in English translation as *The Nazarene*). When the novel first appeared in serialized form in the *Jewish Daily Forward*, both critics and members of the reading public decried the renowned author's sympathetic portrayal of Jesus.[43] As a result, the newspaper discontinued the novel's publication, terminating its longstanding relationship with Asch, and a secular Yiddish school in Brooklyn that had been named in honor of the author removed his name from its building.[44]

The extent to which Christians who have had some contact with Ashkenazim could understand and speak Yiddish is difficult to ascertain, in part due to the multiple variables this entails: the time, place, and context of interaction between particular Christians and Jews, their respective ages, genders, educations, occupations, and so on. On one hand, the Christians who operated the presses that printed the first Yiddish books often relied on converts from Judaism for their knowledge of the language, implying the publishers' limited command of Yiddish.[45] Issuing books to teach Yiddish to Christian German speakers, beginning at the turn of the eighteenth century, evinces both a considerable interest in learning Yiddish and a lack of opportunity to acquire sufficient knowledge of it through interactions with Ashkenazim. On the other hand, the closeness with which Jews and Christians have long encountered one another in daily life as neighbors, in business transactions, and through employment—in particular, Christian women who worked in Ashkenazic homes as servants, starting in the Middle Ages—suggests that there have been considerable opportunities for Christians to become familiar with Yiddish.[46] There are occasional references in memoirs and literary works to Christians' use (and sometimes comic misuse) of Yiddish in eastern Europe, as well as examples of how some Jews developed code words to evade comprehension by Christians, implying their considerable familiarity with the language.[47]

In the United States, non-Jews' ability to speak Yiddish has occasionally been presented as a piquant oddity—such as actor James Cagney's snippet of Yiddish dialogue in a scene from the 1932 gangster film *Taxi*—or as a sign of cross-cultural enrichment, as in US Secretary of State Colin Powell's recalling the Yiddish he learned as a young man in the Bronx while working for a Jewish employer.[48] Now seldom an object of Christian suspicion, Yiddish is increasingly learned, sometimes masterfully, by non-Jewish scholars and performers, for whom the language and its cultural resources provide intellectual stimulation or creative allure.

Beyond its longstanding significance as an index of traditional Ashkenazic piety, Yiddish may be spoken, read, or written today by an ardent Jewish secularist, an agnostic scholar of comparative literature, a disgruntled Hasidic blogger, or an impassioned non-Jewish folksinger. For these individuals as well, Yiddish facilitates a devotion of some kind—to Ashkenazic culture, past or present; to their intellectual pursuits or ideological convictions; or to the Yiddish language itself. As these developments undo the longstanding tautology uniting Yiddish language with its speech community and a way of life, they expand the possibilities of who might turn to the language to embody new notions of *yidishkeyt*.

# 9

# Education

For most of its existence, Yiddish has been acquired by Ashkenazim mimetically as a first language. As is typical of vernaculars, young children in Yiddish-speaking milieus learn from their immediate environment to comprehend and produce the language through imitation and experimentation. They may well acquire other vernaculars simultaneously (if, say, they grow up in multilingual households) or subsequently (for example, as immigrants in contact with new neighbors) and may study additional languages in school or independently. What distinguishes learning Yiddish according to this model, even when it occurs in a multilingual context, is its intimacy as the everyday language of one's home and community, the utterance of Yiddish implicitly identifying the speaker with *yidishkeyt*.

Yiddish is proverbially known as *di shprakh vos redt zikh*—"the language that speaks by itself"—suggesting that it inheres in the native speaker. At the same time, characterizing Yiddish as "speaking by itself" implies that it has an anthropomorphic agency of its own. Traditional practices of learning Yiddish and of using it as a language of instruction long assumed this foundational notion of Yiddish as native, even autochthonic. But as the education of Ashkenazim became more varied, complex, and contentious, the bonds between *yidish* and *yidishkeyt* and between the language and its speakers were loosened, problematizing what it might mean for Yiddish to "speak by itself."

The acquisition of Yiddish in traditional Ashkenazic communities contrasts with learning how to read biblical and liturgical Hebrew, known as *ivre*. In keeping with the general pattern of internal Jewish diglossia, *ivre* entails reading and reciting, rather than conversing. *Ivre* is acquired through schooling, with Yiddish, the students' first language, serving as the language of instruction. Even when learning *ivre* begins at an early age, per traditional Ashkenazic practice, it is through Yiddish that the meaning of holy writ is understood. The engagement with *ivre* centers on language in its written form and is passive, a matter of mastering canonical texts rather than creating new ones. By contrast, vernacular Yiddish entails active, ongoing innovation in the course of its use.

Traditional teaching of *ivre* involves a set of cultural practices that mark the language as instrumental to fulfilling the Jewish male's onus of devotional study. For example, celebrating the first day of a young boy's formal instruction in the Jewish alphabet with a special ritual dates to the Middle Ages among Ashkenazim in German lands, and similar practices were observed in eastern Europe.[1] In contrast to the deliberateness of studying *ivre*, learning Yiddish as one's first language does not involve ceremonial recognition, nor does it require the rigors of instruction. Thus, Max Weinreich asserts, likely with traditional Ashkenazic pedagogy in mind, "No one was ever flogged for not knowing Yiddish."[2]

Yiddish has, of course, long been written as well as spoken. Learning to read or write Yiddish differs from studying *ivre*, which begins with mastering the Jewish alphabet. Among vernacular speakers of Yiddish, by contrast, literacy in the language typically follows some degree of oral fluency. Consequently, learning to read Yiddish—which also uses the Jewish alphabet, though with some key differences—has traditionally been a corollary of studying *ivre*. The practices of reading and writing Yiddish were discussed in some of the earliest published texts in the language, including the translation of *Seyfer mides* (Book of virtues) issued in Isny in 1542 and an edition of *Yosifon* (an expanded adaptation of ancient Jewish history texts by Flavius Josephus) in Yiddish, printed in Zurich in 1546.[3] Composed in the language itself, these guidelines may have been intended to instantiate principles of Yiddish orthography in the then-new medium of print.

Given the ostensibly automatic nature of acquiring Yiddish as an internal vernacular, it is not surprising that the first efforts to provide some kind of formal instruction in the language came from without its speech community. As noted previously, the earliest works devoted to teaching Yiddish are German-language publications by and for Christians, first appearing at the turn of the eighteenth century. The readers of these books were motivated to learn Yiddish for a variety of reasons, including Christian theological studies, business interactions with Jews, efforts to convert them to Christianity, and their policing (this last motive reflecting a longstanding interest in connections between Yiddish and *Rotwelsch*). Jeffrey Grossman notes that all these efforts sought to reform and regulate Jews' lives through external mastery of their vernacular with the ultimate goal not of enhanced engagement with Ashkenazim but of making their "use of Yiddish unnecessary."[4]

In fact, at the same time that instruction in Yiddish gained popularity among these Christians, their Jewish neighbors were beginning to adopt

German as their vernacular. Part of the reason for this change was externally imposed on Yiddish speakers, in the form of laws in the Habsburg Empire and German states requiring the use of German language for documenting business transactions and maintaining Jewish communal records, among other official practices.[5] Educational motives internal to Jews in German lands reinforced this move. The Haskalah's advocacy of pursuing secular knowledge and the new consciousness it prompted regarding Jewish language use inspired the movement's adherents to study European languages of high culture and develop their command of Hebrew as a language for belles-lettres and intellectual exchange. Most *maskilim* did not consider Yiddish worthy of a similar commitment. Indeed, far from maintaining its longstanding role as the vernacular language of instruction in traditional Ashkenazic education, they argued that Jews should reform their approach to the study of sacred texts. Moreover, they deemed knowing Yiddish to be a sign of *Unbildung* (German: "lack of education") and therefore something that should be unlearned, especially given the extent to which the language stigmatized Jews in the eyes of their Christian neighbors.[6]

• • •

In eastern Europe, maskilic derogation of Yiddish did not prompt a large-scale shift away from the language. However, the Haskalah did inform early discussions of how Yiddish might be used to engage modern ideas and practices, including through innovations in education. *Maskilim* as a rule dismissed the notion of Yiddish as a language for modern schooling, conforming to the Russian Empire's prohibition of this possibility except in traditional religious instruction. In fact, the only formal education most eastern European Jews received throughout the nineteenth century took place in a *kheyder* or *talmed-toyre*—private or communally run schools providing traditional elementary education in *ivre* and core devotional texts.[7] Though primarily intended for boys, similar schools for girls (called *meydl-kheyder*) became more common by the turn of the twentieth century.[8]

A small but growing number of wealthier and more worldly eastern European Jews who wished their children to pursue an alternative to traditional Jewish education sent them to gymnasia, secondary schools in which the language of instruction was Russian in the Romanov Empire or German in the Habsburg Empire. Often these schools forbade Jewish students to speak Yiddish.[9] During the mid-nineteenth century, *maskilim* opened a small number of schools that aimed to establish a modern approach to Jewish education. In most of these institutions as well, Yiddish was eschewed, viewed as inimical to modern pedagogy. In the words of *maskil* Shmuel Yosef Fuenn, the language was deemed "an iron wall" that separated Jews from their educated neighbors and "did not allow any ray of scientific light to penetrate."[10] While these modern institutions attracted only a limited number of students, growing numbers of eastern European Jews pursued private study of secular subjects, such as mathematics or other European languages, either on their own or with tutors.

A minority of *maskilim* in eastern Europe did, however, recognize the value of Yiddish for promoting the principles of the Haskalah, and this inspired the first efforts to create modern schools for Jews where Yiddish was either a subject of study or a language of instruction. The earliest of these include the Öffentliche Israelitische Hochschule (Israelite Public High School), established by Joseph Perl in Tarnopol in 1809, and a similar school founded by Avram ben Sholem Hacohen in Brody in 1845.[11] A Jewish girls' school that opened in Vilna in 1830 offered instruction in Yiddish as well as Russian, German, and French.[12] Such efforts testify to the ambivalence with which these *maskilim* regarded Yiddish as an acknowledged presence in Jewish life, on one hand, yet in need of reform through curricularization, on the other hand. More generally, eastern European followers of the Haskalah could not accept Yiddish as it was. Through changes in Jewish education, the language had to be either improved or superseded, consistent with the maskilic view of traditional Ashkenazic life generally.

A more widespread innovation in Yiddish education reached eastern European Jews in the form of *brivnshtelers* ("correspondence manuals"). These books began to appear in the mid-nineteenth century, as letter writing became more prevalent with the development of modern postal systems in Europe. In the course of providing examples of business and personal correspondence in Yiddish, *brivnshtelers* presented models of proper penmanship, orthography, and grammar, thereby teaching Yiddish speakers basic skills for self-expression in the written language. In addition, these books sometimes included lessons in arithmetic (for commercial correspondence) and sample texts for students to copy. Some of these texts addressed topics such as the natural sciences and geography, thereby introducing secular subjects and the possibility of learning about them in the students' vernacular.[13] *Brivnshtelers* were widely used by both men and women for self-study or tutorial instruction. These manuals continued to be published into the early twentieth century on both sides of the Atlantic, as immigrants in the Americas depended on letters to maintain contact with family and other acquaintances in Europe.

Systematic, sustained efforts to use Yiddish in secular classroom settings are a twentieth-century phenomenon, arising from new ideological commitments to the language and changes in its speakers' social and political circumstances. In eastern Europe, advocacy for Yiddish-language schools preceded their realization by several years. In 1906 journalist Yoysef Beker asserted in the Bundist periodical *Folkstsaytung* (People's newspaper) that such schools were necessary because "a child will achieve a measure of normal development only when he is taught in his mother tongue."[14] The following year, a group of progressive Jewish educators in Vilna convened to discuss establishing modern Yiddish-language schools. As the conference was illegal, its participants were arrested, but they continued their meeting in prison.[15] Calls for educating Jewish children in their native language were issued at a landmark conference on Yiddish held in Czernowitz in 1908 and in an official resolution issued by the Jewish Labor Bund in 1910.

Remarkably, these aspirations were first realized during World War I in eastern European territories under German occupation. To counter the hegemony of Russian culture in the region, German forces mandated the establishment of schools in which the children of each ethnolinguistic group were taught in their native language. Creating these Yiddish schools entailed multiple difficulties, including the dearth of both suitable pedagogical materials and qualified teachers fluent in Yiddish. In addition, the schools' advocates faced the challenge of convincing skeptical parents of the feasibility, as well as the value, of a secular education in Yiddish, which was opposed by traditionally observant Jews as well as those who wished to educate their children in a European language of high culture.[16] Though Yiddishists championed modern schools for Jewish children in their first language as "normal," efforts to realize this vision exposed the complexities of eastern European Jews' multilingualism, both instrumentally and symbolically. Indeed, much of the work undertaken to create modern Yiddish-language education did not simply employ this vernacular but transformed it.

• • •

After World War I, the range of educational possibilities available to Jewish children in eastern Europe's newly established nations included a variety of schools run in the Yiddish language. They were made possible by provisions in treaties signed at the 1919 Paris Peace Conference guaranteeing the rights of minority educational and cultural institutions in these countries. Yiddish-language schools were administered either by the state (in Estonia, Latvia, and Lithuania) or by Jewish communities (in Czechoslovakia, Poland, and Romania). In most cases, Jewish political organizations established these schools, forthrightly linking education with ideology. The most extensive Yiddish-language school system in Poland, then home to Europe's largest Jewish community, was the Tsentrale yidishe shul-organizatsye (Central Yiddish School Organization). Known by the acronym TSYSHO, these schools were founded in 1921 by members of the Jewish Labor Bund and left-wing Labor Zionists, who shared commitments to promoting socialism and fostering a secular Yiddish culture. At its peak, TSYSHO enrolled some twenty-four thousand students in over two hundred schools throughout Poland, ranging from kindergarten through high school, and also ran vocational training, a teachers' seminary, and a children's sanatorium. To address this enterprise's manifold newness—socially, politically, and culturally, as well as pedagogically and linguistically—TSYSHO published textbooks for students and issued curricula and educational studies for teachers.[17]

Realizing the ideological commitment to providing modern education in Yiddish tested its limits as a vernacular. These schools needed to create instructional materials and develop new vocabulary for fields of study, such as the natural sciences. Moreover, educators had to establish standards of Yiddish-language usage, from penmanship to grammar. This undertaking involved a population of both students and teachers whose command of Yiddish was sometimes limited. Many Jews who were qualified to teach in these schools spoke little or no Yiddish and acquired expertise in their fields of knowledge at university, where they had become fluent in German, Polish, or Russian and embraced the mainstream secular culture. A growing number of Poland's younger Jews were raised in Polish-speaking homes, and more young Jews were studying the language in the classroom, as mandated in all the nation's schools, including those in which Modern Hebrew or Yiddish was the language of instruction. Thus, when students who spoke only Polish enrolled in the Vilna Jewish Technical School, where all instruction was in Yiddish, they had to learn the language in order to study such subjects as mechanics or applied physics. The students used textbooks with newly developed lexicons for these fields and were often taught by instructors for whom Yiddish was also an unfamiliar language.[18]

The advent of secular Jewish schools in eastern Europe prompted the development of educational alternatives for traditionally observant Jews, using modern pedagogy toward traditional ends. The key innovation concerned girls' education, as boys continued to study in yeshivas. Bais Yaakov schools, founded by Sarah Schenirer in Cracow in 1917, soon educated thousands of girls in Jewish Scripture, ethics, and prayer, while employing innovative pedagogical practices, such as staging plays, going on outdoor excursions, and reading world literature in translation.[19] Yiddish was the language of instruction in these schools. Most Bais Yaakov schools only offered classes in the afternoon, and many of their students attended Polish public schools during the day. Consequently, Bais Yaakov viewed Yiddish as a bulwark against cultural assimilation and fundamental to promoting traditional piety. Supporters of Bais Yaakov asserted that their commitment to Yiddish was different from—indeed, inimical to—that of secular Yiddishists, who were denounced as *apikorsim* ("heretics"). Bais Yaakov's advocates argued that their schools did not "fetishize" Yiddish, unlike TSYSHO and other secularist institutions, but used the language to guarantee "cultural distinctiveness to Jews" while providing "a continuity of generational heritage going back to antiquity." Notwithstanding their divergent ideologies, both TSYSHO and Bais Yaakov adopted modern measures to standardize and curricularize Yiddish, and each felt it necessary to justify maintaining the language as a means of upholding a distinct, proud Jewishness.[20]

Concurrently, Yiddish-language schools figured prominently in the Soviet Union's array of official institutions for its Jewish citizens. In keeping with a policy of the Soviet Union during its early years to offer all children an education in their respective native languages, these schools taught every subject in Yiddish. The language was essential for recognizing Jews as an official national minority in the Soviet Union, as they were understood as not having a defining territory, unlike Armenians, Ukrainians, and other nationalities. Yiddish-language schools both received unprecedented governmental support and were subject to unparalleled state oversight, as was true for other components of Soviet Yiddish culture. Soviet Yiddish schools promoted the state's class-based social and economic revolution and repudiated capitalism and religion. These principles informed all aspects of pedagogy, including Yiddish-language instruction and state-approved curricula on Yiddish literature. Thus, stories in children's primers praised Lenin and Stalin, while demonizing clerics and the bourgeoisie.[21]

At their peak, Yiddish-language schools in the Soviet Union enrolled over a hundred thousand students. However, more Soviet Jews sent their children to Russian-language schools, believing that they offered a superior education and provided children with better professional futures. As state support for national minority cultures was curtailed during the 1930s, the number of Yiddish-language schools declined, as did enrollments. Soviet Yiddish educational institutions were all shuttered during World War II; a limited postwar revival of these schools came to an end by 1951, as part of the state's suppression of all public forms of Yiddish culture.[22]

While only a minority of Jewish children enrolled in these various Yiddish schools, the language played an increasingly important role in adolescent and adult self-education during the twentieth century's first decades, especially among large numbers of laborers and immigrants who lacked opportunities for formal study and had limited command of other languages. Of special note among the array of Yiddish publications for autodidacts are textbooks printed in Poland, the United States, and Palestine for learning other languages, among them Arabic, English, Esperanto, German, Modern Hebrew, Polish, Portuguese, Russian, and Spanish. These include languages spoken by neighbors (or potential neighbors of would-be immigrants) as well as languages of high culture or ideological conviction.[23] Though written to explain the workings of other languages, these textbooks also implicitly taught their readers Yiddish grammar by analogy.

• • •

In the wake of Yiddish-speaking Jews' mass emigration from eastern Europe, schools to teach the language to their children were established during the first decades of the twentieth century in western Europe, the Americas, South Africa, and Australia.[24] These institutions mark a threshold change in learning Yiddish and exemplify the impact of immigration on Yiddish culture generally. Teaching children Yiddish in these new multilingual settings grappled with the larger question of the language's future beyond its role in immigrants' lives as it became, for ensuing generations, something other than their first language and other than a vernacular.

In the United States, home to the largest number of Yiddish-speaking immigrants, the first schools that taught the language to Jewish children were established in the 1910s, several decades after the efflorescence of American Yiddish culture in the form of press, literature, theater, and political activism, all of which served adult immigrants.[25] By 1930 there were four major secular Yiddish school systems in the United States. Then at the height of their popularity, these schools enrolled almost 10 percent of those American children (and some 20 percent in New York City) who received a formal Jewish education.[26] As in Europe, the organizations that established these schools integrated their commitment to Yiddish with a political or cultural ideology: Farband (Labor Zionism), Arbeter Ring (Workers Circle; socialism), Sholem Aleichem Folk Institute (Jewish secularism), and Internatsyonaler arbeter-ordn (International Workers' Order; communism). Adding children's schools to these organizations' other undertakings reflected a growing awareness of the disparity between immigrants' command of Yiddish and that of their children. Almost all of them attended public schools, where English was the sole language of instruction and immigrants' children were often discouraged from speaking their parents' "Old World" languages. A 1920 study on teaching English to the "foreign born" asserted that there is "no question that it is the will of the people that no child in America shall grow into citizenship without mastering the language of America." At the same time, this study noted the challenge educators faced in fulfilling this goal, especially given "the close connection in the alien's mind between language and religion," noting that, for the immigrant, "religious devotion and feeling are inextricably bound up with the native language."[27]

In fact, a commitment to teaching Yiddish to immigrants' children extended beyond secular Jews. Some Orthodox Talmud Torahs, afternoon and weekend schools that taught children to read biblical and liturgical Hebrew, also offered instruction in Yiddish. A primary motive for doing so was to prepare boys to deliver a speech in the language on the occasion of becoming a bar mitzvah. During the first decades of the twentieth century, this practice nominally enacted speaking Yiddish as a sign of coming into Jewish adulthood.[28]

For Orthodox as well as secular American Jews, teaching Yiddish to the next generation figured in larger efforts to negotiate a changing relationship with their European past—which came to seem more remote in the wake of World War I and the subsequent curtailment of mass immigration—and in their concerns for the future of Jewish life in the United States. Immigrants committed to Yiddish may have perceived their native fluency in the language, their solidarity with its speech community, and their devotion to its culture to be innate. But as this appeared increasingly not to be the case for the next generation, these native speakers had to consider how their children might acquire a similar familiarity with Yiddish, and all that it represented, through schooling.

Yiddish primers published in the United States in the decades before World War II, used in both Talmud Torahs and secular schools, reveal how the innovative practice of learning the language in a classroom setting was configured as an extension of linguistic and cultural endurance. For example, many of these primers begin by teaching the same first word—*mame* ("mother")—in conjunction with an illustration of a mother cradling a child. Though these introductory lessons use this iconic image to invoke intimate, intergenerational linguistic continuity, this connection was, in fact, disrupted by the very books in which these lessons appear and the classrooms in which children learned Yiddish. Even though English had become the primary language of many immigrants' children, Yiddish was to be regarded, at least symbolically, as their *mame-loshn*.[29]

Secular Yiddish schools not only transformed the way that the immigrant Jewish child learned the language; they also became centers of communal activity for students' families, presenting programs and celebrations that enacted a new Jewish culture realized in Yiddish. The reach of secular Yiddish education extended further to summer camps, where both children and adults inhabited temporary utopian environments in which Yiddish was the official language for cultural performances as well as routines of seasonal recreation.[30]

• • •

The state of Yiddish after World War II raised unprecedented questions about how the language might be both viable and meaningful for future generations. Within less than a decade, the Holocaust destroyed half of the world's Yiddish speakers as well as their educational and cultural infrastructure. The worldwide displacement of those Jews still alive at the war's end further roiled language continuity. Nevertheless, secular Yiddish education for children continued in the early postwar decades, in both existing venues and new institutions established by survivor communities in Europe (for example, in Paris and Łódź). The fate of these schools has varied, sometimes in response to political circumstances. Such was the case in Poland, where Yiddish education was constrained and eventually shuttered by government policies during the communist period, which culminated in the expulsion of most of the country's Jews in the late 1960s. In immigrant Jewish communities beyond Europe, schools that taught Yiddish were also affected by new social trends, notably a shift toward studying Modern Hebrew at the expense of Yiddish among Jewish communities in the Americas, South Africa, and Australasia. Yet as secular Yiddish pedagogy declined in some locations, it has emerged elsewhere. In 1975, Bundists who were among the Holocaust survivors settling in Melbourne, Australia, established the Sholom Aleichem College, a day school for elementary-level students where Yiddish language and literature continue to be taught as part of the school's commitment to "'veltlekhe yiddishkayt'—a secular approach to Jewish history, traditions and customs, ethics and values."[31] Plans to create "a dual-language Yiddish-English program in a New York City public school" were proposed in 2019, to start the following year.[32]

The postwar dedication of Hasidim to maintaining Yiddish as a language of daily life has engendered an expansive pedagogical apparatus for children. Yiddish remains the language of instruction in most Hasidic yeshivas and is a subject taught in Hasidic girls' schools. Similar to immigrants' creation of American Yiddish schools in the early twentieth century, most Hasidic girls' schools opened decades after Hasidim had established new postwar communities, reflecting their awareness of the intergenerational rupture in linguistic continuity wrought by the Holocaust and postwar migrations. Just as secular Yiddish schools integrated ideological instruction with language learning, Hasidic girls' schools combine lessons in Yiddish with moral edification and preparation for the students' future as pious wives and mothers.[33]

The general postwar decline of secular Yiddish education for children coincided with the advent of courses in Yiddish language in higher education, as part of the rise of Jewish studies in universities in North America and western Europe. In this context, learning Yiddish is a choice young adults make for themselves, rather than a decision parents make for their children. For some students, electing to study Yiddish may be part of their Jewish questing; for others, including students who are not Jews, the choice may arise from scholarly pursuits in history, linguistics, literature, religion, or other fields of study or from an artistic interest in Yiddish as actors, musicians, or writers.

This new configuration for studying the language was set forth in 1949 in Uriel Weinreich's *College Yiddish*, the first book for university-level study of Yiddish published after World War II. As a work of humanistic scholarship, *College Yiddish* does not assume an audience of Jews but one of language students. At the same time, the book validates the tenacity of Yiddish in the wake of the Holocaust, by proclaiming that the language "unites Jews from every country."[34] Weinreich's textbook includes language lessons and supplementary readings that present an interdisciplinary vision of Yiddish studies, embracing history, linguistics, literature, folkloristics, and sociology, among other fields. Inspired by the first generations of modern scholarship on Yiddish, and emulating in particular the agenda of the prewar YIVO Institute, Weinreich's model anticipated the realization of Yiddish studies in postwar universities by decades. In recent years, intensive Yiddish-language programs have been offered, usually in the summer, by institutions of higher education in Australia, Belgium, Canada, England, France, Germany, Israel, Lithuania, Poland, and the United States. These programs attract participants from diverse backgrounds and interests and thereby model expansive possibilities for Yiddish as a language to be studied both as an end in itself—often separate from ethnic, religious, or ideological affiliation—and as a point of entry to further endeavors.

• • •

The dynamics of Yiddish education resemble the plot of a Bildungsroman. Following the trajectory of a sentimental education, an anthropomorphized Yiddish speaks "by itself" in its early years. It then becomes newly self-conscious, as its long, youthful innocence comes to an end with the advent of the Haskalah. Thereafter, Yiddish no longer simply speaks on its own but increasingly requires schooling of some kind—even when the language serves as an instrument of pedagogy. As Yiddish matures, it encounters educational opportunities and challenges posed by new neighbors, ideologies, and governments. It is roiled by war and mass immigration and survives a genocidal assault on its very existence, albeit in a much-altered state, prompting the pursuit of newly concerted efforts of study. If, in its current stage of educational development, Yiddish may speak more deliberately than ever before, it does so perhaps with the wisdom of years, with greater self-awareness.

# 10
# Literacy

Beyond the ability to read, literacy can be reckoned as "a continuum of learning" that enables both personal development and participation in community life.[1] The dynamics of Yiddish literacy, in this expanded sense, entail the advent of new print technologies and cultural practices, as well as transformations of educational opportunities for Ashkenazim, their geographic shifts, and their ideological movements. Following the advent of print in Europe, books and other publications in Yiddish became mainstays of Ashkenazic culture, concomitant with the impact of printing on the rise in use and prestige of other European vernaculars. Print both stabilized Yiddish and endowed it with an elasticity unprecedented in diaspora Jewish vernaculars, eventually enabling it to span northern Europe in a form that transcended local dialects and then to become an international language read by millions. The history of Yiddish publishing over more than five centuries reflects changing understandings of literacy among the language's speakers—that is, notions of who reads Yiddish, what they read, and how and why they do so. Moreover, these developments track the evolving potential of this vernacular to serve as the voice of literate Jews.

Yiddish books and periodicals also evince, if at times obliquely, the shifting constellation of languages engaged by Ashkenazim. Throughout the history of print, they have always had some access to publications in other languages. Translations into and out of Yiddish, as well as multilingual texts that include Yiddish, also figure prominently in Ashkenazic print culture. Issued with few exceptions independent of state support, yet often contending with governmental regulations, Yiddish publications reveal Ashkenazic readers' shifting interests amid a variety of external constraints and opportunities as well as increasing options in multiple languages.

By the end of the sixteenth century a sizeable corpus of books had been published for Yiddish readers in western and central Europe, revealing divergent notions of vernacular literacy among Ashkenazim in the early modern period. Many of these titles extend traditional Jewish study and practice, whether through translations from Hebrew or in original works, including biblical narratives rendered in verse that evince a familiarity with German, Italian, or Hebrew prosody. Alongside these works appeared Yiddish renderings of literature from non-Jewish sources, notably heroic epics adapted from German or Italian texts, including *Bovo Dantona* (Bovo of Antona, first published in 1541) and *Kinig Artis houf* (King Arthur's court, first printed in 1671, following earlier sixteenth-century manuscripts).[2] These works manifest both a sizeable interest among Ashkenazim in the literature of their neighbors and the limited number of Jews who could read these texts in their source languages.[3] As the first presses that printed Jewish books were owned and run by Christians, all Yiddish publications of this period evince the involvement of non-Jews in the fashioning of Ashkenazic literacy—often obliquely, yet sometimes readily apparent, for example, in early Yiddish books' use of illustrations from non-Jewish sources.[4]

Unlike canonical works in *loshn-koydesh*—including editions of the Bible, prayer books, and the Talmud—Yiddish books competed for readers in the marketplace, as promotional notices on the title pages of some of these publications reveal. *Lev tov* (A good heart), a book of moral instruction first published in Prague in 1620, exhorts customers: "Do not tarry, buy it quickly, while you still find it cheap. It also has good paper and ink; even a blind man can see it."[5] The title page of the 1602 edition of the *Mayse-bukh* (Book of tales)—a compendium of morally edifying parables and legends, many translated from rabbinic sources—adjures customers to purchase it "and not read from the *Ku-bukh*," a rival Yiddish publication, or the heroic epics *Dietrich von Bern* and *Meister Hildebrant*, "for they are truly nothing but dirt."[6]

These paratexts also frequently state that Yiddish books were meant for a general Jewish public: adults and children, women and men. Yiddish literacy thus defined a non-elite Jewish readership, distinguished from gentile readers but situated lower in the hierarchy of Jewish learnedness than scholars fluent in *loshn-koydesh*. Nevertheless, Yiddish books could boast that they provide readers something commensurate with rabbinical erudition, if not authority. The aforementioned introduction to the *Mayse-bukh* promises that after the reader has mastered its contents, "the whole world will be astonished at him and every man will say: 'I believe he knows the whole Torah on one foot. As he has such great erudition in the *Gemara*, I believe he knows the whole Torah. Who has seen his like?' "[7] However, the extent to which Jewish legal texts could be translated into Yiddish was subject to rabbinic scrutiny and occasional condemnation. For example, rabbis perceived a transgression of their authority to adjudicate Jewish legal issues when part of the *Shulhan aruch* (Set table), an influential compilation of rabbinic law, was translated into Yiddish in a late eighteenth-century book of moral conduct. They banned the publication, and it was reported to have been publicly burned in Vilna.[8]

As a language that has never stood alone, Yiddish often figures in bilingual or multiglossic reading practices. Among its earliest publications are concordances and glossaries that variously parallel Yiddish with German, Hebrew, Italian, or Latin. Yiddish texts were sometimes integrated into devotional books that are primarily in *loshn-koydesh*, as in the earliest known dated appearance of Yiddish in print: a song inserted into a Passover Haggadah published in Prague in 1526.[9] Bilingual prayer books that juxtapose canonical liturgy with Yiddish translation and, sometimes, commentaries later became mainstays of Ashkenazic publishing.

• • •

Innovations in eastern European Jewish ideology and practice of the late eighteenth century produced new genres of Yiddish publishing and reading practices. Early in the spread of Hasidism, narratives by or about its foundational figures, including *Shivhei ha-Besht* (In praise of the Baal Shem Tov) and the tales of Nahman of Bratslav, were variously published in Hebrew, Yiddish, or bilingual Hebrew/Yiddish editions.[10] These collections reflect the elevated status of vernacular literacy in this spiritual movement, especially the prominent role that storytelling played in Hasidic practice, as part of efforts to democratize Jews' engagements with mysticism and promote the authority of *tsadikim*. Unlike much of earlier Yiddish literature, these Hasidic publications do not translate or adapt biblical and Talmudic narratives or non-Jewish epics but offer original stories, whether accounts of the wondrous actions of the Baal Shem Tov, the movement's progenitor, and later *tsadikim*, or, in the case of Nahman of Bratslav's tales, narratives rich in arcane symbolism. This innovative use of Yiddish storytelling would later be hailed as the beginning of modern Yiddish literature.[11] However, the stories and discourses that *rebeyim* related to their followers in Yiddish were recorded by scribes in Hebrew, reflecting the long-standing complementary relationship in traditional Ashkenazic practice between Yiddish as a primarily oral language and Hebrew as primarily written.[12] Bilingual publications of these early Hasidic works enable readers to engage the orality of the primary act of vernacular storytelling by reading the Yiddish texts aloud, while their

# מעשה א מאבידת בת מלך א

ענה ואמר: בדרך ספורי מעשה ספרתי מעשה שהיה שומעה היה לו הרהור תשובה. וזו היא:

**מעשה** במלך אחד שהיו לו ששה בנים ובת אחת. ואותה הבת היתה חשובה בעיניו מאוד והיה מחבבה ביותר והיה משעשע עמה מאוד. פעם אחת היה מתוועד עמה ביחד באיזה יום ונעשה ברוגז עליה ונזרקה מפיו דיבור שהלא טוב יקח אותך. (דער ניט גוטער זאל דיך נעמן) בלילה הלכה לחדרה. ובבוקר לא ידעו היכן היא והיה אביה מצער מאוד והלך לבקשה אנה ואנה. עמד השני למלכות מחמת שראה שהמלך מצטער מאוד. וביקש שיתנו לו משרת וסוס ומעות על הוצאות. והלך לבקשה. והיה מבקשה מאוד זמן מרובה מאוד עד שמצאה. (עתה מספר איך ביקשה עד שמצאה) והיה הולך אנה ואנה זמן רב ובמדבריות ובשדות וביערים והיה מבקשה זמן רב מאוד. והיה הולך במדבר וראה שביל אחד מן הצד והיה מיישב עצמו באשר שאני הולך כ״כ זמן רב במדבר ואיני יכול למוצאה. אלך בשביל הזה אולי אבא למקום ישוב. והיה הולך זמן רב. אח״כ ראה מבצר (סקורין פגחס) וכמה חיילות היו עומדים שם סביבו. והמבצר היה נאה ומתוקן ומסודר מאד עם החיילות והיה מתיירא מפני החיילות פן לא יניחוהו לכנוס. והיה מיישב עצמו אלך ואנסה. והשאיר הסוס והלך להמבצר והיו מניחים אותו ולא עכבוהו כלל והיה הולך מחדר לחדר בלי עיכוב ובא לפלטין אחד וראה שישב שם המלך בעטורה וכמה חיילות שם וכמה משוררים בכלים לפניו והיה שם. נאה ויפה מאוד והמלך ושום אחד מהם לא שאלוהו כלל. וראה שם מעדנים ומאכלים טובים ועמד ואכל והלך ושכב בזווית לראות מה נעשה שם וראה שהמלך צוה להביא המלכה. הלכו להביא אותה והי׳ שם רעש גדול ושמחה גדולה והמשוררים היו מזמרים ומשוררים מאוד באשר שהביאו את המלכה. והעמידו לה כסא והושיבוה אצלו. והיא היתה הבת מלך הנ״ל והוא (היינו השני למלכות) ראה והכירה. אחר כך הציצה המלכה וראתה אחד ששוכב בזווית והכירה אותו. ועמד׳ מכסאה והלכה לשם

ונגעה

אין וועג האב אויך דער ציילט א מעשה וואס ווער עס האט זוא געהערט הט געהאט א הרהור תשובה:

און דאס איז דיא מעשה

איין מאל איז געוועזן א מלך דער מלך הט געהאט זעקס זון און איין טאכטער. דיא טאכטער איז בייא אים זייער חשוב געוועזן און ער הט זי זייער מחבב געוועזן (כלומר גליבט) און האט זיך מיט איהר זייער משעשע געוועזן. אמאל איז ער מיט איר געוועזן אין איינעם און עפיס אטאג. אין איז אויף איר ברוגז געווארן. האט זיך אים ארוס געכאפט א ווארט דער ניט גוטער זאל דיך אוועק נעמן בייא נאכט. איז זי געגאנגן און איר חדר אריין. און דער פריא האט מען גוט געוויסט וויא זוא איז האט זיך דר פאטער (דהיינו דר מלך) זייער מצער געוועזן און איז געגאנגן זוא זוכן אהין און אהער. איז אויף געשטאנען דר שני למלכות. מחמת ער הט געזעהן. דער מלך האט גרוס צער. און האט געבעטן אז מען זאל אים געבן איין משרת מיט איין פערד. און געלט אויף הוצאות. אין איז געגאנגן זוא זוכן. הט ער זוא זייער גזוכט. זייער אלאנגי צייט ביז ער האט זוא געפונען. (היינט דער ציילט ער וויא אזוי ער הט זוא גזוכט ביז ער הט זי געפונן). איז ער געגאנגן אלאנגי צייט. אין אין מדבריות און אין פעלדער און אין וועלדער אין הט זי גזוכט זייער איין לאנגי צייט. איז ער געגאנגן און אין מדבר. און הט געזעהן א וועג פון דער זייט. הט ער זיך מיישב געוועזן באשר אויך גייא אזוי אלאנגי צייט אין דר מדבר אין קאן זוא ניט געפונען. לאם

אלף

איך גייען אויף דעם וועג. טאמיר וועל אויך קומען צו איין ישוב. און ער געגאנגן אלאנגי צייט דר נאך האט ער געזעהן אשלאס אין אסייך חיילות שטייען ארום. און דער שלאס איז געוועזן זייער שיין אין דוא חיילות זענען ארים געשטאנען כסדר זייער פיין. הט ער מורא געהאט פר די חיילות. טאמר וועלין זייא אים ניט לאזין אריין גיין. האט ער זיך מיישב געוועזן. איך וועל מיך פרובירן. און האט אובר געלאזט דאס פערד אין איז געגאנגן צום שלאס. הט מען אים געלאזט. אין מען הט אים גאר גוט מעכב געוועזן אין ער איז געגאנגן פון איין חדר צום אנדרין אין מען האט אום גיט געווערט. איז ער געקומן צו איין פאליץ האט ער געזעהן. דער מלך זוצט דארט אין איין קרון. און אסייך חיילות שטייען ארום אום. אין איין סך שפילין אויף כלים פאר אום אין עס איז דארט זייער שיין און פיין געוועזן. אי, דער מלך אין קיינער פון זיי הט אום גאר גוט געפרייגט. אין ער הט דארט געזעהן גוטי מאכלים. איז ער געגאנגן און הט געגעסין. און איז געגאנגן אין האט זיך געלייגט אין איין ווינקילי. ער זאל זעהן וואס דארטין וועט זיך טיהן הט ער געזעהן דר מלך האט געהייסן מען זאל ברענגען דיא מלכה. און מען געגאנגן זי ברייגגין. איז דארטין געוועזן איין גרויסער רעש און איין גרוסי שמחה אין דיא קייפעליום האבן זייער געשפילט אין געזונגין. ווייל מען האט געבראכט דיא מלכה. און מען האט איר געשטעלט איין שטול. אין מען הט זוא געזעצט לעבין אום. אין דאס איז געוועזן דיא בת מלך. אין ער הט זוא געזעהן אין הט זוא

דער

The first page of the “Tale of the Loss of the Princess” by Nahman of Bratslav. His collected tales, first published in 1815, are seminal works of Hasidic literature. This bilingual edition, published in Lemberg (now Lviv, Ukraine) in 1902, maintains the practice of printing the Hebrew translation above the Yiddish original. The Yiddish is printed with *nekudes*, a common practice at the time.

rendering in Hebrew imbued these narratives with the imprimatur of sanctity associated with that language. Even though these narratives were first transmitted in Yiddish, bilingual editions of Hasidic tales typically place the Hebrew translation on the top half of the page, above the Yiddish, signifying each language's respective place within Ashkenazic "gradations of sanctity."[13]

The transformation of Jewish literacy advocated by the Haskalah centered on new reading materials and practices that relegated rather than elevated Yiddish. Yet even as *maskilim* in German lands repudiated their traditional vernacular, they sometimes employed Yiddish in their writings, notably in satirical works that ridicule its speakers' worldview and mores. In effect, these *maskilim* turned Yiddish against itself, as part of a larger practice of auto-critique. Isaac Euchel's late eighteenth-century drama *Reb Henekh* exemplifies this deployment of Yiddish. This polyglot text delineates its various characters through different languages and linguistic registers. As Yiddish studies scholar Marion Aptroot notes, non-Jewish characters "speak German, German dialects, or in the case of foreigners, a broken German mixed with elements from their mother tongue." Jewish characters' speech reflects their respective ideologies: traditionally observant Jews, "impervious to the new ideas of the enlightenment, speak Yiddish; the enlightened Jews (and falsely enlightened ones), speak High German; and a character who . . . believes herself to be more enlightened than she really is, occasionally lapses into the local low city dialect" of Berlin.[14] Euchel assumed readers of the play (which was unlikely written to be staged but was perhaps read aloud) would recognize this range of languages and registers and grasp their sociolinguistic implications. Even as *Reb Henekh* ridicules "unenlightened" or superficially enlightened Jews, it requires familiarity with their speech and sensibility. Indeed, their vitality, albeit disparaged, is essential to the drama's plot and its agenda of reforming Ashkenazim.

Reading proved essential to the advance of the Haskalah in eastern Europe, where followers were few in number and often isolated from one another across an expansive region. The circulation of maskilic writings, in both Hebrew and Yiddish, constituted an act of insurgence against a Jewish establishment that generally considered the Haskalah a destabilizing threat. Eastern European *maskilim* made their own innovative, and at times fraught, use of Yiddish literacy to advocate for the Haskalah. *Maskilim* were aware that writing in Hebrew reached an audience limited to a small, largely male elite in eastern Europe, among whom the Haskalah faced stiff opposition. Therefore, some of its advocates turned to Yiddish in order to engage a wider readership. As in an earlier epoch of Yiddish publishing, translation figured prominently in this effort at first. Mendel Lefin rendered selected books of the Bible into Yiddish to encourage eastern European Jews to read Scripture as a maskilic practice. Other *maskilim* decried Lefin's translations as contravening the agenda of the Haskalah, but they were later recognized as pioneering works of modern Yiddish literature.[15] Lefin's Yiddish rendering of Ecclesiastes, prepared during the 1780s, was eventually issued posthumously in 1873, accompanied by his Hebrew commentaries on the text, which were imbued with maskilic principles.[16] This publication juxtaposed two divergent modes of maskilic literacy, exemplifying an unresolved tension regarding language use among *maskilim* in eastern Europe.

Over the course of the nineteenth century, Yiddish publishing in eastern Europe grew in scope and variety, eventually providing a mass readership with a steady supply of books and periodicals. The dynamics of Yiddish literacy reflect larger intellectual, political, economic, and social developments, including shifts in the legality of Jewish publishing. The institution of state censorship in Congress Poland early in the century relied on the judgment of *maskilim*, who attempted to use this regulation to suppress Hasidic publications and books in Yiddish (referred to in an 1820 edict as "the common spoiled language").[17] In the Russian Empire, the number of presses that could print books in Hebrew or Yiddish was severely limited from the 1830s until the 1860s, which ushered in a more liberal era of Jewish culture.

A key figure in the expansion of Yiddish literacy at this time was Ayzik Meyer Dik, subsequently hailed as "the first professional Yiddish writer."[18] Beginning in the 1840s, Dik produced over two hundred books of extraordinary variety, including homilies, romances, satires, parodies, ethnographies, and instructional manuals. Sometimes published anonymously or under a pseudonym, Dik's books included original works as well as adaptations of a wide range of sources (sometimes unacknowledged), from rabbinic narratives to works of fiction and nonfiction originally published in German, Russian, Polish, French, and English. Among these books is a reworking of Harriet Beecher Stowe's abolitionist novel *Uncle Tom's Cabin*, titled *Di shklaferay* (Slavery), issued in 1868. Dik expanded on the maskilic use of Yiddish as a vehicle for satire to write fiction that was both entertaining and morally exhortative. He also produced informational works on history, geography, and mathematics, among other topics. The author's extensive oeuvre introduced Yiddish readers to core principles of the Haskalah: a rationalist approach to piety and the importance of secular knowledge.

Dik's didactic agenda included remaking Yiddish as a literary language. He introduced new terms derived from modern German, sometimes translating them in his texts with words from Semitic and Slavic components of Yiddish that were presumably more familiar to his readers—for example, in an 1865 novel the author glossed *laydenshaft* (cf. German *Leidenschaft*) as *tayve* ("passion") and *geheym* (cf. German *geheim*) as *sakretne* ("secret [adjective]").[19] Dik incorporated Germanisms into Yiddish not to introduce terms for which the language had no equivalent but to fashion it into a suitable vehicle for modern information and concepts by emulating contemporary German and thereby modeling a new notion of Yiddish literacy.

Another pioneer of modern Yiddish culture emerged on the heels of Dik's popularity: Avraham Goldfaden, widely recognized as the founder of modern Yiddish theater. Goldfaden began writing Yiddish plays in the late 1860s and staged his first operettas a decade later, quickly achieving widespread acclaim and establishing theatergoing as a fixture of modern Yiddish culture, a public complement to the private literacy of belles-lettres. Yiddish theater engendered new literacy practices as well, including the publishing of plays (Goldfaden's libretti were issued in Warsaw in the mid-1880s) and the writing of drama criticism.[20]

• • •

The final decades of the nineteenth century witnessed what Benjamin Harshav has termed the "modern Jewish revolution"—that is, eastern European Jewry's abrupt encounter with the opportunities and challenges posed by new social, political, and economic developments: accelerated urbanization and industrialization, the onset of mass emigration out of the region, the rise of radical political movements—all of which demanded that these Jews interrogate assumptions about every aspect of their lives, including their reading and writing.[21] Thus, whereas Dik sought to raise the stature of Yiddish by emulating German, subsequent authors turned to Yiddish because of its distinctive Ashkenazic vernacularity. Most notable among the first to do so are Sholem Yankev Abramovitsh, whom readers associated with his literary persona, Mendele Moykher-Sforim (Mendele the Book Seller), and Sholem Aleichem, Sholem Rabinovitsh's penname, which is the Yiddish equivalent of "Hello!" The unassuming character of their pseudonyms exemplifies the authors' embrace of Yiddish for its quotidian familiarity. Reflecting on his decision to shift from writing in Hebrew to Yiddish, Sholem Aleichem cited its ability to reach a wide public and suggested that the language offered authors an inherent immediacy: "Even when you write in Hebrew, you think in Yiddish—wouldn't it be better for you to write the way you think?"[22]

However, this turn to Yiddish as a literary language was anything but straightforward. Literature scholar Dan Miron notes that almost all Yiddish writers in eastern Europe during this period began their careers in Hebrew or Russian and, when they turned to Yiddish, felt "a compelling need to explain and vindicate themselves" and to defend the language's literary possibilities.[23] Some of these authors continued to write, and occasionally even reworked the same text, in two languages. Most notably, Abramovitsh composed versions of some of his major novels in both Yiddish and Hebrew, the author's movement between the two languages informing his pioneering literary style in each.[24] Shifts among languages continued to shape works by subsequent generations of Yiddish writers. Thus, between 1912 and 1917, S. An-ski (né Shloyme Zaynvl Rapoport) composed different versions of *Der dibek* (The dybbuk), arguably the most famous Yiddish drama, in Russian and Hebrew as well as twice in Yiddish.[25] Philosopher Abraham Joshua Heschel, who also wrote in English, German, and Hebrew, turned to Yiddish at key moments in the beginning, midpoint, and end of his career, spanning the 1930s to the 1970s.[26] These authors' multilingual output did not simply reflect different audiences for their work but juxtaposed different aspects of a polyglot Jewish literacy against one another.

New reading material and practices enabled important developments in the lives of eastern Europe's Jews. Naomi Seidman observes that reading fiction about romantic love helped transform courtship and marriage practices, providing young Jews with greater agency in their choice of marriage partners and redefining expectations of married life.[27] The relationship between literacy and matrimony was reciprocal. Not only did reading romantic literature inform how these Jews approached marriage; they also engaged these intimate experiences through writing, whether in diaries, memoirs, which became an important genre of eastern European Jewish literature during the nineteenth century, or the exchange of courtship letters, which often followed models published in *brivnshtelers.*

By the turn of the twentieth century, reading Yiddish had become an essential practice for a rapidly modernizing eastern European Jewry. Print media constituted a virtual public sphere for an intercontinental Yiddish-speaking diaspora. The flourishing of Yiddish newspapers and other periodicals led the creation of this new print culture and came to epitomize

Jewish modernity. Sporadic efforts to issue Yiddish periodicals in the Russian Empire during the nineteenth century had met with limited success until the laws restricting their publication were liberalized in the first years of the twentieth century. Historian Sarah Abrevaya Stein observes that the Yiddish popular press of this period "changed the texture" of Jewish life by "not only reporting on change but also shaping it."[28] Newspapers established the widespread activity of reading and discussing new information on a daily basis, expanding Yiddish speakers' scope of knowledge and their expectations of literacy. However, "Yiddish newspapers required skill and perseverance" on the part of many speakers whose ability to read the language was limited. "There was no such thing as a casual reader," historian Tony Michels argues. Even carrying a Yiddish newspaper betokened this new form of literacy.[29]

In addition to news, features, and editorials, the Yiddish press published works of literature. During the early decades of the twentieth century, newspapers on both sides of the Atlantic issued weekly literary supplements. Major authors, including Sholem Aleichem, Sholem Asch, and Isaac Bashevis Singer, published serialized versions of long prose works in the press before they were issued in book form. Yiddish newspapers also conducted surveys and contests and printed letters, opinion pieces, recipes, and other submissions from readers, thereby making this new form of literacy an interactive public practice.[30]

As Yiddish book publishing proliferated, it catered to different audiences, reflecting diverging notions of the cultural value of Yiddish literacy. Highbrow aspirations are epitomized by literary anthologies, which strove to curate the best of new writing or establish literary canons of historical depth. Thus, Morris Bassin's anthology of five hundred years of Yiddish poetry, issued in 1917, opens with a *shabes-lid* ("Sabbath song") written in Erfurt in 1410 and concludes with a selection of contemporary poems, followed by linguistic and bibliographic annotations by Ber Borochov.[31]

Concurrently, sensational, lowbrow fiction and drama, collectively referred to as *shund*, proved enormously popular with audiences in eastern Europe and abroad. These works often used lurid plots to address provocative contemporary social issues, such as relations between the sexes, intergenerational conflict, and class struggle.[32] *Shund* became a ready target for writers seeking to establish Yiddish literature as the equal of highbrow European belles-lettres. Sholem Aleichem offered a trenchant critique of *shund* in his 1888 essay "Shomers mishpet" (Shomer's trial), which decried the output of Nokhem Meyer Shaykevitch, known to his readers by the pseudonym Shomer.[33] Nevertheless, Shomer's writings remained popular on both sides of the Atlantic, and his success doubtless inspired other authors to produce new works of *shund*. As the genre continued to flourish, so did its denunciation—for example, in American Yiddish theater criticism during the first decades of the twentieth century and in the interwar Polish Yiddish press.[34]

Many readers of *shund*, especially a largely working-class Jewish public with limited reading skills in other languages, also turned to Yiddish as a vehicle for popular education. Publishers in Europe and the United States produced books for self-study in history, geography, political science, philosophy, mathematics, the natural sciences, and foreign languages. Series of celebrity biographies proved especially popular. In New York at the turn of the twentieth century the Internatsyonale Biblyotek Farlag (International Library Publishing Co.) began issuing books on famous Jewish figures, among other topics, while Warsaw's Farlag Progres (Progress Press) published titles on popular science as well as "lives of significant people."[35] During the interwar years, the Groshn-biblyotek (Penny Library), based in Warsaw, offered dozens of short books on Jewish and world history, political theory, current events (especially the rise of Nazism in Germany), technology, music, and profiles of famous individuals, ranging from Lucrezia Borgia to Mahatma Gandhi.

This burgeoning of publications engendered new reading practices. As books and newspapers proved too costly for many eastern European Jews to purchase for themselves, much of their reading involved shared print material. Libraries, both public and private, became a widespread presence in the Russian Empire beginning in the 1890s, though the public institutions did not carry Yiddish books (and few titles on Jewish subjects in Russian), due to government restrictions, until after the 1905 Revolution. Jewish communities in the Russian Empire also established libraries at this time. Some were connected to a local school, synagogue, or charity, while others were founded by individuals, and Jewish political organizations also ran clandestine libraries.[36] In interwar eastern Europe, professionally run Jewish libraries became fixtures of major cities. Branches of Jewish youth movements in smaller towns often created their own libraries, housed in spaces where members met. In these settings, literacy was a communal activity; young people shared and discussed books as part of their socializing. Periodicals were also frequently shared, whether in cafes and libraries or among neighbors. Literacy became a performative practice, as reading aloud from newspapers was a common social practice on both sides of the Atlantic.[37]

Alongside popular publications, a modernist Yiddish literature emerged in the first decades of twentieth century, rivaling the achievements of European and American avant-garde writers.[38] Even as Yiddish modernists founded their own journals and presses, they often participated in Yiddish mainstream culture as well. Some leading figures of Yiddish literature (for example, Jacob Glatstein, Isaac Bashevis Singer) wrote opinion pieces, features, or sensational fiction for the Yiddish press under pseudonyms. Other major authors wrote extensively for children as well as for adults (Mani-Leib, Kadya Molodowsky, Itzik Kipnis) or translated works of world literature into Yiddish (David Hofstein, Zishe Landau, Leib Naidus, Leon Kobrin). Though some authors may have undertaken these efforts simply to earn a living, others apparently wished to engage the gamut of Yiddish readers, traversing boundaries between elite and popular culture. During the first half of the twentieth century translations of world literature extended the parameters of Yiddish literacy toward the cosmopolitan. For example, the 1925 catalog of titles sold by Farlag B. A. Kletskin, a major publisher of Yiddish books in Poland, included translations of Hans Christian Andersen, Miguel de Cervantes, George Eliot, Maxim Gorky, Heinrich Heine, Jack London, Molière, August Strindberg, Rabindranath Tagore, and Stanisław Wyspiański, among others.[39]

Publishing in Yiddish during this period reflected the speech community's diverging ideological range. At their height during the interwar years, progressive Jewish political parties in Europe and secular Yiddish organizations in America issued a comprehensive array of publications in Yiddish. Recognizing their attraction, especially for younger Jews, Orthodox organizations responded in kind. In interwar Poland, Agudath Israel promoted new works of Yiddish literature that combined "Orthodox content with modern literary form," thereby championing Yiddish literacy as essential to bolstering Jewish piety.[40] This perceived need to argue for the language is telling; for some traditionally observant Jews in interwar eastern Europe, Yiddish literacy could not be taken for granted. Indeed, despite the burgeoning of publishing at this time, the state of Yiddish literacy was often perceived as unstable, even imperiled. Book publishers competed with periodicals for readers. In Poland, both secular Yiddishists and traditionally observant Jews worried that their youth either preferred reading Yiddish translations of world literature to the work of Yiddish authors or were abandoning Yiddish altogether for Polish. Linguistic assimilation was also a concern for Yiddish writers and publishers in the United States, especially following the end of mass immigration from eastern Europe during the early 1920s.[41]

Yiddish publishing did not depend on the vagaries of the marketplace in the Soviet Union. As members of the Soviet Writers Union, Yiddish authors were employed by the state to produce novels, stories, poems, and plays, which were vetted and issued by government presses. The first years of the Soviet Union witnessed a burgeoning of avant-garde publishing in Yiddish, exemplified by the expressionist poetry of Peretz Markish and surreal children's fiction of Itzik Kipnis. Major artists of the period—including Marc Chagall, El Lissitzky, and Issachar Ryback—designed typography and illustrations for Yiddish publications.[42]

From the start, Soviet Yiddish publishing reflected the state's agenda for transforming the Jewish population. In addition to several newspapers (e.g., *Der emes* [The truth], which appeared from 1920 to 1938), the Soviet Union issued an array of periodicals, including some that promoted Marxist values among the young (such as *Zay greyt* [Be prepared], 1928–1937) and a journal that assailed religion (*Der apikoyres* [The heretic], 1931–1935).[43] Like other works of Soviet public culture produced in the 1920s and 1930s, Yiddish literature reflected efforts to address shifts in state-approved aesthetics—for example, moving from more formally experimental writing and illustration to social realism.[44] Tethered to government control, Yiddish publishing in the Soviet Union both rose and fell abruptly. The shuttering of Soviet Yiddish cultural institutions in 1949 and execution of their leading figures in 1952, after being falsely charged and convicted of treason, in effect rendered any public manifestation of Yiddish literacy a crime against the state.[45]

The Soviet Union eventually "rehabilitated" Yiddish in 1959, with its first state-sanctioned publications appearing after a decade of absence. Late Soviet Yiddish publishing is exemplified by *Sovetish heymland* (Soviet homeland), which appeared from 1961 to 1991. Linguist Harald Haarmann characterized this literary journal as a "cultural relic," noting that it included summaries of its contents in Russian, "to assure access [by] non-Yiddish-speaking Jews."[46] During the final years of the Soviet Union, a long-suppressed Russian-Yiddish dictionary was published, as were the first Yiddish textbooks for children to appear since World War II, suggesting that, under perestroika, the language might be afforded greater state support.[47]

• • •

Cover of the August 1932 issue of *Der apikoyres* (The heretic), an anti-religious propaganda magazine, published in Moscow. The spelling of the magazine's name exemplifies the Soviet Union's reform of Yiddish orthography, which renders words from the Semitic component of Yiddish phonetically, rather than the traditional spelling אפיקורות. Images on the cover, designed by Aron Hefter, protest the oppression of the proletariat and mock traditional Jewish religious practices. (Musée d'art et d'histoire du Judaïsme, Paris. Photo: Michel Urtado. © RMN-Grand Palais/Art Resource NY.)

The rise of Nazism galvanized the world of Yiddish letters, which was devastated by the ensuing genocide of European Jewry. Anita Norich notes that Yiddish writers in the United States were at the vanguard of American Jewish attention to the Holocaust, anticipating "wider cultural responses that have become familiar to Americans." During this period, "virtually every writers' conference convened, every new Yiddish publication, every literary symposium . . . was prefaced with a discussion of what it meant to enter into a creative enterprise at this historic moment."[48] The expectation that America's Yiddish speakers must, in effect, be literate in the unfolding catastrophe extended to their children. Magazines published by all four secular Yiddish school systems in America featured stories and poems about the Nazi persecution of Europe's Jews. According to Yiddish studies scholar Naomi Kadar, these schools' leaders viewed children as "partners in despair" and saw literature as strategic to fostering their identification with the genocide.[49]

The destruction wrought by the Holocaust extended beyond the vast human toll to dismantling the cultural infrastructure of presses, booksellers, libraries, and schools in which Yiddish literacy had flourished in Europe. The Nazis' extensive looting of Jewish property included the holdings of communal libraries and archives. After the war, some of these items were recovered by Allied Forces in occupied Germany and sent to new institutions, as Holocaust survivors established new cultural centers, especially in the Americas and Israel.[50]

In the wake of the genocide, Yiddish literacy functioned differently and acquired new cultural significance. This transformation is exemplified by the *Algemeyne entsiklopedye* (General encyclopedia), a project of secular Yiddishists initiated in Europe in 1930 as a general knowledge reference work. During the war the scope of the encyclopedia changed; its final volumes (published between 1939 and 1966) focused exclusively on Jewish history and culture. This shift reflects "changing representational imperatives," notes Barry Trachtenberg. "No longer was the task of Yiddish scholars to edify and educate their readers in the knowledge of the larger world, but instead to make a record of the Jewish world so recently destroyed."[51]

Yiddish culture during the first postwar decades reflects this altered agenda. Literature scholar Jan Schwarz argues that Yiddish writers and cultural activists were energized by a "new set of priorities" centered on "consolidation and continuity."[52] Both established authors and members of the Yiddish-speaking public produced an extensive body of writing to memorialize individuals and communities murdered during the Holocaust and to document their prewar existence. Prominent among these are hundreds of *yizker-bikher*, typically written partially or entirely in Yiddish. Self-published by members of the individual communities whose prewar past was being memorialized, *yizker-bikher* created a distinctively intimate literacy, in which these volumes' authors, subjects, and audiences were largely identical.[53]

Scores of individual memoirs of prewar and wartime experience were published in the Americas, Europe, Israel, and Australia. In the early postwar years the Central Association of Polish Jews in Argentina initiated a series of Yiddish books, titled *Poylishe yidntum* (Polish Jewry), which by the mid-1960s produced more than 160 titles, including histories, novels, poetry, memoirs, biographies, memorial books, and translations.[54] Another monumental publishing project undertaken in Argentina had a different focus: the one-hundred-volume series of anthologies *Musterverk fun der yidisher literatur* (Exemplary works of Yiddish literature), issued between 1957 and 1984 by the Instituto Científico Judío. These anthologies cover the range of Yiddish letters from the 1500s to the mid-twentieth century, including major early works (*Bovo Dantona, Mayse-bukh*), collections devoted to a single author (from *maskil* Shloyme Etinger, the subject of the first volume, to twentieth-century figures such as Max Weinreich and fiction writer Israel Joshua Singer), anthologies of regional Yiddish writing, especially from Latin America, and thematic volumes (e.g., on childhood, humor, Hasidism, the Holocaust). Whereas *Poylishe yidntum* focused primarily on the recent past, the *Musterverk* looked back through the chronology of Yiddish literature as well as forward. On one hand, the series was undertaken to establish "*a biblyotek vos felt*"—a missing library, which implicitly evokes the Holocaust's devastation of Europe's Yiddish book culture. Unlike *Poylishe yidntum*, the *Musterverk* canonized existing Yiddish letters, dating back to the Renaissance, rather than publishing new works. On the other hand, the *Musterverk* was created to serve future generations of Yiddish readers: "those who teach in Jewish secondary schools, in pedagogical seminars, courses on Jewish subjects, readers' clubs, study centers, and . . . who pursue knowledge on their own."[55]

The literary journal *Di goldene keyt* (The golden chain), founded by poet Abraham Sutzkever in Tel Aviv in 1949, similarly sought to instantiate a future for Yiddish literacy in a new context—in this case, the State of Israel. For forty-six years the journal published new works of Yiddish literature, translations into the language, and essays on Jewish literature and culture. As a "golden chain"—a Yiddish idiom associated with the continuity of Jewish life in diaspora—the journal both evoked the prewar efflorescence of Yiddish literary modernism (the journal's name is also the title of an early twentieth-century drama by Peretz) and strove to advance Yiddish literacy at this high level. Moreover, *Di goldene keyt* provocatively added a link to the chain of diaspora Jewish culture at the epicenter of Zionism, flouting the disparagement of Yiddish by state-mandated Hebraism.

As new Yiddish works continue to appear throughout the postwar years, authors have increasingly pondered the rationale for writing in the language. Yiddish abruptly and cruelly lost half of its speakers during the Holocaust and faced an uncertain future. Younger generations of Jews have largely neglected Yiddish and realize their Jewish literacy primarily in the majority languages of their respective countries. One consequence of these developments is the flourishing of self-reflexive Yiddish poetry, in which the subject is the language itself. In contrast to similar works written before World War II, these poems simultaneously affirm the literary richness of Yiddish as they worry for the future of its readership, intimating a disquieting divergence of literary productivity from communal literacy.[56]

The exceptional commitment of Hasidim to Yiddish in their postwar communities has produced their own new literacy practices. Like other fundamentalist groups, Hasidim have embraced the form of certain popular culture genres and imbued them with pious content. Among these are works of what might be termed Hasidic leisure fiction, including historical and adventure novels in Yiddish. These books often open with endorsements from rabbinic authorities and sometimes offer a rationale for this new literature. One introduction explains that reading fiction is a repercussion of modern times that has, regrettably, attracted pious Jews. Rather than leaving them to resort to books in English or secular works in Hebrew and Yiddish, rabbis have encouraged "trustworthy authors" to write engaging works of fiction in Yiddish that are "worthy of being brought into respectable Jewish homes."[57]

The most consequential transformation of Yiddish literacy to come in the wake of the Holocaust is the salient role of translation. Before World War II, almost all readers of Yiddish were native speakers of the language, and relatively little of Yiddish literature was translated into other languages. But soon after the war, the situation reversed: as the numbers of Yiddish readers declined, the audience for its literature in translation burgeoned. In addition to translations of works by individual authors, anthologies established new canons of Yiddish prose and poetry for this readership. Moreover, these collections redefined what it means to be literate in this corpus, informing readers of the significance of Yiddish literature and the culture that produced it through the selection and organization of works and through paratexts—introductions, glossaries, annotations—some of which are extensive.[58] Translators of Yiddish literature regularly grapple with the challenge of rendering culturally specific idioms and allusions in other languages. Notably, Isaac Bashevis Singer proclaimed the English translations of his fiction, which were created with his input, to be "second originals." Meant especially for an audience that did not know Yiddish, they created a new kind of command of Yiddish literature that diverged from the literacy of those who read Yiddish.[59]

Despite this shift, literary translation into Yiddish has continued after World War II, though on a much-diminished scale and toward different ends. In the early postwar period, new renderings of works of world literature into Yiddish for its vernacular readership appeared, sometimes with prefaces noting the symbolic value of these efforts as assertions of the resilience of Yiddish literacy after the Holocaust. Thus, historian Jacob Shatzky writes in his foreword to the 1954 Yiddish translation of the Finnish epic *Kalevala* that in the wake of the Holocaust each translation from world literature into Yiddish "is a prized item and a cause for celebration."[60] Recently, Hebrew writer Etgar Keret's 2018 short-story collection *Takalah bi-ktseh ha-galaksyah* ("Disturbance at the edge of the galaxy"; English title: *Fly Already*) won Israel's Sapir Prize for Literature, which includes commissioning translations of the work into Arabic plus another language of the author's choice. Keret requested a translation into Yiddish, the first author to do so in the prize's history. Keret, who does not speak or read Yiddish, explains his decision as a recognition of "the diaspora Jewishness we Israelis have lost."[61]

A more complex significance has been ascribed to some postwar translations into Yiddish, such as the claim that Joseph Buloff and Luba Kadison's Yiddish rendering of Arthur Miller's drama *Death of a Salesman*, which these actors first performed in Buenos Aires in 1949, constitutes "a disguised original unmasked."[62] The Yiddish version of the 1964 musical *Fiddler on the Roof* involves a more complex movement among Sholem Aleichem's Tevye stories, their translation from Yiddish into English and subsequent adaptation for the American stage, followed by the musical's translation into Yiddish by Shraga Friedman, a Holocaust survivor from Poland, for performance in Israel in 1966. In these examples, translation into Yiddish is perceived as returning works to their linguistic and cultural foundations, thereby recovering an imagined "lost" literacy.

Recently issued Yiddish renderings of renowned works of children's literature—including *The Cat and the Hat, Le Petit Prince*, and *Max und Moritz*—proffer an especially provocative configuration of Yiddish literacy.[63] These translations seem intended less for Yiddish-speaking children who are not literate in English, French, or German than for adults wishing to imagine their childhoods as if they had taken place in Yiddish, including reading beloved works of their youth. Some of these translations Judaize their sources by giving characters Ashkenazic names (thus, Charles Nydorf and Elinor Robinson's Yiddish rendering of *Der Struwwelpeter* is retitled *Pinye shtroykop*) or replacing elements of the text with Yiddish idioms. (For example, in *Vini-der-Pu*, Leonard Wolf's translation of *Winnie the Pooh*, the title character's refrain of "rum-tum-tidl-um-tum" becomes "*haydl-didl, haydl-didl dam.*")[64] Such playfulness is key to these translations, which require familiarity with the original to appreciate the manipulation of translating as a practice in its own right. In these works, Yiddish literacy is defined in relationship with literacy in another language.[65]

Translation is similarly strategic to the transformed literacy of Yiddish in contemporary performance. Presentations of Yiddish plays and songs now seldom assume that their audiences are fluent in the language. As a result, translations are provided through a variety of strategies, including projected supertitles or simultaneous audio transmission received on individual headsets. Singers often incorporate translating into their performances, whether through commentary that introduces a song or by crafting bilingual lyrics that shift between the original Yiddish and its rendering in the audience's vernacular.[66] Translation thereby becomes an integral component of performing Yiddish. As literacy in the language is no longer self-sufficient, its semantic value shifts into other languages, thereby foregrounding the affective qualities of Yiddish apart from its meaning.

Just as the invention of print constituted a threshold in the dynamics of Yiddish literacy some five hundred years ago, the advent of digital media marks a similar watershed. Digitized scans provide greater access to Yiddish publications of the past and preserve rare or fragile archival documents. Thousands of Yiddish titles are available online from a number of sources, including the Yiddish Book Center, while in its Amherst, Massachusetts, headquarters the original volumes have become objects of massed display. The internet enables new writing in Yiddish, whether blogs or online periodicals, to circulate internationally. And translation software promises to enable anyone to become "literate," to some degree, in Yiddish (or any other written language).

Linguist Ross Perlin notes that the presence of Yiddish online is "outsized, . . . with as much activity as languages much more widely spoken." This development, he argues, is due in part to the fact that Yiddish speakers are also readers and writers in the language, and "the Internet gives special prominence to the written word," to the benefit of languages such as Yiddish that "boast unusually high ratios of poets to everyday speakers."[67] The internet's new hybridization of oral and written language redounds to Yiddish practice more generally. Beyond the latest technological innovations, Yiddish literacy, once understood as an extension of its vernacular orality, is now often configured quite differently. The salience of textual literacy has defined modernist Yiddish culture, rivaling and perhaps eventually surpassing oral fluency. Thus, Jonathan Boyarin argues that among secularists the language is increasingly "spoken the way it is written, not written as it is spoken."[68] Indeed, Yiddish literacy can thrive independent of speech (for example, among scholars conducting research in the language) or, given the growing inventory of translations from Yiddish, independent of knowing the language itself. Against these changes is the continued presence of a readership, however configured—or imagined—in pursuit of some interest for which Yiddish literacy contributes to their continuum of learning or personal development.

# 11
# Occupation

As a language of daily life, Yiddish is a language of work. Jews have long spoken Yiddish with fellow workers and clients. Some trades developed their own vocabularies and idioms in the language. The topic of work also appears in a wealth of Yiddish proverbs, folk songs, poems, and political tracts. So extensive is the association of Yiddish with workers that it eventually became emblematic of the Jewish laborer. Non-Jews' interest in and, at times, command of Yiddish emerged in considerable measure from their working relationships with Jews. And in the modern era, Yiddish itself became a form of work, as use of the language was professionalized.

Among the earliest extant Yiddish manuscripts and print publications are a small number of texts that provide details about the livelihoods of some Ashkenazim. These texts include treatises on medical practice from as early as the turn of the fourteenth century, a fifteenth-century note describing artisans' tools, and a sixteenth-century handbook from Italy on laundry.[1] The occasional artifact also yields information regarding Jewish occupations, such as an inventory etched on a fourteenth-century slate, found in Cologne, evincing the use of Yiddish in commercial reckonings of the era.[2] Beyond information on the occupations themselves, these texts provide some insight into the social and economic contexts in which Ashkenazim worked during the late medieval and early modern periods, as do other sources not specifically focused on occupation, such as the memoirs of the seventeenth-century merchant Glikl bas Leyb.

As sources such as these demonstrate, work played a salient role in Jews' contact with their Christian neighbors. Linguistic interactions, inherent in the exchange of goods and services, engendered opportunities for language development, whether enriching the vernacular of Ashkenazim with new vocabulary and idioms or fostering language use intended to insulate Jewish conversations from their neighbors. This contact also inspired some of the first works written about Yiddish by Christian authors. Manuals of self-instruction in the language, published especially for German-speaking Christians who did business with Jews, include overviews of Yiddish grammar; specialized vocabulary, especially in the Semitic component, used for currency, weights and measures, and other mercantile terms; explanations of the *alef-beys* for reading promissory notes and other business correspondence; and sample conversations as guides to pronunciation. These books reveal both extensive contact with Jews and, at the same time, concern about their deception in business dealings through arcane language.[3]

A new form of language use evincing the range of Yiddish speakers' professions emerged during the years between the end of the eighteenth and the middle of the nineteenth century, when Jews in eastern Europe were required to adopt surnames.[4] Yiddish terms for various professions were common sources of surnames that Jews adopted at the time, including the following:

| **Surname** | **Profession** | **Definition** |
|---|---|---|
| Aptekar | *apteker* | pharmacist |
| Becker, Beckerman | *beker* | baker |
| Belfer | *belfer* | *kheyder* teacher's assistant |
| Bonder | *bonder* | cooper |
| Chasen | *khazn* | cantor |
| Cramer, Kramer | *kremer* | shopkeeper |
| Drescher | *dresher* | thresher |
| Drucker | *druker* | printer |
| Einbinder | *aynbinder* | bookbinder |
| Fabrikant | *fabrikant* | manufacturer |
| Farber | *farber* | dyer |
| Fassler | *fasler* | barrel maker |
| Glazer | *glezer* | glazier |
| Kirschner | *kirshner* | furrier |
| Koch | *kokh* | cook |
| Kutscher | *kutsher* | coachman |
| Lehrer | *lerer* | teacher |
| Liwerant | *liverant* | caterer |
| Lomden | *lomdn* | rabbinical scholar |
| Malamud, Milamed | *melamed* | *kheyder* teacher |
| Milner | *milner* | miller |
| Musiker | *muziker* | musician |
| Presser, Pressman | *preser* | presser |
| Schaechter | *shekhter* | kosher slaughterer |
| Schenker | *shenker* | tavernkeeper |
| Scherer, Shearer | *sherer* | barber |

| | | |
|---|---|---|
| Schmuckler | *shmukler* | jeweler |
| Schneider, Schneiderman, Snyder | *shnayder* | tailor |
| Schreiber | *shrayber* | writer |
| Schuster | *shuster* | cobbler |
| Trager | *treger* | porter |
| Weber | *veber* | weaver |
| Zimbalist | *tsimbalist* | hammered dulcimer player |

Some professions inspired a variety of Yiddish surnames, notably garment workers, one of the most common Jewish livelihoods in eastern Europe at the time that family names were adopted. Among these names are Eisen, Ajzenman (cf. *ayzn*, "iron"), Nadler, Nudelman (*nodl*, "needle"), Fingerhut (*fingerhut*, "thimble"), and Schear (*sher*, "scissors"). Other surnames reflect products that Jewish artisans worked with or that Jewish merchants dealt in, such as the following:

| **Surname** | **Product** | **Definition** |
|---|---|---|
| Blech, Blecherman | *blekh* | tin |
| Bronfman | *bronfn* | whiskey |
| Essig, Essikman | *esig* | vinegar |
| Fisch, Fishman | *fish* | fish |
| Fleischer, Fleischman | *fleysh* | meat |
| Fruchter, Fruchtman | *frukht* | fruit |
| Hoberman, Guberman | *hober* | oats |
| Holzman | *holts* | wood |
| Lederer, Lederman | *leder* | leather |
| Mellman | *mel* | flour |
| Seidman | *zayd* | silk |
| Wasserman | *vaser* | water |
| Weiner, Weinerman | *vayn* | wine |
| Weitz, Weitzman | *veyts* | wheat |
| Zucker, Zuckerman | *tsuker* | sugar |

• • •

At the turn of the twentieth century, growing numbers of Yiddish speakers became part of an increasingly politicized work force on both sides of the

Atlantic. Yiddish facilitated union organizing and solidarity among laborers, both in written form (pamphlets, party newspapers, banners displayed at rallies) and in performance (lectures, speeches, choral singing), forging a bond between the language and working-class Jews. The visible and audible presence of Yiddish in the public sphere marked Jews' involvement in strikes, demonstrations, May Day parades, and the like, often alongside the languages of workers from other nationalities. Organized labor and workers' political parties provided Yiddish speakers with a collective presence unprecedented in its scope and mass empowerment of Jews. Yiddishism subsequently became a tenet of Jewish socialist parties. They not only used the language to advance the cause of Jewish workers but also promoted the identification of Yiddish as the language of the labor class.

Work both united a Yiddish-speaking proletariat and engendered professional subcultures reflected in language use. A number of occupations developed their own Yiddish argots, whether to create terminology specific to their trade or as a form of insider language. These idioms eventually attracted interest beyond their respective professions, as folkloristic curiosities. For example, in Sholem Aleichem's 1888 novel *Stempenyu*, about the eponymous charismatic performer of traditional Jewish instrumental music, the author incorporated examples of the slang used by the title character and his fellow *klezmorim* ("musicians"). Aware that readers would likely not know the meanings of these terms, Sholem Aleichem annotated his text with glosses, such as the following: *klive* = *sheyne* ("pretty"), *yaldovke* = *vaybl* ("young woman"), *matret* = *kukt* ("looks"), *zikres* = *oygn* ("eyes"), thereby enabling comprehension of the sentence "*Zi iz dokh take gor a klive yaldovke! Ze nor, ze, vi zi matret mit di zikres!*" ("She's one good-looking woman! Just see how she stares with those eyes!") In doing so, the author provided his audience with entry into the alluringly raffish subculture of *klezmorim*, a linguistic parallel to Stempenyu's seductive appeal for the novel's heroine.[5]

As scholarly study of Yiddish developed in the first decades of the twentieth century, these professional argots attracted the interest of folklorists and philologists, who gathered terminology related to a variety of occupations, including carpenters, bootmakers, tailors, bakers, and house painters, as well as the insider slang of wrestlers and criminals.[6] During the interwar years, the establishment of research centers on Jewish culture in Poland and the Soviet Union elevated folklore collecting from individual pursuits to institutionalized missions, in which scholarship was undertaken both as an end in itself and to support new visions for Jewish culture. Documentation of various occupations' distinctive terminologies appeared in scholarly journals, such as the YIVO Institute's *Filologishe shriftn* (Philological studies). Among the more noteworthy of these collections is Meylekh Gromb's inventory of "two hundred 'street cries' (typical and very remarkable) by which Jewish traders in Warsaw advertise their goods."[7] As these efforts recorded the richness of vernacular Yiddish, they imparted new value to these occupations, hailing them as redoubts of Jewish folk heritage.

Folklorists also collected Yiddish proverbs and songs about work, among other subjects, within a larger effort by scholars of European folkways to celebrate this kind of creativity as ethnic and national patrimony. The act of collecting itself became a new form of work, in which scholars enlisted the general public. In the 1920s, YIVO appealed to eastern European Jews to gather folk materials, characterized as a sacred task: "Tradition is holy. . . . And that is precisely why we must research the life of our people, to learn everything that has come down to us thanks to the strength of our tradition."[8] Concurrently, researchers in the Soviet Union exhorted Jews, "*Forsht ayer shtetl!*" (Study your town!). This undertaking sought to document both religious institutions, characterized as "the remnants of a moldy past," and manifestations of "a new way of life," including the communist youth organization and scouting movement, so as to foster social and economic reform.[9] In the Soviet Union, the work of studying past Jewish mores strove not to transvalue them as heritage but to terminate them and establish in their place a radically new model of Jewish life.

Whether folkways connected to work were documented to ennoble Jews' livelihoods or to revolutionize them, the task of gathering this information shifted it away from its provenance and ensconced it in new venues of research and performance—and thereby in new occupations. Scholars scrutinized proverbs as evidence of linguistic development or indexed them within typologies of traditional lore.[10] Folk songs became part of school curricula or were adapted for performance by choral societies.[11] At the same time, pioneering works of social science scholarship conducted in Yiddish included economic surveys of Jews' means of earning income and ethnographic accounts of bygone Jewish livelihoods, such as those pursued by the shrinking population of rural Jews. In addition to documenting major socioeconomic shifts among eastern Europe's Jews, these studies demonstrated the potential of Yiddish to serve as a scientific language for both retrospective and prospective research.[12]

As Yiddish speakers ventured into new professions, the language was mobilized to provide them with information and support. Efforts to settle Jewish immigrants in agricultural colonies in the Americas, beginning in the late nineteenth century, engendered publications to educate Yiddish speakers in what was, for most, an unfamiliar livelihood.[13] In the United States *Der yidisher farmer* (The Jewish farmer), a monthly publication inaugurated in 1908 by the Jewish Agricultural and Industrial Aid Society, informed subscribers of new developments in farming practices and equipment. This periodical, which continued to appear until 1959, also helped foster a sense of community among its readers, who typically lived at considerable distance from the urban concentrations of most Yiddish speakers.

Concurrently, Jewish philanthropies underwrote efforts to provide young Jews in eastern Europe with vocational training. The Jewish Colonization Association, in agreement with the Russian government, established trade schools in several cities, teaching such skills as carpentry, locksmithing, metalwork, electronics, mechanical drawing, and dressmaking. In 1903, Vilna's Jewish community established Hilf durkh arbet (Help Through Work), an organization that provided vocational education and employment for local Jewish youth and briefly ran an agricultural school at an estate outside the city. After World War I, the community established a technical school, which offered instruction in mechanics and electrical technology, all taught in Yiddish, attracting students from throughout Poland.[14]

The Soviet Union's economic policies regarding its Jewish citizens placed a high priority on abolishing the "nonproductive" vocations by which many Jews earned a living. Soviet Yiddish literature and propaganda publications denounced shopkeepers, wholesalers, brokers, and others whose livelihoods were associated with capitalism. Efforts to transform Soviet Jews into productive workers ranged from valorizing *shloglers* ("shock workers") in Yiddish children's books to resettling thousands of Jews in agricultural colonies. Soviet publications for Jews engaged in new forms of work include Yiddish training manuals on topics such as maintaining a blast furnace or managing a collective farm.[15]

• • •

Expanding uses of Yiddish in different aspects of modern Jewish life engendered professionalization of the language itself. As champions of Yiddish asserted its value for education, works of high culture, and political engagement, they argued for improving both the quality of the language and the proficiency of its users to realize these new applications. Lexicographer and literature scholar Zalman Rejzen issued his *Yidishe gramatik* (Yiddish grammar) in 1908 as both an apologist effort—to demonstrate that the language did, in fact, have a grammar—and an instructional work to guide future generations of writers.[16] In foundational essays on the study of Yiddish language and literature, published in 1914, Ber Borochov called for undertaking research on the history of Yiddish; creating a standardized spelling, lexicon, and grammar; and establishing a language institute to oversee these efforts. For Borochov, this work was integral to the advancement of Jews as a nationality: "As long as a people remain illiterate in their own language," he wrote, "one cannot yet speak of a national culture."[17]

This appeal for new institutions and resources built upon efforts that had been underway during the previous century. Modern Yiddish lexicography, beginning with Shiye-Mordkhe Lifshits's Yiddish/Russian dictionaries, published in 1869 and 1876, strove to establish protocols for spelling and usage as well as provide a lexicon comparable to other European languages.[18] Lifshits's commitment to cultivating Yiddish as a modern literary language reportedly influenced Aleksander Zederbaum's decision to publish *Kol mevaser* (Herald), the first successful Yiddish-language periodical to appear in eastern Europe, beginning in 1862, and informed Sholem Yankev Abramovitsh's choosing to write fiction in Yiddish, starting with his landmark 1864 novella *Dos kleyne mentshele* (The small man). Avraham Goldfaden, whose early work appeared in *Kol mevaser*, founded the first modern Yiddish theater troupe in Romania in 1876. Thus, the 1860s and 1870s witnessed the inauguration of new professions centered on the Yiddish language: editor, novelist, playwright, actor, and lexicographer.

Lifshits's Yiddish dictionaries are far from the earliest such efforts. In fact, the use of Yiddish to gloss terms in another language can be traced back to the oldest manuscript evidence. Elijah Levita, best remembered as the author of the verse epic *Bovo Dantona*, was also an accomplished grammarian, whose wide-ranging achievements include the earliest known published multilingual lexicon to include Yiddish, issued in Isny in 1542.[19] In ensuing centuries, other scholars, Jews as well as Christians, published Yiddish glossaries, varying in form, scope, and intent.[20] In addition to evincing the evolving work of Yiddish lexicographers, these endeavors demonstrate the development of the language as a tool, to be employed parallel to other languages.

Dictionaries glossing Yiddish with other languages reveal the expanding scope of populations working with Yiddish, whether as a source language or a target language, to a variety of ends. For example, the *Sieben-Sprachen-Wörterbuch: Deutsch, Polnisch, Russisch, Weissruthenisch, Litauisch, Lettisch, Jiddisch* (Dictionary of seven languages: German, Polish, Russian, Belorussian, Lithuanian, Latvian, Yiddish), issued by the German military in early 1918, addressed the complex multilingual needs of German forces engaged in eastern Europe during World War I.[21] Dictionaries issued during the interwar years paired Yiddish with Arabic, Modern Hebrew, Portuguese, and Spanish, among other languages, reflecting Yiddish speakers' growing interest in other languages, arising from professional concerns, intellectual undertakings, or ideological convictions, as well as due to the mass emigration of Yiddish speakers out of eastern Europe.[22] In the post–World War II era, still more Yiddish dictionaries have appeared, including reference works glossing the language with Esperanto, French, Hungarian, Italian, Japanese, Polish, Russian, Swedish, and Ukrainian.[23]

More dictionaries have been issued pairing Yiddish with English than with any other language. Among these are the efforts of individuals who dedicated much of their careers to the advancement of Yiddish. In the United States, Alexander Harkavy produced multiple Yiddish dictionaries and other reference works, culminating with the 1928 edition of his trilingual Yiddish-Hebrew-English dictionary. Dovid Katz hails Harkavy for having "almost singlehandedly created an intellectual environment conducive to Yiddish in an assimilation-prone society while masterminding Yiddish lexicography of the twentieth century."[24] Uriel Weinreich's *Modern English-Yiddish / Yiddish-English Dictionary*, published in 1968, set new standards for Yiddish lexicography with the linguist's "most exacting requirements," rooted in his research on semantics and Yiddish dialectology.[25] Most recently, Mordkhe Schaechter's decades-long research on Yiddish terminology was realized posthumously with the 2016 publication of the *Comprehensive English-Yiddish Dictionary*, which contains almost fifty thousand entries and thirty-three thousand subentries, the largest such work.[26] The dictionaries compiled by these three men trace the dynamics of Yiddish lexicography in relation to changes in both the language and its professionalization.

In contrast to the dozens of dictionaries glossing Yiddish with other languages, the inventory of Yiddish lexical resources that are entirely in Yiddish is smaller in number. This not only reflects the constraints of external circumstances but also may indicate a more limited interest in these reference works. Harkavy died in 1939 before completing his *Yidisher folks-verterbukh* (Jewish people's dictionary), and materials for similar dictionaries, collected by interwar research institutes in Minsk and Vilna, were destroyed during World War II.[27] In the early postwar years a group of Yiddish linguists in the United States undertook the creation of an authoritative, comprehensive dictionary that includes documentation of usage, emulating the *Oxford English Dictionary*. The editors of the *Groyser verterbukh fun der yidisher shprakh* (Great dictionary of the Yiddish language) projected a content of 180,000 entries, constituting a comprehensive record of the language that is "all-inclusive as to time, place, and social classification" and thereby offering "an insight into the psychology of the large Yiddish-speaking segment of the Jewish people."[28] However, only four of the dictionary's projected ten volumes were issued.[29] Unlike prewar efforts to create similar dictionaries, the *Groyser verterbukh* was intended to be, in part, a work of salvage ethnography—"a condensed folk encyclopedia" of Ashkenazic Jewry—and a memorial to the murdered Jews of Europe. The publishers note that the dictionary would contain "thousands of words which are not included in literary Yiddish but were acceptable in the spoken language. It was important that this be done now, lest they be relegated to oblivion."[30]

The professionalization of Yiddish culture, which had begun in the mid-nineteenth century with the efforts of enterprising individual authors, performers, publishers, and scholars, soon expanded to become the work of organizations. These include the Hebrew Actors Union (whose members, despite its name, acted in Yiddish), the first performing arts union in the United States, established in 1897, and the Association of Jewish Writers and Journalists in Warsaw, founded in 1916, which served as a trade union as well as a social center for writers, performers, and others engaged in the creation of secular Yiddish culture. Yiddish teachers' seminaries were created both by Orthodox Jews (Bais Yaakov, in 1931) and by secularists in New York (in 1918), Vilna (1921), and Buenos Aires (1940).

Research centers whose missions included the study of Yiddish language and culture were founded with state support in Minsk (Jewish Department of the Institute for Belorussian Culture, in 1924) and Kiev (Institute of Jewish Proletarian Culture, within the Ukrainian Academy of Sciences, 1929) and privately in Vilna (YIVO Institute for Jewish Research, 1925) and Warsaw (Institute for Jewish Studies, 1928). These bodies transformed the study of Yiddish from an idiosyncratic undertaking, often by autodidacts, into a formalized area of research and instruction. At the same time, research on Yiddish melded scholarship in various disciplines with efforts to advance the lives of Yiddish speakers. Thus, Max Weinreich, one of YIVO's founders, explained its commitment to activist scholarship by positing that *visnshaft* ("scientific scholarship") means *visn vos shaft* ("knowledge that creates").[31]

All these research institutions were liquidated during World War II, during which many of their staff, students, supporters, and volunteers were murdered. Nevertheless, their scholarly publications and archival collections endure as the foundation of postwar Yiddish studies. After the war, YIVO was relocated to New York City, and in Warsaw the Jewish Historical Institute was established in the headquarters of the prewar Institute for Jewish Studies. At the initiative of the Jewish National Workers' Alliance in the United States, the Hebrew University in Jerusalem inaugurated a Yiddish studies department in 1952.[32] Following the end of the Soviet Union, archival holdings of Jewish materials in former Soviet republics, long inaccessible, have become available to scholars there and abroad.[33]

The work of Yiddish continues today in universities, research centers, and organizations dedicated to promoting the language and its culture. These include venerable institutions, such as the Arbeter Ring (established in New York in 1900), Kadimah Jewish Cultural Centre and National Library (Melbourne, Australia, 1911), Jewish Public Library (Montreal, 1914), Folksbiene Yiddish Theater (New York, 1915), Fundación IWO (Buenos Aires, 1928), and Bibliothèque Medem (Paris, 1929). The first decades following World War II witnessed the creation of organizations focused on cultivating interest in Yiddish among Jewish youth in the diaspora, including SKIF, the acronym of the Sotsyalistisher kinder farband (Socialist Children's Union; Melbourne, 1950); Hemshekh (Continuity), a Bundist summer camp (upstate New York, 1959); and Yugntruf (Call to Youth, New York, 1964). In Israel institutions were inaugurated to honor the literary heritage of Yiddish, named in memory of prominent writers: Beth Shalom Aleichem (Hebrew: "Sholem Aleichem House") and Leyvik-hoyz (Yiddish: "Leyvik House"), which opened in Tel Aviv in 1966 and 1970, respectively. More recent organizations—the Yiddish Book Center (Amherst, Massachusetts, 1980), Klezkanada (Quebec, 1996), the National Authority for Yiddish Culture (Tel Aviv, 1996), Yiddishkayt (Los Angeles, 1998), Yung-Yidish (Tel Aviv, 2006), and New Yiddish Rep (New York, 2007), among others—promote interest in Yiddish through an expansive range of activities. In addition to language instruction and publishing, these offerings include engagement with Yiddish via other vernaculars, through literature in translation, tourism, performance, and social action.

Shifts in the role of Yiddish in relation to work—from a language in which Jews went about making a living, to a language in which work was celebrated and politicized, and then to a language that became professionalized and itself a subject of work—reflect, to some extent, larger developments in the economic life of Ashkenazim from the early modern period to the present. Moreover, these developments evince changes in the nature of Jewish vernacularity, especially with regard to conjoining daily work and daily speech. Modern notions of work—whether the organizing of labor or the professionalization of writers, performers, and others whose work centers on language—demand a different attention to the possibilities of vernacular language. The multiglossic contexts in which modern Yiddish speakers have worked inform this attention, shaping notions of how Yiddish can be put to work, of the extent to which it requires work, and of Yiddish itself as the object of work.

# 12
# Political Affiliation

As a language of modern political action, Yiddish became the voice of mobilized Jewish masses on an unprecedented scale. The rapid engagement of Yiddish speakers with political activism at the turn of the twentieth century on both sides of the Atlantic coincided with the equally swift efflorescence of modern Yiddish culture. However, this relationship between language and politics was not entirely correlative. The radicalization of Jews in eastern Europe began among small circles of intellectuals who read and spoke Russian, in which most of the region's Jews were not fluent. These activists subsequently turned to Yiddish as they sought to engage the larger Jewish population in political thought and action, a development that transformed the language as well as many of its speakers.

The initial interest in Yiddish among some Jewish anarchists, communists, socialists, trade unionists, and Zionists was largely instrumental, as there was no other language they could employ as effectively to reach most Jews, whether in eastern Europe or in new, growing immigrant communities abroad. Political activists were generally skeptical about the capacity of Yiddish to communicate historical analyses, socioeconomic concepts, and ideological tenets. In fact, political writings in the language expanded its vocabulary primarily by turning to modern German. At the same time, some activists who used Yiddish to propagate their political agendas also drew on traditional Jewish idioms, turning them to new uses. For example, the term *bedikes khomets* ("the search for leavened foods"), a ritual conducted before the start of Passover, was used in the Russian Empire at the turn of the twentieth century to refer to police searches of suspected revolutionaries' homes for illegal documents, which might uncover an analogous form of forbidden ferment.[1] Abraham Cahan, a socialist activist in New York at this time (and eventual editor in chief of the socialist *Jewish Daily Forward*), employed similar idioms when lecturing on politics in Yiddish to immigrant audiences, likening a boycott to *kheyrem* ("excommunication") and the protective value of a union card to that of a mezuzah.[2]

As with earlier uses of Yiddish for popular edification, whether among traditionally pious Jews in the early modern period or by *maskilim* during the nineteenth century, the language was associated with a non-elite audience, whose knowledge base was considered limited. Indeed, Yiddish signified this limitation, marking its readership by default as insufficiently literate in other, more prestigious languages and therefore lacking in sufficient schooling of one kind or another. However, the context and agenda of modern political activism in Yiddish differed from previous didactic turns to the language. Unlike early modern books of moral instruction or guides to ritual observance, political activists' use of Yiddish challenged, rather than validated, rabbinic authority and advocated breaking with traditional beliefs and practices instead of enhancing Jewish piety. In contrast with the liberal, integrationist aspirations of the Haskalah, the activists' movements called for radical change on a grand scale. Moreover, they positioned their audience as central, vital figures in this agenda. Rather than treating them as inferior to an intellectual elite, radicals hailed the Yiddish-speaking masses as a defining force for the Jewish collective and as future leaders of a transformed world.

Nevertheless, most political activists' commitment to Yiddish was provisional at first. Their movements' respective agendas either were universalist—and therefore deemed ethnic and religious loyalties to be of limited worth, if not inimical to their cause—or, in the case of Zionists, were increasingly committed to creating a new Jewish national culture centered on the development of Hebrew as a modern vernacular. Nevertheless, the urgent need to engage a large, rapidly radicalizing population of Yiddish speakers engendered a rich political print culture in the language, manifest in party newspapers and periodicals, ideologists' books and treatises, and election posters and propaganda pamphlets, as well as works of poetry and prose. This literature included the early fiction of Isaac Leib Peretz, whose stories depicting the oppression of impoverished Jews were popular among Jewish revolutionaries, and the poetry of Joseph Bovshover, David Edelstadt, Morris Rosenfeld, and Morris Winchevsky, all of whom immigrated from the Russian Empire to the United States in the 1880s and 1890s. Collectively known as "sweatshop poets," their verses decried the physical and emotional sufferings of beleaguered immigrant workers and exhorted them to action. Some of this poetry was set to music and sung at political gatherings in eastern Europe as well as the United States.[3]

Activists in the Russian Empire soon came to regard Yiddish as valuable in its own right. During the period of reactionary political repression that followed the failed 1905 Revolution, Jewish radical movements turned increasingly to cultural activism. This development entailed contentious debates over Jewish language use, not only among those who advocated variously for Modern Hebrew, Russian, or Yiddish but also internally among the various champions of Yiddish. Members of the Labor Zionist party Poale Zion supported Yiddish as an integral part of Jewish life in the diaspora while also promoting Modern Hebrew as the primary language for Jewish life in Palestine. Under the leadership of Simon Dubnow, the Folkspartey advocated for Jewish autonomy within a liberal democracy and supported Jewish multilingualism, recognizing the value of Hebrew, Russian, and Yiddish. The various Jewish socialist parties—the Jewish Labor Bund, the Fareynikte Yidishe Sotsyalistishe Arbeter Partey (United Jewish Socialist Workers Party), and the Socialist Territorialists—all promoted the use of Yiddish. However, they differed among themselves regarding the ends toward which the embrace of Yiddish should be mobilized—for example, whether cultural activity in the language that did not promote socialism should be encouraged.[4]

The most renowned debates over the use of Yiddish in Jewish cultural politics at this time took place at a conference convened in Czernowitz in 1908, the first such public gathering to discuss the status of Yiddish and plan for its future. The conference attracted a range of individuals committed to the language, including leading ideologists (Nathan Birnbaum, Chaim Zhitlowsky), political activists (Bundist Ester Frumkin [née Khaye-Malke Lifshits], Labor Zionist Lazar Khazanovich, diaspora nationalist Noah Prylucki), and authors (Sholem Asch, Peretz, Abraham Reisen). The conference's agenda raised a series of issues on language development, such as Yiddish pedagogy and standardization, as well as support for various cultural activities. However, debates over the status of the language, especially in relation to Hebrew, dominated the proceedings. Indeed, the conference is best remembered for proclaiming Yiddish to be "a national language of the Jewish people"—thereby accommodating those who insisted that Hebrew also be so recognized—and demanding for Yiddish (and, implicitly, its speakers) "political, social, and cultural equal rights."[5] The signature accomplishment of this conference, therefore, was not strategic but symbolic: a public proclamation of the legitimacy of both Yiddish and its speech community in nationalist terms. At the same time, the conference's agenda demonstrated the ideological value to be invested in the language by raising the needs of standardization, education, and high culture. In this respect, the Czernowitz Conference was comparable to other landmark language conventions of the period, including for Hebrew in 1903, Esperanto in 1904, and Catalan in 1906.[6]

As championing Yiddish became part of the agenda of various eastern European Jewish political movements, the language was no longer regarded simply as an instrument for disseminating information and promoting activism but as a defining emblem of Jews as a political collective. During the first decades of the twentieth century, a number of leading activists in Jewish politics—Ber Borochov, Dubnow, Prylucki, Nokhem Shtif—also made pioneering contributions to the study of Yiddish language and its development. They regarded these efforts as part of a larger project of uplifting eastern European Jews, in which the transformation of their vernacular was integral to their social and political advancement. Barry Trachtenberg writes of Borochov's scholarship and advocacy that his aim was to "turn Yiddish into a state language in the absence of a state. It would therefore be the task of the Yiddish philologist to forge a collective national identity not only by giving Jews a standardized means through which to communicate with one another, but by instilling in them a shared historical narrative, demarcating the nation's borders, and determining—by virtue of fluency—one's status as a 'citizen.'"[7]

Organized support for Yiddish became an ideology—secular Yiddishism—that endowed the language with political agency. Yiddish straddled two distinct aspirations of many eastern European Jewish radicals: participating in a broad-based class revolution with fellow proletarians of all backgrounds and maintaining a distinct Jewish collectivity. Ardently secular in their convictions, they nonetheless refused to assimilate into a Russian cultural mainstream. Yiddish could speak to the large Jewish working class and, moreover, speak for them as the emblematic voice of Jewish labor. At the same time, Yiddish could proclaim Jewish concord across class lines in the face of anti-Semitic attacks (including by some radicals) and signify a distinct Jewish culture as the equivalent of an ethnic nationality. Thus, in 1910 all Jewish political parties in Austria exhorted Jews to list Yiddish as their first language in the census as a signifier of Jewish solidarity.[8]

As their ideological embrace transvalued the language, Yiddishists demanded that Jewish radicals who had become estranged from Yiddish engage it with new attention to its significance. Some argued for the language's vital presence in the Jewish body politic, articulated in a corporeal discourse. In 1897 Zhitlowsky exhorted a group of radical Jewish students in Basel to return to Yiddish and thereby "reunite yourselves with the masses. Unify the separated limbs of our people. Return it to its senses!"[9] Nor were such convictions exclusive to Yiddishists; writing in Hebrew to his fellow Zionists in 1903, Mordecai ben Hillel Hakohen insisted: "Only by means of the Jargon [i.e., Yiddish], can we understand the internal life of the Jewish masses. . . . As long as we do not understand Jargon, we will not feel the pulsebeat of the masses or train our ears to hear . . . the masses when they address us or each other. Nor will we have the real key . . . to the people's heart."[10]

This purposeful embrace of Yiddish is exemplified by the fact that it was not the native language of several leaders of Yiddishist political movements. Nathan Birnbaum (autonomism), Borochov (Poale Zion), and Vladimir Medem (Bund) all had limited, if any, command of Yiddish until they became politically active as young men, at which time they began studying it. This new consciousness about the language among the most politically active Jews redounded to eastern Europe's Yiddish-speaking masses, who subscribed to political movements' periodicals, joined their youth movements and labor unions, participated in their rallies, and attended other public events.

As Jewish political movements evolved, Yiddishism increasingly diverged from Zionism. Like cultural Zionists, Yiddishists envisioned secular activities, centered on language, as having the capacity to unite Jews as a nationality. But cultural Zionism promoted Hebraism, which required that the Jewish masses learn what was, in effect, a new language: not the language of *ivre* but what in Yiddish is called *hebreish* ("Modern Hebrew"). Instead, Yiddishists advocated embracing the longstanding vernacular shared by millions of Jews as a language to be cultivated, rather than condemned. Moreover, Yiddishists viewed the diaspora not as degrading but as having defining value for Jewish life, thereby putting them at odds with political Zionists, who prioritized establishing a Jewish sovereign state.

Yiddishists' convictions about language and diaspora were conjoined in the political principle of *doikeyt*. The familiarity of Yiddish exemplified the geographical imminence of *doikeyt*. At the same time, *doikeyt* transvalued the places where Jews lived and the language they spoke with one another in the course of daily activities as defining sources of national consciousness and pride. One's milieu, physical as well as linguistic, was not to be regarded as inferior, nor was it simply to be taken for granted. Rather, it should be embraced and thereby revolutionized.

After World War I, the redrawn map of eastern Europe enabled unprecedented possibilities for political activity in Yiddish. New republics created by the Paris Peace Conference of 1919 transformed subjects of the former Romanov and Habsburg Empires into citizens of new countries. The conference made special provisions for their ethnic minorities, including the right to form political parties that could publish and convene public meetings in their native languages. Jewish political parties—religious and secular, Zionist and diaspora nationalist—employed Yiddish to communicate with the Jewish public and to operate youth movements, school systems, workers' associations, public health organizations, and amateur sports clubs.[11]

Yiddish was central to the Soviet Union's recognition of Jews as a national minority. In tandem with the endorsement of Yiddish, the state repudiated Hebrew for its association with religion and Zionism. During its first decades, the Soviet Union both underwrote and supervised minority language activity—including press, theater, publishing, education, and research—thereby providing Yiddish writers, performers, educators, and scholars with unprecedented governmental attention that was both supportive and constraining. The state mobilized Yiddish to regulate daily life—for example, providing legal forms in Yiddish, as was done with other minority languages—and to realize large-scale efforts to transform Jewish life ideologically, socially, and economically. Under the aegis of the Soviet Union, every public use of Yiddish was imbued with political meaning, reflected in form as well as content.[12]

As Yiddish manifested Jews' public presence in the Soviet Union, the fate of the language, its culture, and its communal leadership was tied to shifts in state policy toward national minorities. Public Yiddish culture declined under Stalin's leadership in the 1930s, as part of larger efforts to centralize state authority. Yet after the outbreak of World War II, the Soviet Union mobilized Yiddish culture to promote the international struggle against fascism, including visits to Jewish communities in England and North America by writer Itzik Feffer and actor Solomon Mikhoels as representatives of the Jewish Anti-Fascist Committee in 1943. Shortly after the war's end, however, the Soviet Union liquidated public Yiddish culture. Schools and other institutions were shut down; leading writers and activists were arrested in 1948, falsely convicted of anti-Soviet activities, and executed in 1952.[13] Akin to a political prisoner, Yiddish was "rehabilitated" in the late 1950s, as part of a larger cultural thaw under Khrushchev, and maintained a limited public presence in the Soviet Union until its collapse in 1991.

In the United States, by contrast, the lack of state regulation afforded Yiddish-speaking political activists expansive opportunities to organize

"Worker—Your newspaper is the *Folkstsaytung*." This 1936 poster advertises the *Folkstsaytung* (People's newspaper), which was published by the Yidisher Arbeter Bund (Jewish Labor Bund) in Warsaw from 1921 to 1939. Both the poster's slogan and the artwork by H. Cyna link this Yiddish newspaper with the Jewish working masses and with public activism, which would be reinforced by the poster's display in city streets. (From the Archives of the YIVO Institute for Jewish Research.)

and publish. At the turn of the twentieth century, immigrant Jewish radicals printed political materials not only for domestic distribution but also to be smuggled into Russia, where such works would not receive the censors' approval.[14] Immigrant political movements promoted their respective ideologies through their own Yiddish newspapers, some of which had long runs, especially the anarchist *Freie Arbeiter Stimme* (1890–1979) and the socialist *Jewish Daily Forward* (1897–1986).[15] Over the years, these papers' editors negotiated ideological changes wrought by major events—including wars, massacres, economic turmoil, the collapse of regimes and creation of new countries—using a medium that can, in effect, reinvent itself on a daily basis. Throughout these upheavals, the Yiddish language served as a constant, both instrumentally and symbolically. At the same time, the trajectories of the American Yiddish press also reflect generational dynamics, shaped by immigration and education as well as language use and political convictions.

As social media platforms, these American Yiddish newspapers were at the hub of activities that included political action (strikes, elections, rallies) and cultural events (lectures, excursions, balls). Alongside the press, a politically charged American Yiddish performance culture developed in the first decades of the twentieth century, including choruses affiliated with political organizations, radical theater productions staged by ARTEF (acronym of the Arbeter teatr-farband [Worker's Theater Union], 1925–1940), and comical left-wing sketches performed by Modicut (1925–1933), a puppet theater created by Yosl Kotler and Zuni Maud.[16] Efforts to engage immigrants' children in political activism centered on secular Yiddish schools run by the Labor Zionist Farband, socialist Arbeter Ring, and communist Internatsyonaler arbeter-ordn. Summer camps run by these movements (named Kindervelt, Kinder-ring, and Kinderland, respectively) strove to provide youngsters with utopian environments in which Yiddishist political and cultural ideals were imparted in conjunction with athletics, crafts, and performances.

• • •

Jewish political activists dealt with Yiddish as a subject of opprobrium as well as support. Yiddishism took shape in eastern Europe within a *shprakhnkamf*, in which advocates for Yiddish wrangled with both Hebraists and language assimilationists. The contending arguments for or against various languages were rooted in new ideologies of Jewish nationalism, which were informed by ongoing political discourses in Europe. Language use was central to nineteenth-century discussions of nationalism among ethnic groups in the Romanov and Habsburg Empires. As historian Raymond Pearson notes, the region's minorities "seized upon language as the criterion which granted their nationalism equal status with any other."[17] These groups maintained that a single, shared language and its attendant culture (literature, press, education, theater, folklore) defined a nationality both inclusively—uniting speakers across regional and class differences—and exclusively, distinguishing one nation from another. Many eastern European Jewish nationalists embraced this model, flouting Jews' traditional internal diglossia, their widespread geography across ethnolinguistic boundaries, and their growing interest in mastering the languages of their neighbors—Hungarian, Polish, and Romanian, among others—as well as languages of culture with which they may not have had any direct contact, including English, French, and German.[18]

External efforts to encourage eastern European Jews to abandon Yiddish as their vernacular and turn to state languages had been underway in some locations since the late eighteenth century, fostered by government endeavors through education and bureaucratic regulation. Joseph II issued edicts in the 1780s intended to transform Jewish life in the Habsburg Empire, such as permitting Jews' admission to secular schools where German was the language of instruction and mandating the use of German in official documents and records. In 1844 the Romanov Empire opened schools that taught Russian language and secular subjects to Jewish children.[19] Magyarization of Jewish education was instituted in 1867 in Hungary, following the establishment of its semi-independent status within the Habsburg Empire.

Results of these efforts varied within each country, reflecting differences in language use correlated to region, class, education, and religiosity. In the western provinces of the Russian Empire, Jews' linguistic assimilation was largely confined to small but influential groups of intellectuals, professionals, and members of the upper economic strata. By the turn of the twentieth century, the majority of Jews in Hungary spoke Hungarian. In many cases, they spoke German as well, though census data counted Yiddish as German; Hasidim in particular were distinguished by continuing to speak Yiddish.[20] In Romania, Jews living in major urban centers, especially Bucharest, tended to adopt Romanian as their vernacular, while Jews in provincial locales were more likely to maintain the use of Yiddish. Even as these states strove to promote an official monolingualism, eastern European Jewish populations evolved new configurations of their longstanding multiglossia, especially in communities located at political and cultural frontiers. For example,

Jews in Czernowitz, the capital of Bukowina under the Habsburgs, evolved a complex "mixture of languages (German, Yiddish, Romanian, Ruthenian, Russian) that resulted in a characteristic local jargon," which was maintained even after the region came under Romanian control following World War I and Romanian was proclaimed the official language.[21]

Like Yiddishists, Hebraists resisted linguistic assimilation in the name of establishing a modern Jewish national culture centered on language use. However, informed by both maskilic principles and Zionist ideologies, Hebraists typically viewed Yiddish as inimical to Jewish nationalism, associating the language with their portrayal of the diaspora as exile, in which Jews were detached from their ancient cultural and political roots. Ahad Ha'am (né Asher Zvi Hirsch Ginsberg), the founder of cultural Zionism, argued that only Hebrew had ever been the Jews' national language. He insisted not only that Yiddish lacked the dignity or respect for this level of prestige, but that it was "an alien tongue acquired in a strange land." The fallen state of exile, he maintained, had reduced Jews to a weakened condition, in which they resorted to Yiddish "only under compulsion" and would doubtless soon rid themselves of this "external and temporary medium of intercourse."[22] Literature scholar Avraham Novershtern notes that the *shprakhnkamf* was severest in sites of the most radical transformations of Jewish life: the Zionist settlement in Palestine, where Hebraists' "efforts to deny any place for Yiddish sometimes took ugly and even violent forms," and the Soviet Union, where "all manifestations of Hebrew culture were banned," in part "due to the active intervention of the Jewish communists, who considered Yiddish the only legitimate language of the 'Jewish working masses.'"[23]

As Hebraism became a central aim of Zionism, efforts to establish Hebrew as a language of daily life focused on Jewish settlers in Palestine. There the "rebirth" of vernacular Hebrew paralleled the mission to establish a Jewish state on the site of ancient Israel as a response to the onerous conditions of Jewish life in the diaspora. Hebraists linked the creation and mastery of their new vernacular with suppressing the diaspora languages spoken by Jewish immigrants to British Mandate Palestine. This undertaking entailed the equivalent of military action: Hebraists organized the Gedud megine ha-safah (Battalion of the Defenders of the [Hebrew] Language) and the Igud le-hashlatat ha-ivrit (Organization for the Enforcement of Hebrew) to police Jewish settlers' language use. Historian Liora Halperin suggests that Hebraists' persecution of Yiddish was due, in part, to fears that "the British, who had granted Hebrew official status, would renege on this commitment if they came to believe that Hebrew was not the real mother tongue of many Jews." Anti-Yiddish activity included campaigns against showing talking films in the language—most infamously, a 1930 protest against a presentation of *Mayn yidishe mame* (My Jewish mother) in Tel Aviv, during which members of the Gedud megine ha-safah disrupted the film with noise and threw ink and "foul smelling objects" at the screen. As a compromise, the film was shown without sound—in effect, staging a performance of the silencing of both the *yidishe mame* and the audience's mother tongue.[24]

Historian David Shneer notes that the suppression of Hebrew in the Soviet Union had been "part of the internal Jewish battle for more than a decade to create a monolingual, modern Jewish culture, a battle taken on by—not created by—the Communist Party and Soviet state." In this context, advocacy for Yiddish and against Hebrew was articulated in terms of class conflict. Thus, Shneer observes, in 1926 the Central Jewish Bureau of the Council for National Minorities likened the use of Latin in Christian Europe to that of Hebrew as a language associated with "materially privileged segments of the Jewish population." These Jews "had a contemptuous attitude toward Yiddish, the language spoken by the Jewish poor," which therefore "reflected the needs of the exploited classes."[25] As a consequence of this view of Hebrew, journalist Yehoshua Gilboa reports, the Soviet Union banned all activity in the language, including "communist and explicitly pro-Soviet publications. . . . Even the 'Internationale' in a Hebrew translation" was deemed "counter-revolutionary."[26]

• • •

The outbreak of World War II roiled and eventually undid Jewish political life in eastern Europe. Stripped of their basic rights as citizens in Nazi-occupied territories, Jews struggled for their very survival. German forces confined Jews in ghettos and established *Judenräte* (German: "Jewish councils") to govern these imprisoned populations under German supervision. These councils used Yiddish to communicate with ghetto inhabitants; at the same time, the language played a vital role in organizing underground resistance movements and covert projects to document both the German persecution of Jews and their resilience. Interwar Jewish political activism provided a foundation for these efforts, exemplified by Emanuel Ringelblum, whose youthful experience as a member of Poale Zion inspired his career as a historian and community activist in the years before the war. In the Warsaw ghetto, Ringelblum organized an extensive clandestine project to collect records of Jewish life and death in the ghetto.[27] Jews undertook similar efforts to document their persecution in other ghettos and also composed Yiddish poems and songs that gave voice to suffering and inspired resistance.[28] The language was "written . . . with blood," as Hirsh Glik, a poet of the Vilna ghetto, famously stated in his "Partisans' Hymn." This was no mere metaphor, as documented by a photograph taken by Zvi Kadushin in the Kovno ghetto. During a raid, as one of his neighbors lay dying, the man wrote on the floor in his own blood the words *Yidn nekome!* ("Jews—revenge!").[29] In the early postwar years, examples of how Yiddish had served as a means of resistance to persecution during the Holocaust—through songs, poems, jokes, sayings, and other expressions—were collected and published by writers Szmerke Kaczerginski and Yisrael Kaplan, among others.[30]

On June 26, 1941, a man shot during an attack in the Kovno ghetto wrote the words *Yidn nekome!* ("Jews, revenge!") on the floor, using his own blood. His message was photographed by Zvi Kadushin (George Kadish), a math and science teacher who secretly documented the ghetto using handmade cameras. (From the United States Holocaust Memorial Museum.)

The political uses of Yiddish that had flourished in the first half of the twentieth century were either greatly weakened or terminated altogether in the wake of the war. Beyond the mass murder of Yiddish speakers throughout Europe, this decline was due in part to the much-altered social and political circumstances in which Jews around the world now found themselves, as well as to rapid changes in their language use: the suppression of Yiddish culture in the Soviet Union and constraints on its use in countries under Soviet domination, the repudiation of Yiddish by the State of Israel, and extensive linguistic assimilation among Ashkenazim living in the Americas, western Europe, and elsewhere, as a result of both external pressures and internal desires to integrate successfully in these countries. Notwithstanding these developments, some prewar Jewish political organizations continued to advocate for Yiddish or used it to communicate with constituents in the postwar period. A case in point is the Jewish Labor Bund, which, historian David Slucki notes, was transformed into a transnational movement after the war, extending its principle of *doikeyt* to Yiddish-speaking communities in major cities in Argentina, Australia, France, Israel, Mexico, and the United States, among other countries.[31]

In the decades since the Holocaust, Yiddish has emerged as a political voice in new ways, involving a variety of populations, ideologies, and agendas as well as different ideas of the language's symbolic value. The subaltern status of Yiddish in Israel tacitly marked public use of the language in print and performance as acts of resistance against the state's language policy and its implications for Jewish culture in the new country. Sometimes the political significance of using Yiddish in Israel was more overt. For example, actors Shimen Dzigan and Yisroel Shumacher, famous for their comic satires in interwar Poland, settled in Israel in the 1950s, where they continued to perform in Yiddish. Yiddish studies scholar Diego Rotman observes that the duo "sought to invert, deprecate, and thus subvert" Israel's "political elites" and their "vaunted self-image" by taking the "national Hebrew narrative" and relating it "in the Yiddish vernacular."[32]

The postwar reconstitution of Hasidic communities in locations far from their eastern European origins—London, Antwerp, Montreal, Jerusalem, Melbourne, and especially New York—engendered new uses of Yiddish as a political language. Hasidic leaders employ Yiddish to promote political action within their communities, for example, when endorsing candidates for whom their followers should vote in elections. Conversely, local politicians and government agencies sometimes make use of Yiddish to engage

Hasidim. In addition to the instrumental value of communicating in the language to disseminate public health information or notices about changes in mass transit, as has been done in New York, this practice implicitly acknowledges the importance of Hasidim as constituents. Their use of Yiddish has also figured in debates concerning the limits of their political power. In 1994 the Supreme Court of the United States ruled against the Satmar Hasidim of Kiryas Joel, located in Orange County, New York, who sought to create a separate state-funded school district, exclusively for their children, within the town. Though the court's majority ruling was based on the principle of the separation of church and state, a dissenting minority opinion questioned whether the issue at hand concerned culture rather than religion, given the community's extensive use of Yiddish as their language of daily life.[33]

The advent of Yiddish as a subject of study at university has attracted some students whose interest in the language is overtly political. In the United States, this was notably the case in the 1970s, as some young activists on the New Left were interested in learning about earlier generations of Jewish radicals. Studying Yiddish enabled these students to acquire information about this history and forge a symbolic bond with earlier progressive activists. University students continue to be drawn to Yiddish because of its association with various Jewish social and political alternatives. Some opt to learn Yiddish over Modern Hebrew, whether rejecting its association with Zionism or as a reaction against the State of Israel's history of asserting a Hebrew hegemony by marginalizing and oppressing diaspora Jewish languages and cultures. This valuation of Yiddish has even attracted interest among young Jews in Israel, such as members of the Israeli group Hemshekh-dor (Generation of Continuity), who promoted the study of Yiddish at the turn of the twenty-first century as part of a call to their generation of Israelis to connect with Ashkenazic heritage. The group argued that this rethinking of their identity as Israelis not only would be to their own benefit but also could have a positive impact on their relations with Palestinians and the Arab world.[34]

Concurrently, cities in Europe have become home to Yiddish language courses, publishers of Yiddish translations, and performances of klezmer music and Yiddish song. These cultural endeavors, in which non-Jews play a significant, often leading, role, have noteworthy political implications. For example, Jewish heritage activist Ruth Ellen Gruber argues that "playing klezmer and Yiddish music in Germany and Poland presents a symbolic attempt to right wrongs: to reconstitute Jewish culture destroyed in the Holocaust, to 'bring back,' to 'resurrect,' to 'heal.' "[35] Engaging Yiddish culture in this context recalls Europe's Jewish past both as an important subject in itself and in order to address challenges that Europeans now face with regard to multiculturalism.

All of these recent activities complicate the once self-evident tautology conjoining Yiddish language, Ashkenazic culture, and Jews. Far from the turn to Yiddish as an expedient for engaging masses of native speakers in political thought and action, as was the case little more than a century earlier, the language is now used to test the limits of what might constitute Yiddish culture and its relation to a public, thereby creating new possibilities for Yiddish to find a political voice.

# 13
# Personality

Attributing a personality to a language may yield its most imaginative anthropomorphizations. Doing so turns attention away from the language as a means of sharing information, opinions, feelings, speculations, and so on, and instead centers on the language as having some inherent signifying power, above and beyond the semantic content of what is uttered or written in it. The language's scope as a signifier is both diminished and expanded by this attribution. On one hand, it suggests that the language is inherently constrained by its character, which inhibits or skews the ability to use the language comprehensively. On the other hand, a language's personality implicitly imbues anything conveyed in the language with an extra register of meaning. Languages are more likely to be assigned a personality when they are engaged at some remove from their vernacular imminence and presumed role as routine conduits of meaning—for example, when encountered as a foreign language, a language juxtaposed against other languages, a partial language, an endangered language, or a language under critical scrutiny.

All of these possibilities pertain to Yiddish, to which a remarkable range of personalities has been ascribed. Benjamin Harshav attributes this propensity to the language's foundational vernacularity. He argues that associations with its orality and cultural intimacy inform the "semiotics of Yiddish," regardless of how it is employed:

> In the twentieth century, Yiddish has been used for many kinds of discourse, often quite contradictory to whatever might be its "inherent" or accepted nature. This "oral" and popular language has been successfully harnessed to impressionist prose, historiography, linguistic and statistical research, political propaganda, and "ivory tower" poetry. Nevertheless, in social perception, the language did carry a cluster of characteristic features, developed in its unique history and crystallized in its modern literature. The very fact that native speakers may assign such emotive qualities to the language, rather than seeing it as a neutral vehicle for communication, speaks for itself.[1]

Though this phenomenon has a longer history, ascribing a personality to Yiddish has become more expansive and perhaps more urgent in the decades following World War II. This practice is particularly prevalent when devotees employ other languages to extol the distinct character of Yiddish in order to convey its significance to audiences unfamiliar with the language. These accolades sometimes appear in books that compile selected glosses of Yiddish terms, historical information, explanations of traditional customs, or translations of anecdotes—all in an effort to celebrate the scope of Yiddish culture. Consider, for example, Endel Markowitz's 1980 *Encyclopedia Yiddishanica*, a soi-disant "anthology of Jewish history, culture, religion, language, idioms, colloquialisms and teachings," which begins as follows:

> The Yiddish language can only be described as a conglomeration of ageless, paradoxical sentiment transfused into emotional reaction due to the constant pressure and recrimination heaped upon the Jews through the centuries. Steeped in irony and sarcasm; stained and spattered by bitterness and despair, the poignant Jewish existence, painfully accepted as their destiny, reveals itself through the subtlety of sardonic expressions, which, strangely enough, enabled them to retain their sanity and continue to survive.[2]

The preface to *The Joys of Yiddish*, Leo Rosten's "relaxed lexicon" of the language, offers a more overtly anthropomorphic characterization: "I think Yiddish a language of exceptional charm. Like any street gamin who has survived unnamable adversaries, it is bright, audacious, mischievous. . . . I think it a tongue that never takes its tongue out of its cheek. . . . In its innermost heart, Yiddish swings between *shmaltz* [here, 'mawkishness'] and derision."[3] Maurice Samuel's 1971 book *In Praise of Yiddish* also addresses "the inside feel of Yiddish," which, he asserts, "is a mirror of the total Jewish condition of the last two thousand years." However, aware of other characterizations of the language, Samuel first cautions against "those who harbor a sentimental but uninstructed affection for Yiddish as a quaint patois which has somehow produced a number of gifted writers" as well as "those Jews whose vestigial Yiddish is of the kind cultivated by borsht-circuit comedians posing as experts." With this caveat Samuel suggests, if inadvertently, that these more limited and distorted perceptions of Yiddish are also part of its character, as a language whose significance is often misunderstood or underestimated.[4]

The practice of imparting a personality to Yiddish engages the language in what I have termed the postvernacular mode, which privileges the language's secondary, symbolic level of signification over its primary level of communicating information. In the postvernacular mode, the fact that something is written or said in Yiddish, as opposed to some other language, is as important as the information being conveyed, if not more so.[5] Postvernacular engagement with Yiddish long predates the Holocaust, but in its wake this mode of engaging the language comes to the fore. The deliberate, self-conscious nature of postvernacular Yiddish facilitates conceiving of the language as having a personality. After World War II, the notion that Yiddish embodies a distinctive character, shaped by the travails and tenacity of its speakers, addresses the implicit question of why one might turn to the language at a time when its use has diminished and its future seems uncertain.

Assessments of the personality of Yiddish often arise in discussions of what are perceived as either its deficits or its excesses, in both cases intimating a defining imbalance of character. Regarding the former, Samuel's portrait of Yiddish includes what he considers to be its "blind side." He posits that although the language possesses words for flora and fauna, it lacks a sensibility for the natural world "such as we find in no other language," notwithstanding the fact that until the late nineteenth century "the major part of Yiddish-speaking Jewry lived in townlets and villages in close proximity to, though not in, nature." Similarly, he argues, Yiddish does not have a feel for the gentile world, whether Christian or pagan. This lack, he insists, "is not a matter of vocabulary; even if an equivalent or near-equivalent could be found for every word and idiom," addressing these topics in Yiddish, he asserts, "would seem . . . to belong to an unintelligible world."[6] Samuel thereby suggests that the language is both thorough in its expression of the "Jewish condition" and, at the same time, limited to this sensibility.

This argument does not square with the views of Yiddishists who vaunt the language's comprehensive breadth, exemplified by the extensive vocabulary for flora and fauna in Nahum Stutchkoff's Yiddish thesaurus and the hundreds of terms for plant life in Mordkhe Schaechter's dictionary of Yiddish botanical terminology.[7] But the notion of the language's inherent weaknesses (and the implicit corresponding limitations of its speakers) is hardly new, having featured frequently in attacks on Yiddish by *maskilim* and even on occasion by some of its champions.

Indeed, this critique figures provocatively in a landmark work of Yiddish literature by one of its most ardent champions, Isaac Leib Peretz's "Monish." (Initially published in 1888, it is sometimes identified as the first modern Yiddish poem.)[8] "Monish" relates a mock cautionary tale of the eponymous pious Jewish youth led astray by his attraction to a foreign woman, who is actually a sinister demon in disguise. Midway through the poem, Peretz interrupts the narrative with a disquisition on the incapacity of Yiddish to address the subject:

> How differently this song is sung
> For gentiles, in a gentile tongue.
> But not for Jews, not in *zhargon*;
> It doesn't have the proper tone
> For love or feelings. Not one word
> That suits the subject can be heard.[9]

Peretz's meta-discourse on the character of Yiddish archly echoes the established maskilic trope that the language lacks, among other things, the capacity for expressing romantic love. Following this sequence (which continues for another five stanzas), the tale of Monish resumes. The poem recounts how he succumbs to his temptress, who exhorts the youth to swear his love by articles of Jewish piety, including his *peyes* ("sidelocks") and the *paroykhes* ("curtain covering the ark in which Torah scrolls are kept in a synagogue"), and ultimately by God's name, which dooms Monish to perdition. His demise is not only the result of this blasphemy, having been seduced by a femme fatale who represents the forbidden enticements of Western culture. Monish is also damned because of his inability to articulate romantic sentiments properly, given the limitations of his native language, which is implicitly emblematic of a larger cultural deficit among its speakers. Moreover, by offering this playfully double-edged critique in a Yiddish poem that is modern in its form and worldview, even as it draws on a trove of traditional Jewish lore, Peretz suggests new possibilities for the language as the voice of irony.

Whereas some observers regard the personality of Yiddish as deficient in certain areas, others view it as plentiful in different aspects, especially after the Holocaust. As part of the beatified portrait of prewar Yiddish culture presented in their 1952 book *Life Is with People: The Jewish Little-Town of Eastern Europe*, anthropologists Mark Zborowski and Elizabeth Herzog explain that Yiddish "is rich in terms for referring to a learned man" and list ten examples, noting that "these are only a few of the terms used in everyday speech" to denote traditional Jewish erudition.[10] But far more attention has been paid to the abundance of piquant Yiddish idioms, especially proverbs and curses, which have been anthologized repeatedly, both in the original language and in translation.[11] Linguist James Matisoff introduces his 1979 study of Yiddish psycho-ostensives—conventionalized idioms voicing "blessings, curses, hopes, and fears"—by asserting that "Jews have always admired articulate, flavorful speech" and that "Yiddish has the deserved reputation of being a highly expressive language." Like Samuel, Matisoff seeks to correct others' portrayals of Yiddish as he proffers his own characterization of the language: "This 'funkiness' has been sentimentalized over with insistent vulgarity by some popular writers. At the other extreme we find the somewhat solemn academic approach of the professional Yiddishist, for whom the Yiddish language is primarily a vehicle for high-minded scholarly endeavor, a precious jewel to be preserved intact for an ever-dwindling cultural élite."[12]

To determine just what gives the language its "considerable emotive power," Matisoff advocates studying "the earthier side of Yiddish." He identifies the richness of the idioms at hand, centered on "attitudes toward good and evil," as a riposte against the onerous existence of eastern European Jewry, described as culturally isolated, economically impoverished, and socially oppressed: "For Jews with limited access to the mainstream of Western culture in the *shtetlekh* of Eastern Europe, the outside Gentile world was often rather hostile, cold, and intimidating. The inner Jewish world, in compensation, despite its material poverty and frequent pettiness, was at least full of overt demonstrations of feeling: heartfelt loves and hatreds, fears and hopes received constant outward expression in the language of the people."[13] For Matisoff, this aspect of Yiddish is noteworthy not merely for its histrionics but more significantly for providing its speakers with a defiant source of empowerment and a means of voicing moral convictions in the face of frequent injustices.

• • •

Especially complex characterizations of Yiddish are offered by some Ashkenazim who were not native speakers of the language but were at some remove, if only by a generation or two, from its speech community. Among German-speaking Jews at the turn of the twentieth century, this relationship was shaped by the longstanding perspective of Germanists who pathologized both Yiddish and its speakers. The discomfort produced by these Jews' attenuated relationship with the language engendered an understanding of its character that exposed their own definitional ambiguity about Jewishness.

Sigmund Freud's references to Yiddish, particularly in his 1905 study *Der Witz und seine Beziehung zum Unbewußten* (Jokes and their relation to the unconscious), exemplify this complexity. Yiddish is an essential element of some of the jokes Freud analyzes, and this has prompted scholars to probe the psychoanalyst's relationship to Jewishness.[14] Among others, linguist Christopher Hutton notes Freud's "clear association of Yiddish with 'the natural,' the true self that is suppressed in the process of transition (and translation)"—that is, the dynamic in Freud's family from his ancestors' traditionally observant life in provincial Galicia to his cosmopolitan, secular life in Vienna, marked by a shift in vernacular language. Hutton also links the suppression of Yiddish with the denial of "the feminine and the sexual in [Freud's] nature, this being in part symbolized by Yiddish."[15]

Consequently, "linguistic insecurity cannot have been absent from Freud's personality," Hutton posits. "The slip from German to Yiddish which would betray 'the hidden self' underneath would have been an important factor in the genesis of Freud's sensitivity to the revealing nature of small deviations from normative behaviour." Hutton argues that the use of Yiddish in the jokes Freud cites in his study are linguistic slips that "control" this regression. The language is employed as "a sign of the wish or the need for this repressed inner self to be revealed" and therefore constitutes for the Jewish tellers of these jokes "a kind of therapy."[16]

Franz Kafka offered a more playfully contradictory enactment of this fraught characterization of Yiddish in a lecture on the language that the author delivered in conjunction with a recitation of Yiddish poetry by actor Yitskhok Levi in Prague's Jewish Town Hall in 1912. Speaking in German, Kafka famously confronted his audience's anxieties about Yiddish by asserting "how much more Yiddish you understand than you think." Kafka's remarks on the nature of Yiddish, which are so laden with errors that they appear coyly deliberate, characterize the language as "tangled," lacking in "lucidity," its grammar undocumented (and undocumentable), and consisting "solely of foreign words" and "only of dialect." On one hand, he admonishes the audience that "you will not understand a word of Yiddish. . . . You will try to make out what you know already, and you will miss what is really there." On the other hand, Kafka assures his listeners that they nevertheless have an inherent ability to understand Yiddish "intuitively. . . . If you relax, you suddenly find yourselves in the midst of Yiddish." This will prove so powerful that the audience members will no longer be afraid of Yiddish but of themselves—which Yiddish can help them overcome.[17] Kafka provocatively suggests that it is precisely the tension between the anxieties associated with the language's otherness and the allure of its potential accessibility that defines his audience's equivocal Jewishness. Like Freud, Kafka characterized Yiddish as emblematic of both a Jewish pathology and its cure.

Evelyn Torton Beck argues that Kafka's perception of "the highly connotative nature of Yiddish," a consequence of his intense interest in Yiddish theater in the years 1910–1912, informed his distinctive literary style: "Especially rich in idiom and nuance, the Yiddish language is characterized by warmth and intimacy, a fact which Kafka himself observed when he wrote that to call the Jewish mother by the German *Mutter* is to create a false image, since the German language is colder and more formal than the Yiddish." According to Beck, Kafka's attention to the multivalent signification that inheres in the language may be reflected in "his vocabulary, which often suggests several layers of meaning behind each word."[18] Though written in German, she intimates, Kafka's prose was haunted by the personality of Yiddish, a reminder of the problematic fit between the author and his literary language.

Not all German-speaking Jews attributed to Yiddish a characterization that reflects their own anxieties about an ineluctable Jewish otherness. Martin Buber, for example, introduced his 1903 translation of a Yiddish play by David Pinski into German by explaining that Yiddish was "not just a rich but a supple language—less abstract but warmer than the Hebrew which it has enriched. Yiddish may lack the pure spiritual pathos of Hebrew, but it is replete with incomparably softer and sturdier, tender and rough inflections. In Yiddish the very substance of the people has in itself become a language."[19] Defined explicitly in contrast to the elevated stature of Hebrew—and implicitly, like Kafka, against the affectively cool constraints of the assimilated Jew's German—Yiddish incarnated for Buber an emotionally vibrant folkhood. He reported being drawn to Yiddish folktales because they "seem to live only by virtue of the unique inflections of that inimitable language of East European Jewry."[20]

Other Jews whose relationship to Yiddish was similarly attenuated have been drawn to study the language in order to connect with its distinctive vernacularity. Author Richard Fein offers an extensive account of this undertaking is his 1986 memoir, *Dancing with Leah: Discovering Yiddish in America*. Fein recounts his childhood engagement with Yiddish in a multigenerational household, where the language "was not so much spoken" but served "as a point of reference" among adults. Consequently, he explains, he grew up with a dislocated Yiddish: "Rhythms without a vocabulary," the language "was in my bones but hidden from my tongue." As an adult, Fein resolved to study Yiddish, initiating a relationship with the language that he describes in powerful anthropomorphic terms. He writes that he "succumbed to Yiddish" (the inverse of Monish's fate), which "was all the time waiting patiently for me," having "autochthonous powers of claiming me." The forceful agency that Fein attributes to an anthropomorphic Yiddish is echoed in his characterization of the language's "incantatory sounds" and "muscular flexing."[21] For Fein, like Buber, Yiddish has a personality of compelling energy, rooted in its ethnic authenticity.

• • •

The slogan "If you can't say anything nice, say it in Yiddish" might seem to have been lifted from Peretz's aforementioned disquisition on the language in "Monish." However, this is the title of one of the more recently issued English-language collections of Yiddish curses, and the sentence also appears emblazoned on T-shirts, coffee mugs, and lapel buttons, among other mass-produced items available for purchase.[22] This pithy characterization of Yiddish extends to other publications and material objects, appearing primarily in the United States after World War II, which present Yiddish as a language of invective, histrionics, and vulgarity. These phenomena include an array of comic dictionaries, which provide playful glosses and amusing anecdotes to selected Yiddish terms. Some of these books—such as *Drek!: The Real Yiddish Your Bubbe Never Taught* and *Dirty Yiddish: Everyday Slang from "What's Up?" to "F*%# Off!"*—present Yiddish as the idiom par excellence for imprecation.[23] Other examples, titled *Yiddish for Yankees* and *Every Goy's Guide to Common Jewish Expressions*, suggest that they are especially meant to provide cultural outsiders with access to Yiddish arcana.[24] But the front cover of the latter book reads, under the title, "Also recommended for Jews who don't know their punim ['face'] from their pupik ['navel']." Here, the non-Jewish reader serves as the rationale for a dictionary also intended for Jews bereft of Yiddish literacy, not unlike the role of women as the emblematic readers of early Yiddish literature that was, in fact, also for men who lacked the erudition of the learned elite.

Similar to these books is an assortment of mass-produced ephemera imprinted with one or more Yiddish words, almost always romanized, and often in a "kosher-style" font. Though sometimes evoking sentimentality (e.g., *mameleh*, "mommy"), the preponderance of words on these objects are provocative: *alter kocker* ("old fart"), *yenta* (here, "gossip"), *chutzpah* ("audacity"), *meshuganah* ("crazy"), *shiksa* (pejorative term for "non-Jewish woman"), among others.[25] In these manifestations, Yiddish—always appearing in fragmentary form, as isolated words rather than a whole language—is a signifier of the flamboyant, irrational, truculent, or salacious, but never the dispassionate. Stand-up comedians made similar use of selected Yiddishisms, first performing for fellow American Jews in "Borsht Belt" resorts, located in the Catskills and Poconos, and later for national audiences on comedy albums and television.[26]

Thus, after World War II, Yiddish shifts from being a sign of Jewish vernacularity to more of an emblem of linguistic and cultural obstinacy or alterity. Uriel Weinreich noted this shift in Yiddish use and signification in the early 1950s. In postwar America, he posited, the language was "losing its main communicative role" and seemed "destined to acquire peculiar connotations," especially "comic associations," through a selective "borrowing of its lexical elements," notably "colorful idiomatic expressions . . . with strong affective overtones, whether endearing, pejorative, or . . . obscene."[27] This practice has continued into the present, imparting the sensibility of Yiddish-speaking immigrants' children, who came of age in the middle decades of the twentieth century, to future generations. They, in turn, receive Yiddish as a mock heritage, understood as inherently fragmentary, unrestrained, and carnivalesque, and preserve it by perpetuating this limited Yiddish vocabulary in the modes of sentimentality, ridicule, and indelicacy.

Assessments of the character of Yiddish inevitably approach it selectively, as a result of either a limited familiarity with its full scope or a deliberate focus on those aspects of the language considered the epitome of its distinctive nature. Those who strive to describe the personality of Yiddish sometimes juxtapose their observations against others', an indication of how contingent and subjective these assessments can be. In light of the wide range of characteristics attributed to Yiddish—pious, vulgar, histrionic, ironic, ludic, constrained—it may be tempting to think of the language as suffering from multiple personalities. But such a diagnosis reflects an expectation that Yiddish ought to be consistent across speech communities as well as in the eyes and ears of all those attending to it, when, in fact, this is not the case.

Native speakers' efforts to attribute a character to Yiddish may reveal their sense of change in its value as a widely shared vernacular among Ashkenazim. For those who claim Yiddish as an ancestral language and engage it later in life, imbuing it with a character becomes an implicit exercise in self-scrutiny,

The cover story of the Summer 2011 issue of *Chutzpah* (Audacity), a magazine about Jewish culture published in Pennsylvania, examines the place of Yiddish in contemporary American life. Listed on the magazine's cover is a selection of popular Yiddish words, predominantly expressions of suffering, exuberance, sentiment, contempt, and appetite. Along with the magazine's name, this inventory presents Yiddish as especially rich in terms for voicing the histrionic and the extravagant, as opposed to a language of routine communication. (With permission of Andrew Cantor, publisher/creative director, *Chutzpah* magazine.)

refracted through the prism of a language that is both at a remove and, in some way, connected to them. Not only is the scope of their engagements with Yiddish frequently limited to isolated words or idioms taken out of context; they appear in formats other than vernacular language use: staged performances, anthologies, material goods.

Often, it is precisely those attributes of Yiddish that were reviled by earlier generations—its signification of ethnic particularism, irrational religious fervor, scholarly pietism, or unrefined earthiness—that attract subsequent enthusiasts. Their interest is rooted in a desire to engage a form of Jewishness understood as arcane or lost; it is envisioned as organic, authentic, and comprehensive, realized in the intense expressivity of vernacular speech. This devotion to Yiddish is different from that of secular Yiddishists, for whom the language is emblematic of national legitimacy and vitality, or from that of contemporary Hasidim, who value Yiddish for defining their communities' constituency and their borders. Rather, this is a postvernacular attachment, informed by a distance from Yiddish as a language of daily life. This distance is not only, or even primarily, a limitation, but is instead what animates the interest in Yiddish—and, moreover, imbues the language with a sense of liveliness that takes on a personality, embodying the desires that those who engage with Yiddish seek to fulfill.

# 14
# Life Expectancy

Discussing the demise of a language can be even more fraught than making claims for its time and place of birth, given the charged anthropomorphic terms employed and their extralinguistic implications. To speak of a language as dead, linguist David Crystal asserts, "is like saying that a person is dead."[1] Referring to languages as endangered suggests they are akin to rare species of animals or plants. The implied threat is not merely to their existence but to the planet's as a whole. Describing a language in these terms portends the disruption of a larger linguistic and cultural ecosystem, a loss for humankind generally. Even when languages are remote from our own community, or we have never even heard of them, their disappearance diminishes "the variety of world views embodied in those languages."[2]

Not all of the scholarly literature on dying or endangered languages mentions Yiddish—which may seem surprising, given the extent to which popular discussions of the language so often characterize it as being on the verge of expiring.[3] But sociolinguistic definitions of dying and endangered languages refer to speech communities so reduced in number that the possibility of there being no one alive who can speak, or even understand, their languages is imminent. Often, these languages have always had a small number of highly localized speakers and may not exist in an indigenous written form, their only documentation being an anthropologist's transcriptions or audio recordings. Conversely, there are ancient languages known to us only from a written record that is no longer decipherable. In both cases, the separation of languages from their users betokens a cultural fatality.

Yiddish is not in such dire straits. Nevertheless, as linguist Netta Avineri notes, the contemporary discussion of Yiddish "endangerment" entails both "a phenomenological reality and a discursive strategy."[4] Though statistics on the current state of its use are approximate, the language is currently understood, spoken, read, or written by hundreds of thousands of people across multiple generations and in numerous locations. While this is too robust a prognosis for a dying language, the current population of Yiddish speakers is exponentially smaller than it was less than a century ago. This rapid decline is due, foremost, to the Nazi-led murder of half of the world's Yiddish speakers during World War II. Other persecutions from without—notably, the suppression of Yiddish culture in the Soviet Union during the years following the war—are also responsible, as are abandonments from within. Jews' voluntary desertion of Yiddish includes non-*haredi* communities in the Americas, Australasia, and South Africa, where a more general shift among immigrants and their descendants away from "Old World" vernaculars to the languages of mainstream cultures has prevailed. Among Ashkenazic Jews in postwar Europe, their maintenance or abandonment of Yiddish reflects similar convictions about integration into a majority culture. In the case of Israel, what appears to be a similar shift is complicated by a state repudiation of Yiddish as part of the construction of an Israeli national culture that negates the diaspora and promotes the ideal of Modern Hebrew monolingualism.

Therefore, the decline in Yiddish speakers after the Holocaust is tied to larger transformations of Jewish life, beginning with geographic relocations on a grand scale: the diminution of Europe as a centuries-old redoubt of world Jewry and the emergence of two new, powerful centers in the United States and Israel. This development has in turn altered the longstanding practice of maintaining diaspora Jewish languages as in-group vernaculars, alongside some familiarity with Hebrew and Aramaic as devotional languages, as well as the languages of neighbors, states, or high culture, all interrelated within a complex multiglossia. Instead, Jews are increasingly monolingual, employing the mainstream languages of the nations in which they live for internal and external communication, as well as for religious study and sometimes even worship.

The most widely used language among Jews today is English, reflecting their extensive settlement in Australia, Canada, South Africa, the United Kingdom, and the United States. Moreover, given the stature of English as a world language of unparalleled reach, many Jews living in Europe, Israel, or Latin America also have at least some command of the language. Modern Hebrew, once envisioned by cultural Zionists as uniting world Jewry, has relatively few speakers outside of Israel, though there are strong symbolic attachments to the language, primarily reflecting a loyalty to Zionism.[5] Therefore, implicit in the contemporary discourse of Yiddish as dying is the larger issue of what it now means to speak or write as a Jew.

This discourse has, so to speak, taken on a life of its own. In the post–World War II era, the fate of Yiddish is often tied to the genocide of European Jews in memorial gestures. Anita Norich writes, "One of the lesser tragedies of the Holocaust has been that the dead cannot be allowed to rest in peace. We are forever trying to listen to them. . . . They are presumed to be calling out to us in Yiddish . . . , and Yiddish is presumed to have died with them."[6] Some Holocaust survivors address this close association of Yiddish with victims of the genocide forthrightly. For example, Dov Lewanoni explains at the beginning of his interview for the Shoah Visual History Archive, recorded in 1996, that he chose to speak in Yiddish "because it was the language spoken by most of the six million Jews murdered during the war." Other survivors interviewed for this archive recite poems or sing songs in Yiddish, even when their interviews are otherwise conducted in another language. In this context, performing in Yiddish constitutes "an act of defiance. Through these recitals, survivors implicitly insist that their lives be realized, and be heard, not only in the context of destruction and loss but also in terms of Jewish cultural persistence and creativity in their first language."[7] The demise of Yiddish also figures in humor that acknowledges, if somewhat wistfully, the passing of a generation of Jews for whom the language was their vernacular. Thus, a character in Cynthia Ozick's 1969 short story "Envy; or, Yiddish in America" tells a joke about a funeral cortege passing the offices of a struggling Yiddish newspaper on the Lower East Side. One of the paper's editors looked out the window, "saw the funeral passing by and called to his colleague: 'Hey, Mottel, print one less!' "[8]

In response to this pervasive sense of its decline, there has been considerable speculation as to what the use of Yiddish might be like today, had millions of its speakers not been murdered during the Holocaust. Some observers posit that even if there had been no genocide, Yiddish would have become obsolescent in eastern Europe. Sociologist Celia Heller, for example, argues that "had Poland not been defeated and had Jews lived on there, within two or three generations Polish would have probably replaced Yiddish as their predominant language."[9] However, historian Samuel Kassow maintains that such a community of Polish Jews would have continued to rely on Yiddish to communicate with relatives and other Jews living elsewhere (as was the case during the early postwar years).[10]

Yiddishists tend to respond to claims that the language is dying with ripostes in kind, insisting on its endurance and vitality. Thus, the title of linguist Joshua Fishman's 1981 compendium of essays, which provides an overview of "a thousand years of Yiddish life and letters," exhorts readers to "never say die!"[11] Fishman also defiantly responds to those who characterize Yiddish as moribund that doing so "merely reflects how dead it is to the claimants and how dead *they are* to its continued speakers."[12] In the aftermath of World War II, flouting widespread sentiments of the language's demise emerged as an important theme of Yiddish literature, in which continuing to write in the language often became an interrogation of itself. In Abraham Sutzkever's poem titled "Yiddish," composed shortly after his arrival in the new State of Israel, the author challenges the assertion that "my mother tongue is about to disappear" by demanding that the contender "show me *just where* is this language disappearing to?" The poet then proclaims that he will "swallow this vanishing language— / swallow and awaken every generation with my growl!"[13] Jacob Glatstein offers a similarly defiant response to those who declared that Yiddish is dying by defending it as "a language for eternity, not for the meantime" and mocking the lugubrious posturing of his fellow Yiddish speakers in America: "These prophets of doom are having themselves a genuine *good time*. . . . You can recognize it in their ecstasy, in their pathos, in the lovely Yiddish words they use to depict the end of their language, . . . creating an orgy of death and destruction. . . . They are all permeated with the sensation that they've heard a final Yiddish word."[14]

Remarkably, the trope of Yiddish as dying predates the Holocaust by decades, and not only among its opponents, such as Ahad Ha'am, who alleged in 1902 that "there is . . . no doubt that before long Yiddish will cease to be a living and spoken language."[15] (By contrast, maskilic detractors of Yiddish had bemoaned its unruly robustness only decades earlier.) At the turn of the twentieth century, some champions of the language also saw its demise as imminent. In 1899, Leo Wiener predicted that in the Western Hemisphere the language's "lease of life is commensurate with the last large immigration to the new world," while in Europe Yiddish would endure only "as long as there are any disabilities for the Jews."[16] Two years earlier, Morris Rosenfeld, whose Yiddish poetry Wiener promoted, claimed that the language "has no future" in America. Rosenfeld predicted that within a quarter century "even the best works in this language will only be literary curiosities" and bemoaned the future of a people "unable to utter their thoughts and feelings in a living tongue."[17]

Perhaps it seems confounding that such sentiments were voiced at a moment when the number of Yiddish speakers was greater than ever and they were extending their reach beyond Europe to major communities on other continents; when Yiddish literature, theater, and press were burgeoning, and the language was becoming a voice for mass political organizing and attracting support as a defining force for Jewish nationality. Yet it may be that some people perceived these very developments as destabilizing phenomena, disrupting the established vernacularity of Yiddish through geographic dislocation on a grand scale, the embrace of radical ideologies, and the advent of new cultural practices. Characterizing Yiddish as near its end at the turn of the twentieth century therefore marks a telling shift in the discourse surrounding the language, raising for the first time the possibility of its mortality, less a reflection of its use than a response to the uncertain future of its significance.

• • •

Beyond the tropes of Yiddish as either terminal or thriving are discussions of the language's state of being as transcending mortality. In response, Norich warns that "Yiddish has suffered terribly from and in the twentieth century, but part of its suffering at the beginning of the twenty-first century results from this turn to anthropomorphizing it, seeing it as an entity that can feel pain, die, rise phoenix-like from the ashes. Yiddish comes metonymically to stand for the people whose tears we cannot see, perhaps because, unlike them, it may be imagined to have a future."[18] Similarly, literature scholar Janet Hadda argues that the "tenacity and pluckiness" of Yiddishists "do not bestow immortality" on the language and that their convictions constitute a denial of its passing as a psychological defense against acknowledging that "an era has ended."[19]

Yet discourses that situate Yiddish beyond living or dying may be key to understanding how, in the wake of the catastrophic losses of the Holocaust and other assaults on the language, people conceive a future for Yiddish, however altered from its prewar existence. Rather than dismiss such sentiments as deluded or as magical thinking, it is worth considering the power of investing in the expansive possibilities suggested by the supernatural. For example, Max Weinreich offered this oft-cited explanation, when asked about his commitment to Yiddish in the postwar era, despite its widely perceived obsolescence: "Because Yiddish has magic, it will outwit history."[20] Adrienne Cooper explains the title of her 1997 recording of songs, titled *Dreaming in Yiddish*, as indebted to another of Weinreich's characterizations of the language's uncanny power: "Yiddish is the language of the Jewish unconscious in which every modern Jew will eventually dream. When that Yiddish dream comes to them, they will need an interpreter."[21] Other performers of Yiddish engage in similar subjunctive exercises to conjure approaches to the language and its culture that speak to contemporary audiences. Alicia Svigals, a founding member of the Klezmatics, explains that the band developed its approach to transforming the klezmer repertoire through a provocative speculation: If there hadn't been a Holocaust, "there would be Yiddish rock bands today, playing the kind of music we play."[22]

Perhaps the most famous discussions of Yiddish that situate it beyond mortality come from Isaac Bashevis Singer. In his remarks on receiving the Nobel Prize for Literature in 1978, Singer offered this roguish explanation for writing in Yiddish: "I like to write ghost stories, and nothing fits a ghost better than a dying language. The deader the language, the more alive is the ghost. Ghosts love Yiddish; they all speak it."[23] At the conclusion of his acceptance speech, however, Singer asserted that "Yiddish has not spoken its last word. It contains treasures that have not been revealed to the eyes of the world."[24] Indeed, Singer regularly reminded English-speaking audiences that when it came to the well-being of Yiddish, there was a significant difference between a dead language and a dying one. In an interview included in a 1986 documentary on his life and work, he remarked, "When I was a child, they told me that Yiddish was dying. They spoke about Yiddish dying fifty years ago, a hundred years ago. But Yiddish keeps on dying for at least the last two hundred years. It began to die the moment it was born. What is true about Yiddish is true in a way about the Jewish people. While we die we keep on being born again."[25]

Singer's comments recall literature scholar Simon Rawidowicz's characterization of Jews as "the ever-dying people," a notion he first addressed in Hebrew in 1948. Tracing this trope in texts from the Bible to the modern era, Rawidowicz argues that "Jewry has indulged so much in the fear of its end that its constant vision of the end helped it to overcome every crisis, to emerge from every threatening end as a living unit, though much wounded and reduced. In anticipating the end, it became its master. . . . Our incessant dying means uninterrupted living, rising, standing up, beginning anew."[26] Yet despite Singer's intimations of the language's immortality, he has been much vaunted as a vestigial figure, "the last great Yiddish writer,"[27] notwithstanding the fact that other accomplished Yiddish authors born in Europe before World War II—Binem Heller, Blume Lempel, Yenta Mash, Chava Rosenfarb, Sutzkever, among others—both lived and wrote longer than Singer did.

Moreover, the eventual passing of this cohort has given way to younger creators of Yiddish culture, most of them born after the war. Their work takes on new formats and themes, even as it is indebted to earlier generations of Yiddish speakers and is informed, if obliquely, by the phenomenon of their loss. Some of this work engages Yiddish in relation to other languages: performer Daniel Kahn's bilateral translations of song lyrics, variously involving English, German, and Yiddish;[28] media/performance pieces by Sala-Manca Group, in which artists Lea Mauas and Diego Rotman juxtapose Yiddish with Modern Hebrew as well as other languages;[29] artist Yevgeniy Fiks's 2016 *Soviet Moscow's Yiddish-Gay Dictionary*, which integrates glossaries of Russian gay slang and Yiddish to project an imagined solidarity between "two marginal communities";[30] and *Hatuey: Memory of Fire*, a 2017 opera in English, Spanish, and Yiddish by composer Frank London and librettist Elise Thoron, based on Yiddish author Ascher Penn's epic poem of 1931 about the eponymous Taíno chieftain who fought against the Spanish invasion of Cuba in the early sixteenth century.[31] These interlinguistic juxtapositions both recall earlier works of Yiddish culture in which contact with other languages was a defining feature and situate Yiddish in new multicultural configurations, in which the unlikeliness of its presence often constitutes a provocation.

Contemporary Yiddish culture increasingly involves people who are not native speakers of the language and whose connection to it does not conform to a conventional model of a heritage language. They frequently offer rationales for their interest in Yiddish, a practice that has, in effect, become a significant part of contemporary Yiddish culture. Consider, for example, Shane Baker, whose commitment to the language includes serving as executive director of the Congress for Jewish Culture, a secular Yiddish organization founded in New York in 1948, and performing in productions of the New Yiddish Rep. Baker has billed himself on the troupe's website as "the foremost Episcopalian on the Yiddish stage today," explaining that he "did not grow up with Yiddish, but plans on growing old with it."[32] Among Baker's performances is an autobiographical monologue, in which he recounts his early curiosity about Yiddish as a young man in Kansas City, Missouri, and drolly explains that after he began studying the language, he was visited "by the ghost of a Yiddish vaudevillian named Ludwig Zats, who urged him to become a star of Yiddish theater in New York."[33]

Even those with a more direct biographical connection to Yiddish recount the trajectory of their creative devotion to the language. Yermiyahu Ahron Taub, an American poet who writes primarily in English, explains that he also chooses to write in Yiddish "because I refuse to be denied my cultural heritage." Though he grew up among Yiddish speakers, it is not his first language, a fact that he describes as providing him entry into "a world that's familiar and also alien." Taub admits that there is an "audacity needed to create literary work in a language that is not one's first" and characterizes the effort as an act of defiance, flouting not only those who question why he would write in a language with a diminished readership but also the larger assumption that Yiddish culture is no longer accessible: "I'm staking a claim for Yiddish as a current, dynamic, ever-evolving language for literary creation and my own tiny tent within it. . . . Simply put, I can't let Yiddish go."[34] More than a manifesto declaring Taub's decision to write in Yiddish, this statement is part of his working through the challenges that doing so poses for him, revealing the effort that is part of his artistry.

• • •

The study of Yiddish today juxtaposes unrivaled opportunities with unprecedented challenges. At present, scholars at universities in Europe, North America, Israel, and Australia participate in the multidisciplinary study of Yiddish, publishing their scholarship in English, French, German, Hebrew, Polish, and Russian, among other languages.[35] Even as these endeavors expand on pioneering studies of Yiddish language, literature, and culture undertaken in Europe during the first half of the twentieth century, they differ in substantive respects that entail both gains and losses. Contemporary scholars of Yiddish seldom need to defend its intellectual legitimacy in the academy. Yet at the same time, these scholars are typically at further remove from vernacular speakers and their cultural as well as linguistic fluency. On one hand, the field benefits from scholarship in a broad range of intellectual perspectives, and the study of Yiddish is generally less driven by the ideologies of its speech communities. On the other hand, much of what researchers would once have found more easily accessible and perhaps have more readily understood has been lost or obscured by time and manifold cultural breaches. This is, of course, a challenge that scholars of many languages and cultures face; in the case of Yiddish studies, the loss is definitional, if often implicit. Its magnitude and enormity pose daunting challenges even as it inspires efforts to document and analyze the language, its speakers, and their ways of life.

Consider, for example, the consequences of digital humanities projects that provide readier access not only to Yiddish manuscript collections and print materials but also to audio and video documentation of native speakers, now digitized, catalogued, and accessed on the internet. This material includes sound recordings made in the immediate postwar years by individual researchers, such as thirty-two of psychologist David Boder's pioneering interviews on magnetized wire of Holocaust survivors, conducted at various sites in Europe in 1946.[36] That year, folklorist Ruth Rubin began recording Yiddish folk songs from informants in Canada and the United States, an undertaking she continued into the 1970s; another folklorist, Ben Stonehill, collected over one thousand wire recordings of Yiddish songs performed by Holocaust survivors in New York in 1948.[37] Audiotaped interviews for the Language and Culture Atlas of Ashkenazic Jewry, initiated in the 1950s, are available online, as are digitized scans of its extensive paper archive.[38] More recent projects documenting native speakers of Yiddish born in prewar Europe include the World of Yiddish: The Voice and The Image, a collection of "video testimonies given in Yiddish in which informants talk about their lives in Jewish Eastern Europe before the Holocaust," a project begun in the 1990s by the Yiddish Department of the Hebrew University in Jerusalem,[39] and AHEYM, the Archives of Historical and Ethnographic Yiddish Memories (the acronym means "homeward" in Yiddish), which videotaped interviews with nearly four hundred of "Eastern Europe's last native speakers of Yiddish," launched in 2002 by linguist Dov-Ber Kerler and historian Jeffrey Veidlinger at Indiana University.[40] In addition to recent projects specifically intended to document this cohort of Yiddish speakers, hundreds of interviews of Holocaust survivors have been recorded in the language, including over six hundred videos made in the 1990s for the Shoah Visual History Archive. Though not undertaken to document language use, these recordings nonetheless provide additional resources for the study of Yiddish as well as valuable insights into the role of language in offering personal history and Holocaust remembrance.[41]

These audio and video resources endow the Yiddish speech of waning generations with a kind of afterlife. Like all such recordings, they preserve moments of liveness, even as they transmute vernacular language use through the recording media and these various collecting projects' protocols. Here, too, there are gains and losses. On one hand, these recordings provide access to narratives, discussions, and performances from a bygone era, enabling one to listen to them repeatedly or excerpt them, thereby providing unprecedented opportunities for close study of oral language use. On the other hand, the recordings fix speech acts, the most evanescent and mutable of cultural productions, in suspended time. Even as they provide incomparable access to Yiddish orality of the past, these collections of recordings also serve as reminders of its loss, bringing the listener speech acts that can be audited, but not joined.

The threshold moment in the dynamics of Yiddish defined by the passing of its prewar native speakers coincides with new thinking about studying the language, some of which is motivated by recent changes in its use. The model of postvernacularity, while applicable to Yiddish language and culture well before World War II, is inspired by developments of the postwar period. Particularly notable among these developments is Queer Yiddishkeit, which, as a phenomenon of LGBT culture, offers a provocative model for rethinking the possibilities of Yiddish culture more generally. Instead of emulating an ideal of cultural continuity modeled on the biological relationship of parents and children, queer culture is the product of modern coming-of-age cohort groups. Moreover, it is distinguished by an intergenerational *dis*continuity that is "valued as an energizing force. . . . The queer paradigm of culture is that of a dynamic proving ground, its constancy comprising an ongoing breaking down and rebuilding of cultural practices and sensibilities." This model is fitting for the study of modern Yiddish culture as realized by its own cohort generations, "manifest in youth organizations, religious movements, political parties, trade unions, literary circles, educational institutions, various immigrant, refugee, and survivor associations, and so on." Rather than adhering to the paradigm of a "golden chain" of linked biological generations, Queer Yiddishkeit suggests that Yiddish culture is defined by "a tenacious discontinuity that, far from resisting disruption, thrives on it."[42]

The discontinuous nature of modern Yiddish culture also entails losses and gains. On one hand, none of the children of the *klasiker*—Sholem Yankev Abramovitsh, Sholem Aleichem, Peretz—spoke Yiddish. On the other hand, some of the leading Yiddishists of the first half of the twentieth century, including Max Weinreich, had limited or no native knowledge of the language but mastered it later in life. Nor is disruption only found in secular Yiddish culture. The Yiddish spoken by contemporary Hasidim not only varies considerably in substance from the language of their prewar ancestors; it is also used today as a barrier, rather than a bridge, between Hasidim and other Jews. Indeed, the pattern of discontinuity extends throughout the history of Yiddish, marked by periods of efflorescence—for example, the language's "Italian century," extending from the late 1400s to the early 1600s, during which there was "a veritable explosion" of innovative cultural activity among

Ashkenazim in northern Italy[43]—that eventually subside, only to be followed by other moments of thriving, involving different sites, genres, and agendas.

Complementing this diachronic model of linguistic and cultural discontinuity are new paradigms of synchronic language hybridity. As a rubric for the study of multilingualism, the concept of "translanguaging" challenges the conventional understanding of languages as discrete, parallel entities. Noting that "named languages are social, not linguistic, objects," linguists Ricardo Otheguy, Ofelia García, and Wallis Reid define translanguaging as "the deployment of a speaker's full linguistic repertoire without regard for watchful adherence to the socially and politically defined boundaries of named (and usually national and state) languages."[44] Translanguaging is an especially apt model for the study of Yiddish, whose speakers are always in some way multilingual. Moreover, given the demotic, diasporic character of Yiddish, as well as its varied history of recognition as a legitimate language and the contentious efforts to standardize it, the model of translanguaging suggests possibilities for analyzing Yiddish usage from the vantage of its speech communities rather than externally imposed criteria.

The notion of a contingent language hybridity, as opposed to the paradigm of the discrete, named language, also informs linguist Sarah Bunin Benor's approach to the study of Jewish language use in terms of a "distinctively Jewish linguistic repertoire"—that is, the ability to draw on "the linguistic features Jews have access to that distinguish their speech or writing from that of local non-Jews." Benor proposes this model in response to questions that have bedeviled the study of Jewish languages: Which (if any) vernaculars spoken by diaspora Jewish communities can be deemed languages, as opposed to dialects, and by what criteria? How does calling a Jewish community's demotic a "language" encompass its internal variations? Is the identity of a language as "Jewish" compromised when it is also spoken by non-Jews—for example, when "Christians who lived and worked in close proximity with Jews in densely Jewish areas sometimes picked up Yiddish as a second language?" Benor's model shifts attention away from languages as systems in the abstract and toward individual speakers and their linguistic agency. She writes that "Jews in any given time and place make selective use of their distinctive repertoire, in combination with the repertoires used by non-Jews, as they construct their identity."[45] Conceiving of language use as a process of individuated discernment redounds to the modern concept of the Jewish self as an ongoing, idiosyncratic project. Indeed, the rubric of identity, which figures extensively in discussions of contemporary American Jewish culture, may have inspired this model for examining Jewish language use generally.

Benor's study of Jewish languages includes considerable attention to Jewish English, which, per her model, is distinguished from the English of non-Jews by incorporating features of other languages, including Yiddish loanwords and constructions that calque Yiddish grammatical structures (for example, "She's staying by us"). This is "a widespread phenomenon among contemporary American Jews," who inflect their English with Yiddish "to indicate facets of their ethnic and religious selves, even when their parents and grandparents do not."[46] These "echoes" of Yiddish, as Benor terms them, constitute a kind of afterlife for the language. Studies of other contemporary languages—including Dutch, German, and especially Israeli Hebrew—perceive Yiddish as a similarly vestigial reverberation.[47] Linguist Ghil'ad Zuckermann argues that Yiddish is not merely a lingering presence in Israeli (as he terms the Hebrew now spoken in Israel) but plays a foundational, if largely unacknowledged, role in its formation. Whereas revivalists consider Israeli Hebrew a Semitic language, given its vaunted continuity with ancient Hebrew, Zuckermann "defines Israeli as Indo-European: Yiddish *relexified*, i.e., Yiddish, most revivalists' *mame loshn* (mother tongue), is the substrate, whilst Hebrew is the superstrate providing lexicon and frozen, fossilized, lexicalized morphology." Despite the fact that Hebrew revivalists envisioned their efforts as "a campaign for linguistic purity" that would negate "the Yiddish 'jargon,' . . . the Diaspora, and the diasporic Jew," the language they created "mirrors the very hybridity and foreign impact they [sought] to erase."[48]

Yiddish studies is galvanized by these threshold developments in the study of language and in the Yiddish language itself. Since World War II, Yiddish has shifted rapidly from a mass language to a niche language; from a language rooted in eastern Europe to a language based in multiple, disparate locations, most of them remote from its erstwhile center; from a native language to one increasingly acquired later in life, and therefore from a seemingly inevitable demotic to an elected language (by Jews whose ancestors abandoned Yiddish, by Jews who are not the descendants of Yiddish speakers, and by non-Jews); a language of shared vernacularity to a language of deliberate opposition—to the consequences of genocide, to assimilation, to Zionism, to Hebraism, to heteronormativity, or to some other status quo. In light of these developments, those studying Yiddish need to be open-minded with regard to both the practice and the theorization of Yiddish, past as well as present.

Perhaps, in the end, it is better not to speak of the life of Yiddish, but of its lives, as manifest in its multiple names, its geographic migrations, its shifting place within changing constellations of languages, its varied status as a language, and the range and dynamics of how it has been used. This may seem to contradict the anthropomorphism implicit in a biography of the language, but it affirms the foundational relationship of Yiddish with those who have used or engaged it in some way. For how can one think of a language without thinking of its speakers, even when they are gone? At the turn of the twentieth century, discussions of the relationship between Yiddish and its speech community often centered on the need to transform the language in order to improve the lives of its many native speakers. This impetus resulted in divergent strategies for reconceiving Yiddish and its speech community, initiated by revolutionaries and Orthodox Jews, diaspora nationalists and Zionists, champions of the avant-garde and purveyors of *shund*, those who wished to enshrine the Yiddish-speaking past and those who wished to subvert it. Today, discussions of Yiddish may center more on the language's need for speakers, as is the case among other languages whose future is considered uncertain. What is in danger of being lost is not language per se—lexicon, grammar, sound recordings, works of poetry and prose—but people for whom the language is part of their way of life.

• • •

As is also the case for others who work in the field of Yiddish, I am often asked what the language's future will be—a question that can only invite speculation or a shrug of the shoulders. But my answer is this: expect the unexpected. I began my work in Yiddish studies in the early 1980s; the years since have witnessed a number of developments that would then have surprised me and, no doubt, many of my mentors and colleagues: The burgeoning of interest in Yiddish among young scholars and enthusiasts, most of whom are not Jews, in Germany, Poland, and other European countries. New opportunities for contact between Yiddish speakers in countries that were once part of the Soviet Union with those in the West, as well as access to archives in former Soviet republics that had been shuttered for decades. The role of the klezmer revival in prompting international interest in Yiddish song and folkways, and the advent of *klezmorim* as authoritative spokespersons for the history of Yiddish-speaking Jewry. The attraction Yiddish holds for some younger Jews in Israel, part of that nation's evolving understanding of its relationship to the Jewish diaspora. The expanding role of Yiddish among Hasidim, including meta-discussions of its place in their lives and the language's use to voice dissent by the growing numbers of people breaking with *haredi* communities. The embrace of Yiddish as a voice of Jewish alterity by lesbian, gay, bisexual, and transgender people. The performance of Yiddish in contemporary media series, whether portraying multigenerational *haredi* family life in Jerusalem (*Shtisel*) or facilitating the irreverent comedy of two sparring pals in Montreal (*Yidlife Crisis*). The many possibilities for creating and sharing materials in or about Yiddish through the internet, as well as its potential for fostering communion among Yiddish speakers across geographic, generational, and ideological divides. In sum, there are more chapters yet to be written in the biography of Yiddish. It awaits new people drawn to the language for one reason or another and is limited only by their sense of its possibilities.

# Notes

## Introduction

1. On the estimated percentage of Jews who are Ashkenazim, see, e.g., Joël Zlotogora, "Mendelian Disorders among Jews and Population Screening for Reproductive Purposes," in *Focus on Genetic Screening Research*, ed. Sandra R. Pupecki (New York: Nova Science, 2006), 59. In 2001 sociolinguist Joshua A. Fishman estimated that there were about 250,000 Yiddish speakers in the United States, approximately the same number in Israel, and another approximately 100,000 elsewhere in the world. Paul Glasser, email message to author, May 14, 2003. Fishman discusses the challenge of determining the number of Yiddish speakers in "How Many Jews Speak Yiddish?" [Yiddish], *Afn shvel* 316 (October–December 1999): 22.

## Chapter 1

1. See Johann Gottfried Herder, "Treatise on the Origin of Language," in *Herder: Philosophical Writings*, ed. and trans. M. N. Forster (Cambridge: Cambridge University Press, 2002), 152. See also Jeffrey A. Grossman, *The Discourse on Yiddish in Germany from the Enlightenment to the Second Empire* (Rochester, N.Y.: Camden House, 2000), 28–74.
2. As cited in Solomon A. Birnbaum, *Yiddish: A Survey and a Grammar*, 2nd ed. (Toronto: University of Toronto Press, 2016), 46.
3. Ruth von Bernuth, *How the Wise Men Got to Chelm: The Life and Times of a Yiddish Folk Tradition* (New York: New York University Press, 2016), 81. See also Aya Elyada, *A Goy Who Speaks Yiddish: Christians and the Jewish Language in Early Modern Germany* (Stanford, Calif.: Stanford University Press, 2012), 1–2.
4. Elyada, *A Goy Who Speaks Yiddish*, 189.
5. Grossman, *Discourse on Yiddish in Germany*, 107, 106.
6. Jerold C. Frakes, *The Politics of Interpretation: Alterity and Ideology in Old Yiddish Studies* (Albany: State University of New York Press, 1988), 28–29.
7. See Steven E. Aschheim, *Brothers and Strangers: The East European Jew in German and German Jewish Consciousness, 1800–1923* (Madison: University of Wisconsin Press, 1982).
8. Cited in Wolf Moscovich, "Postwar Soviet Theories on the Origins of Yiddish," in *Origins of the Yiddish Language: Winter Studies in Yiddish*, vol. 1, ed. Dovid Katz (Oxford: Pergamon, 1987), 105.

9. Birnbaum, *Yiddish*, 57. On Birnbaum's life and work, see essays by David and Eleazar Birnbaum, Kalman Weiser, and Jean Baumgarten, ix–lxxviii.
10. Birnbaum, *Yiddish*, 13.
11. Max Weinreich, *History of the Yiddish Language*, ed. Paul Glasser, trans. Shlomo Noble and Joshua A. Fishman, vol. 1 (New Haven, Conn.: Yale University Press, 2008), 3.
12. See Philippe Wolff, *Western Languages AD 100–1500*, trans. Frances Partridge (New York: McGraw-Hill, 1971).
13. Weinreich, *History of the Yiddish Language*, 1:45.
14. Max Weinreich, "The Reality of Jewishness versus the Ghetto Myth: The Sociolinguistic Roots of Yiddish," in *To Honor Roman Jakobson: Essays on the Occasion of His Seventieth Birthday* (The Hague: Mouton, 1967), 2204.
15. On Dubnow, see Sophie Dubnov-Erlich, *The Life and Work of S. M. Dubnov: Diaspora Nationalism and Jewish History*, trans. Judith Vowles (Bloomington: Indiana University Press, 1991); on Medem, see Vladimir Medem, *The Life and Soul of a Legendary Jewish Socialist*, ed. and trans. Samuel A. Portnoy (New York: Ktav, 1979).
16. Weinreich, *History of the Yiddish Language*, 1:2–3.
17. Weinreich, *History of the Yiddish Language*, 1:6.
18. On proto-Yiddish, see Weinreich, *History of the Yiddish Language*, 2:658–718; for a more concise overview, as well as discussion of the critique of conceptualizing proto-Yiddish, see Neil G. Jacobs, *Yiddish: A Linguistic Introduction* (Cambridge: Cambridge University Press, 2005), 22–40.
19. Leo Fuchs, "The Romance Elements in Old Yiddish," in Katz, *Origins of the Yiddish Language*, 23–25.
20. Robert D. King, "Early Yiddish Vowel Systems: A Contribution by William G. Moulton to the Debate on the Origins of Yiddish," in *Field of Yiddish: Studies in Language, Folklore, and Literature, Fifth Collection*, ed. David Goldberg (Evanston, Ill.: Northwestern University Press, 1993), 88–89.
21. Dovid Katz, "The Proto Dialectology of Ashkenaz," in Katz, *Origins of the Yiddish Language*, 54.
22. David L. Gold, "Has the Textbook Explanation of the Origins of Yiddish and of Ashkenazic Jewry Been Challenged Successfully?" *Mankind Quarterly* 26, nos. 3–4 (1986): 339–363.
23. Erika Timm, "The Early History of the Yiddish Language," in *The Jews of Europe in the Middle Ages (Tenth to Fifteenth Centuries)*, ed. Christoph Cluse (Turnhout, Belgium: Brepols, 2004), 354, 356.
24. Alexander Beider, *Origins of Yiddish Dialects* (Oxford: Oxford University Press, 2015), xxxi–xxxiii.
25. Charles Nydorf, "The Role of Crimean Gothic in the Formation of the Eastern Yiddish Dialects," *Gothic Yiddish* (blog), December 2, 2014, http://gothicyiddish.blogspot.com/2014/12/the-role-of-crimean-gothic-in-formation.html.
26. Paul Wexler, *Two-Tiered Relexification in Yiddish: Jews, Sorbs, Khazars, and the Kiev-Polessian Dialect* (Berlin: De Gruyter Mouton, 2002), 64, 9, 7, 67.
27. Charles Nydorf, "Spectacular Genomic Confirmation of Max Weinreich's Babylonian Renaissance," *Gothic Yiddish* (blog), July 31, 2017, http://gothicyiddish.blogspot.

com/2017/07/the-13th-century-pivot-genomic.html. On Weinreich's notion of a "Babylonian renaissance" in Ashkenaz, see his *History of the Yiddish Language*, 2:376–377.

28. Ranajit Das, Paul Wexler, Mehdi Pirooznia, and Eran Elhaik, "Localizing Ashkenazic Jews to Primeval Villages in the Ancient Iranian Lands of Ashkenaz," *Genome Biology and Evolution* 8, no. 4 (April 2016): 1132.
29. Pavel Flegontov et al., "Pitfalls of the Geographic Population Structure (GPS) Approach Applied to Human Genetic History: A Case Study of Ashkenazi Jews," *Genome Biology and Evolution* 8, no. 7, (July 2016): 2259–2265; Marion Aptroot, "Yiddish Language and Ashkenazic Jews: A Perspective from Culture, Language, and Literature," *Genome Biology and Evolution* 8, no. 6 (June 2016): 1948–1949. For response in the general press, see, e.g., Jordan Kutzik, "Don't Buy the Junk Science That Says Yiddish Originated in Turkey," *Forward*, April 28, 2016.
30. Cherie Woodworth, "Where Did the East European Jews Come From? An Explosive Debate Erupts from Old Footnotes," *Kritika: Explorations in Russian and Eurasian History*, n.s., 11, no. 1 (Winter 2010): 110.
31. Uriel Weinreich, William Labov, and Marvin Herzog, "Empirical Foundations for a Theory of Language Change," in *Directions for Historical Linguistics*, ed. W. P. Lehmann and Y. Malkiel (Austin: University of Texas Press, 1968), 188.

## Chapter 2

1. Lily Kahn and Aaron D. Rubin, eds., *Handbook of Jewish Languages* (Leiden: Brill, 2015), has entries on twenty-three languages; Bernard Spolsky, *The Languages of the Jews: A Sociolinguistic History* (Cambridge: Cambridge University Press, 2014), also lists twenty-three languages; a list of thirty Jewish languages appears in Joshua L. Miller and Anita Norich, eds., *Languages of Modern Jewish Cultures: Comparative Perspectives* (Ann Arbor: University of Michigan Press, 2016), xi–xii. The Jewish Language Research Website lists entries or links to entries for twenty-six languages (https://www.jewish-languages.org, accessed February 25, 2018).
2. On Judezmo, see Bryan Kirschen, ed., *Judeo-Spanish and the Making of a Community* (Newcastle upon Tyne, UK: Cambridge Scholars Publishing, 2015).
3. See Paul Wexler, "Terms for 'Synagogue' in Hebrew and Jewish Languages: Explorations in Historical Jewish Interlinguistics," *Revue des études juives* 140, nos. 1–2 (1981): 123–127; Max Weinreich, *History of the Yiddish Language*, ed. Paul Glasser, trans. Shlomo Noble and Joshua A. Fishman, vol. 1 (New Haven, Conn.: Yale University Press, 2008), 106.
4. Weinreich, *History of the Yiddish Language*, 1:30.
5. Alexander Beider, *Origins of Yiddish Dialects* (Oxford: Oxford University Press, 2015), xxxi.
6. On translating *Haskalah* as "Jewish Enlightenment," see Olga Litvak, *Haskalah: The Romantic Movement in Judaism* (New Brunswick, N.J.: Rutgers University Press, 2012), 26–28.

7. "Introspectivism [Manifesto of 1919]," trans. Anita Norich, in *American Yiddish Poetry: A Bilingual Anthology*, ed. Barbara Harshav and Benjamin Harshav (Berkeley: University of California Press, 1986), 774, 775, 780.
8. Weinreich, *History of the Yiddish Language*, 1:29–30.
9. Robert D. King, "Early Yiddish Vowel Systems: A Contribution by William G. Moulton to the Debate on the Origins of Yiddish," in *Field of Yiddish: Studies in Language, Folklore, and Literature, Fifth Collection*, ed. David Goldberg (Evanston, Ill.: Northwestern University Press, 1993), 87–98; Beider, *Origins of Yiddish Dialects*, xxxii, 52.
10. See Tal Hever-Chybowski, "The Semitic Component in Yiddish and Its Ideological Role in Yiddish Philology," *Philological Encounters* 2 (2017): 368–387.
11. For more information on Yiddish grammar, see Neil G. Jacobs, *Yiddish: A Linguistic Introduction* (Cambridge: Cambridge University Press, 2005); Dovid Katz, *Grammar of the Yiddish Language* (London: Duckworth, 1987); Solomon A. Birnbaum, *Yiddish: A Survey and a Grammar*, 2nd ed. (Toronto: University of Toronto Press, 2016).
12. R. J. Zwi Werblowsky and Geoffrey Wigoder, eds., *The Encyclopedia of the Jewish Religion* (New York: Holt, Rinehart & Winston, 1966), 409.
13. Morris Rosenfeld, *Songs from the Ghetto* (Boston: Small, Maynard, 1900). The glossary was prepared by Leo Wiener.
14. On *davenen*, see Weinreich, *History of the Yiddish Language*, 2:650; David L. Gold, "More on the Etymology of Yiddish *doynen/davnen/davenen*," *Jewish Language Review* 5 (1985): 162–178, 173–180. Beider writes that *davenen* "is of uncertain, most likely Hebrew, origin" (*Origins of Yiddish Dialects*, 337).
15. See Weinreich, *History of the Yiddish Language* 2:351–354; Jacobs, *Yiddish*, 41–44; Dovid Katz, "The Phonology of Ashkenazic," in *Hebrew in Ashkenaz: A Language in Exile*, ed. Lewis Glinert (New York: Oxford University Press, 1993), 46–87.
16. Jacobs, *Yiddish*, 296.
17. Benjamin Harshav, *The Meaning of Yiddish* (Berkeley: University of California Press, 1990), 40.
18. Hirsz Abramowicz, *Profiles of a Lost World: Memoirs of East European Jewish Life before World War II*, trans. Eva Zeitlin Dobkin (Detroit: Wayne State University Press, 1999), 69, 70. Bracketed text in original.
19. Maurice Samuel, *In Praise of Yiddish* (Chicago: Henry Regnery, 1971), 124, 128.
20. Jacobs, *Yiddish*, 19.
21. H. L. Mencken, *The American Language: An Inquiry into the Development of English in the United States*, 2nd ed. (New York: Knopf, 1921), 405, 406.
22. Mordecai Kosover, *Arabic Elements in Palestinian Yiddish: The Old Ashkenazic Community in Palestine, Its History and Its Language* (Jerusalem: Rubin Mass, 1966), 252, 256, 162, 168, 271.
23. Miriam Isaacs, "Contentious Partners: Yiddish and Hebrew in Haredi Israel," *International Journal of the Sociology of Language* 138 (1999): 114.
24. Weinreich, *History of the Yiddish Language*, 2:418.

25. This expression was used by both Noah Prylucki and Max Weinreich. See, e.g., Maks Vaynraykh, "There's No Need for Germanicisms" [Yiddish], *Yidish far ale* [Yiddish for everyone] 1 (1938): 105.
26. Raymond Pearson, *National Minorities in Eastern Europe 1848–1945* (London: Macmillan, 1983), 26.
27. Noyekh Prilutski, "Methodological Remarks on the Problem of Germanicisms" [Yiddish], *Yidish far ale* [Yiddish for everyone] 1 (1938): 201–209; Vaynraykh, "There's No Need for Germanicisms," 97–106. See also Steffen Krogh, "*Dos iz eyne vahre geshikhte* . . . On the Germanization of Eastern Yiddish in the Nineteenth Century," in *Jews and Germans in Eastern Europe: Shared and Comparative Histories*, ed. Tobias Grill, New Perspectives on Modern Jewish History 8 (Berlin: De Gruyter Mouton, 2018), 88–114, and Martina Niedhammer, "Codified Traditions? YIVO's *filologishe sektsye* in Vilna and Its Relationship to German Academia," in Grill, *Jews and Germans in Eastern Europe*, 115–124.
28. See Rakhmiel Peltz, "The Undoing of Language Planning from the Vantage of Cultural History," in *Undoing and Redoing Corpus Planning*, ed. M. Clyne (Berlin: Mouton de Gruyter, 1997), 339–348.
29. Harshav, *Meaning of Yiddish*, 61, 73.

## Chapter 3

1. On Jewish life in German lands during the Middle Ages, see Elisheva Baumgarten, *Practicing Piety in Medieval Ashkenaz: Men, Women, and Everyday Religious Observance* (Philadelphia: University of Pennsylvania Press, 2014). On Jewish settlement in Poland and Lithuania, see Bernard D. Weinryb, *The Jews of Poland: A Social and Economic History of the Jewish Community in Poland from 1100–1800* (Philadelphia: Jewish Publication Society, 1972).
2. On demographics, see Weinryb, *Jews of Poland*, 308–320.
3. On eastern European Jewish surnames, see Alexander Beider, *A Dictionary of Jewish Surnames from the Russian Empire* (Teaneck, N.J.: Avotaynu, 1993); Alexander Beider, *A Dictionary of Jewish Surnames from the Kingdom of Poland* (Teaneck, N.J.: Avotaynu, 1996).
4. Steven Lowenstein, "The Shifting Boundary between Eastern and Western Jewry," *Jewish Social Studies*, n.s., 4, no. 1 (1997): 60–61.
5. Solomon A. Birnbaum, *Yiddish: A Survey and a Grammar*, 2nd ed. (Toronto: University of Toronto Press, 2016), 34.
6. Maks Vaynraykh, "Yidish," *Algemeyne entsiklopedye* [General encyclopedia], vol. *Yidn: beys* (Paris: Dubnov-fond, 1940), col. 25; Birnbaum, *Yiddish*, 41.
7. See, e.g., statistics for interwar Poland in Lucjan Dobroszycki and Barbara Kirshenblatt-Gimblett, *Image before My Eyes: A Photographic History of Jewish Life in Poland, 1864–1939* (New York: Schocken, 1977), 257–263.
8. Mikael Parkvall, *Sveriges språk: Vem talar vad och var?* [Sweden's languages: Who speaks what and where?], RAPPLING 1. Rapporter från Institutionen för lingvistik

vid Stockholms universitet (Stockholm: Institutionen för lingvistik, Stockholms universitet, 2009), 68–72; see also "National Minorities and Minority Languages" [Yiddish] Faktablad, Justitiedepartamentet, November 2004, http://www.manskligarattigheter.se/dynamaster/file_archive/050216/24a99c86fd734f-15c9f722b343cc152e/FaktaJu_0415ji.pdf, accessed July 7, 2018.

9. Central Bureau of Statistics, "Selected Data from the 2011 Social Survey on Mastery of the Hebrew Language and Usage of Languages," http://www.cbs.gov.il/reader/newhodaot/hodaa_template.html?hodaa=201319017, accessed July 7, 2018. On Yiddish in Israel, see Rachel Rojanski, *Yiddish in Israel: A History* (Bloomington: Indiana University Press, 2020).
10. On interwar travel, see Daniel Soyer, "Revisiting the Old World: American-Jewish Tourists in Inter-War Eastern Europe," in *Forging Modern Jewish Identities; Public Faces and Private Struggles*, ed. Michael Berkowitz, Susan L. Tananbaum, and Sam W. Bloom (London: Vallentine Mitchell, 2003), 16–38.
11. Kh[ayem] Zhitlovski, "In a Jewish/Yiddish Nation" [Yiddish], in *Geklibene verk* [Selected works], ed. Yudl Mark (New York: CYCO, 1955), 321–323. This essay was first printed in *Yidishe velt* [Jewish/Yiddish world] in 1913, with the subtitle "How I became a Yiddishist." My translation.
12. See Jeffrey Shandler, *Adventures in Yiddishland: Postvernacular Language and Culture* (Berkeley: University of California Press, 2005), 33–34.
13. Benedict Anderson, *Imagined Communities: Reflections on the Origin and Spread of Nationalism*, rev. ed. (London: Verso, 1991), 68.
14. A. Almi, "Yidish" [Yiddish], in *Far yidish: a zamlbukh* [For Yiddish: An anthology], ed. Sh. Edberg (New York: National Council of Young Israel, 1930), 59–60. My translation.
15. Sidra DeKoven Ezrahi, *Booking Passage: Exile and Homecoming in the Modern Jewish Imagination* (Berkeley: University of California Press, 2000), 14, 10.
16. J. Hoberman, *Bridge of Light: Yiddish Film between Two Worlds* (New York: Schocken, 1991), 5.
17. On *doikeyt* and the concept of diaspora nationalism generally, see Ezra Mendelsohn, *On Modern Jewish Politics* (Oxford: Oxford University Press, 1993).
18. Samuel Kassow, "Travel and Local History as a National Mission: Polish Jews and the Landkentenish Movement in the 1920s and 1930s," in *Jewish Topographies: Visions of Space, Traditions of Place*, ed. Julia Brauch et al. (Hampshire, UK: Ashgate, 2008), 248.
19. See Gabriel Davidson, *Our Jewish Farmers: The Story of the Jewish Agricultural Society* (New York: L. B. Fischer, 1943); Jonathan Dekel-Chen, *Farming the Red Land: Jewish Agricultural Colonization and Local Soviet Power, 1924–1941* (New Haven, Conn.: Yale University Press, 2005).
20. On Birobidzhan, see Robert Weinberg, *Stalin's Forgotten Zion: Birobidzhan and the Making of a Soviet Jewish Homeland* (Berkeley: University of California Press, 1998).
21. On recent travel to Birobidzhan, see, e.g., Shelley I. Salamensky, "'Jewface' and 'Jewfaçade' in Poland, Spain, and Birobidzhan," in *The Routledge Handbook of Contemporary Jewish Cultures*, ed. Laurence Roth and Nadya Valman (London:

Routledge, 2015), 213–223; Yale Strom, dir., *L'chayim, Comrade Stalin!* (Los Angeles: Blackstream Films, 2002).

22. On *yizker-bikher*, see Jack Kugelmass and Jonathan Boyarin, eds., *From a Ruined Garden: The Memorial Books of Polish Jewry* (New York: Schocken, 1983).
23. Kalman Weiser, *Jewish People, Yiddish Nation: Noah Prylucki and the Folkists in Poland* (Toronto: University of Toronto Press, 2011), 187–188.
24. Mordecai Veinger, *Forsht yidishe dialektn!: Program farn materyalnklayber* [Research Yiddish dialects!: Guide for collectors] (Minsk: Yidopteyl fun Invayskult, 1925).
25. Marvin Herzog et al., *The Language and Culture Atlas of Ashkenazic Jewry*, vol. 3: *The Eastern Yiddish–Western Yiddish Continuum* (Tübingen: Max Niemeyer, 2000), 156–157, 304–305.
26. On the questionnaire, see Marvin Herzog et al., *The Language and Culture Atlas of Ashkenazic Jewry*, vol. 1: *Historical and Theoretical Foundations* (Tübingen: Max Niemeyer, 1992), 6. For a list of interviewee locations, see Marvin Herzog et al., *The Language and Culture Atlas of Ashkenazic Jewry*, vol. 2: *Research Tools* (Tübingen: Max Niemeyer, 1995), 95–100.
27. Other scholars of Yiddish dialectology distinguish additional regions of Yiddish speech. For example, see Birnbaum, *Yiddish*, 94–105.
28. Herzog et al., *Language and Culture Atlas of Ashkenazic Jewry*, 1:114.
29. Herzog et al., *Language and Culture Atlas of Ashkenazic Jewry*, 1:107.
30. Herzog et al., *Language and Culture Atlas of Ashkenazic Jewry*, 1:64.
31. Uril Vaynraykh, "On a New Yiddish Language and Culture Atlas" [Yiddish], *Di goldene keyt* [The golden chain] 37 (1960): 5.
32. Uriel Weinreich, "Mapping a Culture," *Columbia University Forum* 6, no. 3 (1963): 18.
33. An early example is the innkeeper Reb Shmuelke Troyniks in Solomon Ettinger's early nineteenth-century maskilic comedy *Serkele*. See Alyssa Pia Quint, "The Currency of Yiddish: Ettinger's 'Serkele' and the Reinvention of Shylock," *Prooftexts* 24, no. 1 (Winter 2004): 106.
34. James A. Matisoff, *Blessings, Curses, Hopes, and Fears: Psycho-Ostensive Expressions in Yiddish* (Philadelphia: Institute for the Study of Human Issues, 1979), 44; see also Max Weinreich, *History of the Yiddish Language*, ed. Paul Glasser, trans. Shlomo Noble and Joshua A. Fishman, vol. 1 (New Haven, Conn.: Yale University Press, 2008), 180–181.
35. Lowenstein, "Shifting Boundary between Eastern and Western Jewry," 62.
36. Uriel Weinreich, "Is a Structural Dialectology Possible?," *Word* 10, no. 2–3 (1954): 388–400.
37. Weinreich, "Mapping a Culture," 17–19.
38. See Ruth von Bernuth, *How the Wise Men Got to Chelm: The Life and Times of a Yiddish Folk Tradition* (New York: New York University Press, 2016).
39. Sholem Aleichem, *Tevye the Dairyman and the Railroad Stories*, trans. Hillel Halkin (New York: Schocken, 1987), 1–131; Perets Markish, *Nit gedayget: poeme* [No worries: Narrative poem] (Kharkov: Tsentrfarlag, Alukrainishe opteylung, 1931); Perets Markish, *Erd: Dramatishe varyant fun der poeme "Nit gedayget"* [Earth: Dramatic version of the narrative poem "No worries"] (Moscow: Emes, 1933).

40. Herzog et al., *Language and Culture Atlas of Ashkenazic Jewry*, 1: *12; questionnaire page 007, questions 080–085.
41. See Max Weinreich, "The Reality of Jewishness versus the Ghetto Myth: The Sociolinguistic Roots of Yiddish," in *To Honor Roman Jakobson: Essays on the Occasion of His Seventieth Birthday* (The Hague: Mouton, 1967), 2199–2211.
42. See, e.g., Louis Wirth, *The Ghetto* (Chicago: University of Chicago Press, 1928).
43. See Daniel B. Schwartz, *Ghetto: The History of a Word* (Cambridge, Mass.: Harvard University Press, 2019).
44. Dan Miron, *The Image of the Shtetl and Other Studies of Modern Jewish Literary Imagination* (Syracuse, N.Y.: Syracuse University Press, 2000), xii.
45. See Jeffrey Shandler, *Shtetl: A Vernacular Intellectual History* (New Brunswick, N.J.: Rutgers University Press, 2014).
46. Yiddish Farm, "About Us," https://yiddishfarm.org/history/aboutus, accessed November 30, 2017.
47. See Joshua B. Friedman, "Yiddish Returns: Language, Intergenerational Gifts, and Jewish Devotion" (PhD diss., University of Michigan, 2015).
48. Tsvi Sadan, "Yiddish on the Internet," *Language and Communication* 30, no. 2 (May 2011): 105.

## Chapter 4

1. Jerold C. Frakes, *The Politics of Interpretation: Alterity and Ideology in Old Yiddish Studies* (Albany: State University of New York Press, 1989), 23.
2. See Jerold C. Frakes, *Early Yiddish Texts, 1100–1750* (Oxford: Oxford University Press, 2004), 1–3.
3. Other biblical references to Ashkenaz: Jeremiah 51:27; 1 Chronicles 1:6. How Ashkenaz came to be the Jewish term for German lands is uncertain, though theories abound; see, e.g., Max Weinreich, *History of the Yiddish Language*, ed. Paul Glasser, trans. Shlomo Noble and Joshua A. Fishman, vol. 1 (New Haven, Conn.: Yale University Press, 2008), A4.
4. Israel Zinberg, *A History of Jewish Literature*, vol. 7: *Old Yiddish Literature from Its Origins to the Haskalah Period*, trans. Bernard Martin (Cincinnati: Hebrew Union College Press, 1975), 49–50.
5. Ruth H. Sanders, *German: Biography of a Language* (New York: Oxford University Press, 2010), 93.
6. Zinberg, *History of Jewish Literature*, 7:148; 7:21n60.
7. Zinberg, *History of Jewish Literature*, 7:87. See also Jean Baumgarten, *Introduction to Old Yiddish Literature*, ed. and trans. Jerold C. Frakes (Oxford: Oxford University Press, 2005), 69.
8. Weinreich, *History of the Yiddish Language*, 1:317–318.
9. Weinreich, *History of the Yiddish Language*, 1:315.
10. Weinreich, *History of the Yiddish Language*, 1:317.
11. Nokhem Stutshkov, *Oytser fun der yidisher shprakh* [Thesaurus of the Yiddish language] (New York: YIVO, 1950), section 369.

12. Weinreich, *History of the Yiddish Language*, 1:322.
13. E.g., Johann Heinrich Callenberg, *Kurtze Anleitung zur Jüdischteutschen Sprache* [Short guide to the Judeo-German language] (Halle, 1733); Wilhelm Christian Just Chrysander, *Jüdisch-Teutsche Grammatik* [Judeo-German grammar] (Leipzig & Wolfenbüttel, 1750); Carl Wilhelm Friedrich, *Unterricht in der Judensprache und Schrift: Zum Gebrauch für Gelehrte und Ungelehrte* [Instruction in Jewish speech and writing: For use by the educated and uneducated] (Prentzlow, 1784).
14. Weinreich, *History of the Yiddish Language*, 1:69.
15. See Sander L. Gilman, *Jewish Self-Hatred: Anti-Semitism and the Hidden Language of the Jews* (Baltimore: Johns Hopkins University Press, 1986), 140–141; Jeffrey Grossman, *The Discourse on Yiddish in German Literature from the Enlightenment to the Second Empire* (Rochester, N.Y.: Camden House, 2000), 139.
16. Dan Miron, *A Traveler Disguised: A Study in the Rise of Modern Yiddish Fiction in the Nineteenth Century* (New York: Schocken, 1973), 34–66.
17. Weinreich, *History of the Yiddish Language*, 1:285.
18. Dovid Katz, *Yiddish and Power* (New York: Palgrave Macmillan, 2014), 116.
19. Emanuel S. Goldsmith, *Architects of Yiddishism at the Beginning of the Twentieth Century: A Study in Jewish Cultural History* (Rutherford, N.J.: Fairleigh Dickinson University Press, 1976), 77–78.
20. E.g., Y. Y. Inditski, *Ha-metargem: Mikhtamim, pitgamim, ma'amre Hazal, ma'amarim ketsarim ve-divre hakhamim ve-hidotim la-safah ha-meduberet (zhargon)* [The translator: Epigrams, proverbs, essays, and words of wisdom and riddles in the spoken language (Jargon/Yiddish)] (Warsaw, 1896); *Derashah le-var mitsvah bi-shene halakim: Ha-helek ha-rishon ba-lashon ha-medubar benenu (zhargon) ve-ha-helek ha sheni bi-leshon ha-kodesh u-vi-leshon rusya ve-ashkenazit* [Bar mitzvah sermons in two parts: First in the language spoken among us (Jargon/Yiddish) and second in Hebrew and Russian and German] (Vilna: Bi-defus Rozenkrants ve-Shriftzettser, 1914).
21. A. L. Bisko, *Milon male ve-shalem zargoni-ivri* [Comprehensive Jargon/Yiddish-Hebrew dictionary] (London: Bi-defuso shel Y. Naroditski, [1913]); A. G. Gordon, *Milon tanakhi, ivrit-yahadut: Verterbukh oyf gants tanakh . . .* [Bible dictionary, Hebrew-Yiddish: Dictionary for the entire Bible . . . ] (Warsaw: T. Jakobson & M. Goldberg, 1926).
22. Sholem Aleichem, ed., *Di yidishe folks-biblyotek: A bukh far literatur, kritik un visnshaft* [The Jewish people's library: A book for literature, criticism, and scholarship], vol. 1 (Kiev, 1888).
23. Shimen Frug, "Poems in the Jewish Jargon" [Yiddish], *Ale shriftn fun Sh. Frug* [Complete works of S. Frug], vol. 3 (New York: Hebrew Publishing Company, 1910), 205–217.
24. Sophie Dubnov-Erlich, *The Life and Work of S. M. Dubnov: Diaspora Nationalism and Jewish History*, trans. Judith Vowles (Bloomington: Indiana University Press, 1991), 196.
25. George Wolfe, "Notes on American Yiddish," *American Mercury*, August 1933, 478.
26. Weinreich, *History of the Yiddish Language*, 1:322.
27. Jonathan Boyarin, *Thinking in Jewish* (Chicago: University of Chicago Press, 1996), 1.

28. E.g., *New Yiddish Jokes* (Cleveland: Arthur Westbrook, [ca. 1900?]).
29. See, e.g., "Yiddish Dance," http://aviamoore.com/yiddish-dance/, accessed September 14, 2017.
30. Gitl Schaechter-Viswanath and Paul Glasser, eds., *Comprehensive English-Yiddish Dictionary (Based on the Lexical Research of Mordkhe Schaechter* (Bloomington: Indiana University Press, 2016), 823.
31. Leo Rosten, *The Joys of Yiddish* (New York: McGraw-Hill, 1968), xi, 49, 264.
32. Chaim M. Weiser, *Frumspeak: The First Dictionary of Yeshivish* (Northvale, N.J.: Jason Aronson, 1995), xxxii.
33. Chaim Dalfin, *LubavitchSpeak: A Dictionary of Chabad-Lubavitsh Hasidim: Words, Sayings, and Colloquialisms*, 2nd ed. (Brooklyn: Jewish Enrichment Press, 2015), viii.
34. Weinreich, *History of the Yiddish Language*, 1:325, 324.

## Chapter 5

1. For more information on the gendering of nouns and the forming of diminutives, see Neil G. Jacobs, *Yiddish: A Linguistic Introduction* (Cambridge: Cambridge University Press, 2005), 166–168; Dovid Katz, *Grammar of the Yiddish Language* (London: Duckworth, 1987), 47–53; Solomon A. Birnbaum, *Yiddish: A Survey and a Grammar*, 2nd ed. (Toronto: University of Toronto Press, 2016), 227–228.
2. Uriel Weinreich, "The Seven Genders of Yiddish" (typescript), paper delivered at the Linguistic Society of America, Chicago, December 29, 1961, available online at https://yivo.org/The-Seven-Genders-of-Yiddish.
3. Alexander Harkavy, *Yiddish-English-Hebrew Dictionary*, 2nd ed. (1928; repr., New York: Schocken/YIVO, 1988).
4. Steffen Krogh, "How Satmarish Is Haredi Satmar Yiddish?," *Yidishe shtudyes haynt / Jidistik heute / Yiddish Studies Today,* vol. 1, ed. Marion Aptroot, Efrat Gal-Ed, Roland Gruschka, and Simon Neuberg (Düsseldorf: Düsseldorf University Press, 2012), 489.
5. Per email to author from Jordan Kutzik, December 27, 2017.
6. Max Weinreich, *History of the Yiddish Language*, ed. Paul Glasser, trans. Shlomo Noble and Joshua A. Fishman, vol. 1 (New Haven, Conn.: Yale University Press, 2008), 274, 277, 274.
7. Israel Zinberg, *A History of Jewish Literature*, trans. Bernard Martin, vol. 7: *Old Yiddish Literature from Its Origins to the Haskalah Period* (Cincinnati: Hebrew Union College Press, 1975), 157.
8. Weinreich, *History of the Yiddish Language*, 1:274.
9. Jean Baumgarten, "Listening, Reading and Understanding: How Jewish Women Read the Yiddish Ethical Literature (Seventeenth to Eighteenth Century)," *Journal of Modern Jewish Studies* 16, no. 2 (2017): 257.
10. Zinberg, *History of Jewish Literature*, 7:124–125.
11. Weinreich, *History of the Yiddish Language*, 1:276. See also Chava Weissler, *Voices of the Matriarchs: Listening to the Prayers of Early Modern Jewish Women* (Boston: Beacon, 1998), 38–44.

12. Miriam Stark, "Translator's Preface," in *Tz'enah Ur'enah: The Classic Anthology of Torah Lore and Midrashic Comment*, trans. Miriam Stark Zakon (Brooklyn: Mesorah, 1983), vii.
13. Jean Baumgarten, *Introduction to Old Yiddish Literature*, ed. and trans. Jerold C. Frakes (Oxford: Oxford University Press, 2005), 80.
14. Weissler, *Voices of the Matriarchs*, 9.
15. See Naomi Seidman, *A Marriage Made in Heaven: The Sexual Politics of Hebrew and Yiddish* (Berkeley: University of California Press, 1997), 40–53.
16. Iris Parush, *Reading Jewish Women: Marginality and Modernization in Nineteenth-Century Eastern European Jewish Society* (Waltham, Mass.: Brandeis University Press, 2004), 146.
17. Seidman, *Marriage Made in Heaven*, 42.
18. See Dan Miron, *A Traveler Disguised: The Rise of Modern Yiddish Fiction in the Nineteenth Century* (New York: Schocken, 1973), 14; Seidman, *Marriage Made in Heaven*, 44–47.
19. Cited in Miron, *Traveler Disguised*, 18.
20. See Seidman, *Marriage Made in Heaven*, 31–35.
21. See, e.g., "I. L. Peretz's Folksy Novel" [Yiddish], *Der groyser kundes* [The big prankster], June 16, 1911; "Ruvn Braynin in the *Tageblat*" [Yiddish], *Der groyser kundes*, November 3, 1916. See also Joshua A. Fishman, "Cartoons about Language: Hebrew, Yiddish, and the Visual Representation of Sociolinguistic Attitudes," in *Hebrew in Ashkenaz: A Language in Exile*, ed. Lewis Glinert (New York: Oxford University Press, 1993), 151–166.
22. See, e.g., "The Mover of Our Movement: Dr. Chaim Zhitlowski" [Yiddish], *Der groyser kundes*, October 22, 1922; "Three in One: Mendele the Book Seller" [Yiddish], *Der groyser kundes*, December 29, 1916.
23. Y. Lerner, "The Yiddish Muse" [Yiddish], *Hoyzfraynd* [Home Companion] (St. Petersburg, 1889), as cited in Emanuel S. Goldsmith, *Architects of Yiddishism at the Beginning of the Twentieth Century: A Study in Jewish Cultural History* (Rutherford, N.J.: Fairleigh Dickinson University Press, 1976), 54.
24. See Daniel Boyarin, *Unheroic Conduct: The Rise of Heterosexuality and the Invention of the Jewish Man* (Berkeley: University of California Press, 1997).
25. Kathryn Hellerstein, *A Question of Tradition: Women Poets in Yiddish, 1586–1987* (Stanford, Calif.: Stanford University Press, 2014), ch. 2.
26. See *Glikl: Memoirs, 1691–1719*, ed. Chava Turniansky, trans. Sarah Friedman (Waltham, Mass.: Brandeis University Press, 2019).
27. Janet R. Hadda, *Yankev Glatshteyn* (Boston: Twayne, 1980), 13–14.
28. E. Korman, ed., *Yidishe dikhterins: Antologye* [Yiddish women poets: Anthology] (Chicago: L. M. Stein, 1928).
29. Anita Norich, introduction to Kadya Molodovsky, *A Jewish Refugee in New York*, trands. Anita Norich (Bloomington: Indiana University Press, 2019), xii–xiii.
30. Joanna Lisek, "Orthodox Yiddishism in *Beys Yakov* Magazine in the Context of Religious Jewish Feminism in Poland," in *Ashkenazim and Sephardim: A European

*Perspective*, ed. Andrzej Katny, Izabela Olszewska, and Aleksandra Twardowska (Frankfurt am Main: Peter Lang Edition, 2013), 135. See also the discussion of this literature, 148–152.

31. Kalman Weiser, "The Capital of 'Yiddishland?,'" in *Warsaw, The Jewish Metropolis: Essays in Honor of the 75th Birthday of Professor Antony Polonsky*, ed. Glenn Dynner and François Guesnet (Leiden: Brill, 2015), 315. The appellation *shmendrikizm* was inspired by the title character of Avraham Goldfaden's play *Shmendrik* of 1877; see also Alyssa Quint, *The Rise of the Modern Yiddish Theater* (Bloomington: Indiana University Press, 2019), 99.
32. Asya Vaisman, "English in the Yiddish Speech of Hasidic Women," *Yiddish* 15, no. 3 (2008): 17–28.
33. Ayala Fader, *Mitzvah Girls: Bringing Up the Next Generation of Hasidic Jews in Brooklyn* (Princeton, N.J.: Princeton University Press, 2009), 128.
34. See Weissler, *Voices of the Matriarchs*, 156–171.
35. For a bibliography of Yiddish female authors in English translation, see Amanda Siegel, "Women in Translation Month: Yiddish," New York Public Library blog, August 17, 2016, https://www.nypl.org/blog/2016/08/17/women-translation-yiddish, accessed July 30, 2018. In addition to modern Yiddish poetry and prose, the list includes translations of *tkhines*.
36. Irena Klepfisz, *Dreams of an Insomniac: Jewish Feminist Essays, Speeches and Diatribes* (Portland, Ore.: Eighth Mountain, 1990), 156–157.
37. See Irena Klepfisz, *A Few Words in the Mother Tongue: Poems Selected and New (1971–1990)* (Portland, Ore.: Eighth Mountain, 1990), 213–236.
38. *Vaybertaytsh* website, "About," http://www.vaybertaytsh.com/about-1/, accessed July 18, 2018.
39. See Klepfisz, *Dreams of an Insomniac*.
40. Alisa Solomon, "Notes on Klez/Camp," *Davka* 1, no. 3 (Winter 1997): 29–31.
41. See Jeffrey Shandler, "Queer Yiddishkeit: Practice and Theory," *Shofar* 25, no. 1 (2006): 90–113.
42. League for Yiddish, "'Words of the Week': Trans and Non-binary," email, March 31, 2019.

## Chapter 6

1. Andreas Feininger, *New York in the Forties* (New York: Dover Publications, 1978), 126, 122.
2. See, e.g., Lajb Fuks and Chaim Gininger, "On the Oldest Dated Work in Yiddish Literature," in *The Field of Yiddish: Studies in Language, Folklore, and Literature*, vol. 1, ed. Uriel Weinreich (New York: Linguistic Circle of New York, 1954), 267–274.
3. Solomon A. Birnbaum, *Yiddish: A Survey and a Grammar*, 2nd ed. (Toronto: University of Toronto Press, 2016), 107–109.
4. Solomon A. Birnbaum, "Two Methods," in *Origins of the Yiddish Language: Winter Studies in Yiddish*, vol. 1, ed. Dovid Katz (Oxford: Pergamon, 1987), 7–11.

5. On the fonts used for Yiddish in the early years of publishing, see Herbert C. Zafren, "Variety in the Typography of Yiddish: 1535–1635," *Hebrew Union College Annual* 53 (1982): 137–163. On the names used for these fonts, see Neil G. Jacobs, *Yiddish: A Linguistic Introduction* (Cambridge: Cambridge University Press, 2005), 47.
6. Jacobs, *Yiddish*, 301.
7. On Soviet Yiddish language policy, see Gennady Estraikh, *Soviet Yiddish: Language Planning and Linguistic Development* (Oxford: Clarendon, 1999).
8. *Takones fun yidishn oysleyg* [Rules of Yiddish spelling] (Vilna: YIVO, 1937).
9. Birnbaum, *Yiddish*, 200–215. See Kalman Weiser, "The 'Orthodox' Orthography of Solomon Birnbaum," *Studies in Contemporary Jewry* 20 (2004): 275–295.
10. Joana Lisek, "Orthodox Yiddishism in *Beys Yakov* Magazine in the Context of Religious Jewish Feminism in Poland," in *Ashkenazim and Sephardim: A European Perspective*, ed. Andrzej Katny, Izabela Olszewska, and Aleksandra Twardowska (Frankfurt am Main: Peter Lang, 2013), 141–148.
11. See Sore-Rokhl Schaechter, "That Time We Picketed the Forward" [Yiddish], *Yiddish Daily Forward*, online edition, April 27, 2017, http://yiddish.forward.com/articles/203344/that-time-we-picketed-the-forward/?p=all#ixzz4xIeLwYsT.
12. Satoko Kamoshida, "The Variations of Yiddish Orthographical Systems in the Present Hasidic Newspapers," *European Journal of Jewish Studies* 2, no. 2 (2009): 299–312.
13. Adele Kronick Shuart, *Signs in Judaism: A Resource Book for the Jewish Deaf Community*, illus. Ruth E. Peterson, ed. Muriel Strassler (New York: Bloch, 1986); Elena Hoffenberg, "Making Sense of Squiggles: Teaching and Learning Yiddish Stenography," *In geveb* [In the network], October 2017, https://ingeveb.org/blog/making-sense-of-squiggles-teaching-and-learning-yiddish-stenography, accessed May 31, 2018.
14. David Efron, *Gesture, Race and Culture: A Tentative Study of Some of the Spatio-Temporal and "Linguistic" Aspects of the Gestural Behavior of Eastern Jews and Southern Italians in New York City, Living under Similar as Well as Different Environmental Conditions* (The Hague: Mouton, 1972), 98–99.
15. See Mark Slobin, *Tenement Songs: The Popular Music of the Jewish Immigrants* (Urbana: University of Illinois Press, 1982).
16. Leo Wiener, *The History of Yiddish Literature in the Nineteenth Century* (New York: Charles Scribner's Sons, 1899). Wiener states that "the main intention of the present Chrestomathy is to give a transcription of the literary value of Judeo-German literature, and not of its linguistic development" (257).
17. Immanuel Olsvanger, ed., *Rosinkess mit Mandlen: Aus der Volksliteratur der Ostjuden; Schwänke, Erzählungen, Sprichwörter, Rätsel* [Raisins and almonds: From the folklore of eastern European Jews; Jokes, stories, sayings, riddles] (Basel: Verlag der Schweizerischen Gesellschaft für Volkskunde, 1920); Immanuel Olsvanger, ed., *Rêjte Pomeranzen: Ostjüdische Schwänke und Erzählungen* [Red oranges: Eastern European Jewish jokes and stories] (Berlin: Schocken, 1936). These collections were reissued, using a different Romanization system, in the United States in the 1940s and have been frequently reprinted.
18. On Zamenhof, see Esther Schor, *Bridge of Words: Esperanto and the Dream of a Universal Language* (New York: Metropolitan Books, 2016), 68.

19. Jacobs, *Yiddish*, 303.
20. See Jeffrey Shandler, *Adventures in Yiddishland: Postvernacular Language and Culture* (Berkeley: University of California Press, 2005), ch. 5.

## Chapter 7

1. See Aya Elyada, *A Goy Who Speaks Yiddish: Christians and the Jewish Language in Early Modern Germany* (Stanford, Calif.: Stanford University Press, 2012), 1–15.
2. Jeffrey A. Grossman, *The Discourse on Yiddish in Germany from the Enlightenment to the Second Empire* (Rochester, N.Y.: Camden House, 2000), 20.
3. See Sander Gilman, *Jewish Self-Hatred: Anti-Semitism and the Hidden Language of the Jews* (Baltimore: Johns Hopkins University Press, 1986), 70–81.
4. Elyada, *Goy Who Speaks Yiddish*, 13.
5. Adolf Hitler, *Mein Kampf* (excerpt), in Anson Rabinbach and Sander Gilman, *The Third Reich Sourcebook* (Berkeley: University of California Press, 2008), 171.
6. Grossman, *Discourse on Yiddish in Germany*, 44.
7. Elyada, *Goy Who Speaks Yiddish*, 8.
8. On the history of Reform Judaism, see Michael A. Meyer, *Response to Modernity: A History of the Reform Movement in Judaism* (Detroit: Wayne State University Press, 1995).
9. See Grossman, *Discourse on Yiddish in Germany*, 77–79.
10. John M. Efron, *German Jewry and the Allure of the Sephardic* (Princeton, N.J.: Princeton University Press, 2016), 58.
11. Gilman, *Jewish Self-Hatred*, 17–19.
12. Gilman, *Jewish Self-Hatred*, 279, 286.
13. Arnold Zweig, *The Face of East European Jewry*, ed. and trans. Noah Isenberg (Berkeley: University of California Press, 2004), 20, 22, 27–28.
14. Benjamin Harshav, *Language in Time of Revolution* (Berkeley: University of California Press, 1993), 157.
15. Efron, *German Jewry and the Allure of the Sephardic*, 29.
16. Harshav, *Language in Time of Revolution*, 157.
17. See Arye L. Pilowsky, "Yiddish alongside the Revival of Hebrew: Public Polemics on the Status of Yiddish in Eretz Israel, 1907–1929," in *Readings in the Sociology of Jewish Languages*, ed. Joshua A. Fishman (Leiden: E. J. Brill, 1985), 104–124.
18. Yael Chaver, *What Must Be Forgotten: The Survival of Yiddish in Zionist Palestine* (Syracuse, N.Y.: Syracuse University Press, 2004), 20.
19. Liora R. Halperin, *Babel in Zion: Jews, Nationalism, and Language Diversity in Palestine, 1920–1948* (New Haven, Conn.: Yale University Press, 2015), 17, 73, 56.
20. Harshav, *Language in Time of Revolution*, 160–161.
21. Jacob A. Riis, *How the Other Half Lives: Studies among the Tenements of New York* (New York: Dover Publications, 1971), 85.
22. On dialect humor, see, e.g., Esther Romeyn, *Street Scenes: Staging the Self in Immigrant New York 1880–1924* (Minneapolis: University of Minnesota Press, 2008),

ch. 6; on Henry Adams and Henry James, see Irving Howe, *World of Our Fathers: The Journey of the East European Jews to America and the Life They Found and Made* (New York: Harcourt Brace Jovanovich, 1976), 405–408.

23. Deborah Dash Moore, *At Home in America: Second Generation New York Jews* (New York: Columbia University Press, 1981), 90, 100.
24. See Baila R. Shargel, "The Texture of Seminary Life during the Finkelstein Era," in *Tradition Renewed: A History of the Jewish Theological Seminary of America*, ed. Jack Wertheimer, vol. 1 (New York: Jewish Theological Seminary, 1997), 524–525.
25. Leo Wiener, *The History of Yiddish Literature in the Nineteenth Century* (New York: Charles Scribner's Sons, 1899), 12.
26. Michael Brenner and Gideon Reuveni, eds., *Emancipation through Muscles: Jews and Sports in Europe* (Lincoln: University of Nebraska Press, 2006), 4.
27. See Dan Miron, *A Traveler Disguised: The Rise of Modern Yiddish Fiction in the Nineteenth Century* (New York: Schocken, 1973), 26–31.
28. Naomi Seidman, *A Marriage Made in Heaven: The Sexual Politics of Hebrew and Yiddish* (Berkeley: University of California Press, 1997), 42.
29. Roman Jakobson, preface to Uriel Weinreich, *College Yiddish: An Introduction to the Yiddish Language and to Jewish Life and Culture* (New York: YIVO, 1949), 7–8.
30. See Harald Haarmann, *Language in Ethnicity* (Berlin: Mouton de Gruyter, 1986), ch. 3.
31. Barry Trachtenberg, *The Revolutionary Roots of Modern Yiddish, 1903–1917* (Syracuse, N.Y.: Syracuse University Press, 2008), 122.
32. Maks Vaynraykh, "There's No Need for Germanicisms" [Yiddish], *Yidish far ale* [Yiddish for Everyone] 1 (1938): 97–106.
33. Mordkhe Schaechter, "The 'Hidden Standard': A Study of Competing Influences in Standardization," in *Never Say Die! A Thousand Years of Yiddish in Jewish Life and Letters*, ed. Joshua A. Fishman (The Hague: Mouton, 1981), 672.
34. Y. M. Lifshits, "The Four Classes" [Yiddish], *Kol mevaser* [Herald], 1863, no. 2., reprinted in Fishman, *Never Say Die!*, 259–265.
35. As cited in Emanuel S. Goldsmith, *Architects of Yiddishism at the Beginning of the Twentieth Century: A Study in Jewish Cultural History* (Rutherford, N.J.: Fairleigh Dickinson University Press, 1976), 143.
36. Jacobs, *Yiddish*, 17.
37. Uriel Weinreich, "Is a Structural Dialectology Possible?," *Word* 10, no. 2–3 (1954): 388–400.
38. Dovid Katz, *Yiddish and Power* (New York: Palgrave Macmillan, 2014), 272.
39. The term "fabulous invalid" comes from the eponymous 1938 play by George S. Kaufman and Moss Hart, about the ongoing struggles of Broadway's New Amsterdam Theatre.

## Chapter 8

1. See Miriam Isaacs, "Contentious Partners: Yiddish and Hebrew in Haredi Israel," *International Journal of the Sociology of Language* 138 (1999): 101–121.

2. See Chone Shmeruk, "The Versified Old Yiddish Blessing in the Worms 'Mahzor,'" in *Worms "Mahzor," MS. Jewish National and University Library Heb 4° 781/1*, ed. Malachi Beit-Arié (Jerusalem: Jewish National and University Library, 1985), 100–103.
3. Jerold C. Frakes, *Early Yiddish Texts, 1100–1750* (Oxford: Oxford University Press, 2004), nos. 37, 73.
4. See Yosef Hayim Yerushalmi, *Haggadah and History* (Philadelphia: Jewish Publication Society, 1997), plates 19, 20, 34, 37, 51, 52, 62, 77, 79.
5. On the challenges of defining these early Yiddish texts as works of "popular religion," see Michael Stanislawski, "Toward the Popular Religion of Ashkenazic Jews," in *Mediating Modernity: Challenges and Trends in the Jewish Encounter with the Modern World*, ed. Lauren Strauss and Michael Brenner (Detroit: Wayne State University Press, 2008), 93–106.
6. On early Bible translations into Yiddish, see Jean Baumgarten, *Introduction to Old Yiddish Literature*, ed. and trans. Jerold C. Frakes (Oxford: Oxford University Press, 2005), ch. 5; Israel Zinberg, *A History of Jewish Literature*, trans. Bernard Martin, vol. 7: *Old Yiddish Literature from Its Origins to the Haskalah Period* (Cincinnati: Hebrew Union College Press, 1975), 87–139.
7. See Morris M. Faierstein, ed. and trans., *Ze'enah u-Re'enah: A Critical Translation into English* (Berlin: De Gruyter, 2017).
8. On the publishing history of *Tsene-rene*, see Dorothy Seidman Bilik, "*Tsene-rene*: A Yiddish Literary Success," *Jewish Book Annual* 51 (1993): 96–111; Morris M. Faierstein, "The 'Se'enah U-Re'enah': A Preliminary Bibliography," *Revue des Études Juives* 172, nos. 3–4 (2013): 397–427.
9. Jerold C. Frakes, ed. and trans., *Early Yiddish Epic* (Syracuse, N.Y.: Syracuse University Press, 2014), 15.
10. See Zinberg, *History of Jewish Literature*, vol. 7, ch. 12; Baumgarten, *Introduction to Old Yiddish Literature*, 35–85.
11. On Hasidic practice, see Aaron Wertheim, *Law and Custom in Hasidism*, trans. Shmuel Himelstein (Hoboken, N.J.: Ktav, 1992); Jerome R. Mintz, *Hasidic People: A Place in the New World* (Cambridge, Mass.: Harvard University Press 1994).
12. Jacob Katz, *A House Divided: Orthodoxy and Schism in Nineteenth-Century Central European Jewry*, trans. Ziporah Brody (Hanover, N.H.: Brandeis University Press / University Press of New England, 1998), 48.
13. See Gershon C. Bacon, *The Politics of Tradition: Agudat Yisrael in Poland, 1916–1939* (Jerusalem: Hebrew University Magnes Press, 1996).
14. See Miriam Isaacs, "Haredi, *Haymish* and *Frim*: Yiddish Vitality and Language Choice in a Transnational, Multilingual Community," *International Journal of the Sociology of Language* 138 (1999): 99–130.
15. Samuel Heilman, *Sliding to the Right: The Contest for the Future of American Jewish Orthodoxy* (Berkeley: University of California Press, 2006), 211.
16. *Di yidishe shprakh, undzer tsirung: Lern [un] leyen bukh* [The Yiddish language, our jewel: Textbook and reader], part 1, rev. ed. (Brooklyn: Ohel Torah, 2002), 2. My translation.
17. See Mark Kligman, "On the Creators and Consumers of Orthodox Popular Music in Brooklyn," *YIVO Annual* 23 (1996): 259–293.

18. See Isaacs, "Haredi, *Haymish* and *Frim*."
19. "Mendel's Haymish Brand" (promotional brochure) (Brooklyn, [1985?]). Collection of the author.
20. See Ayala Fader, *Mitzvah Girls: Bringing Up the Next Generation of Hasidic Jews in Brooklyn* (Princeton, N.J.: Princeton University Press, 2009); Isaacs, "Haredi, *Haymish* and *Frim*"; Lewis Glinert, "We Never Changed Our Language: Attitudes to Yiddish Acquisition among Hasidic Educators in Britain," *International Journal of the Sociology of Language* 138 (1999): 31–52.
21. Fader, *Mitzvah Girls*, 98–99.
22. Collection of the author.
23. On Jewish English, see David Gold, "Jewish English," in *Readings in the Sociology of Jewish Languages*, ed. Joshua A. Fishman (Leiden: E. J. Brill, 1985), 280–298; Sarah Bunin Benor, "Echoes of Yiddish in the Speech of Twenty-First-Century American Jews," in *Choosing Yiddish: Studies in Language, Culture, and History*, ed. Lara Rabinovitch, Shiri Goren, and Hannah Pressman (Detroit: Wayne State University Press, 2012), 319–323.
24. "Letters to the Editor" [Yiddish], *Mayles* [Virtues] 6, no. 68 (2002): 3, my translation. On recent efforts to standardize Hasidic Yiddish in this publication, see Yeshue Kahane, "The First Magazine to Aim to Standardize Hasidic Yiddish" [Yiddish], *yiddish.forward.com*, January 31, 2019.
25. Adam Vardy, dir., *Mendy* (2003); Eve Annenberg, dir., *Romeo and Juliet in Yiddish* (2010), Pearl Gluck, dir., *Where Is Joel Baum?* (2012), Maxime Giroux, dir., *Félix et Meira* (2014), Joshua Weinstein, dir., *Menashe* (2017), Maria Schrader, dir., *Unorthodox* (2020).
26. Ayala Fader, "The Counterpublic of the J(ewish) Blogosphere: Gendered Language and the Mediation of Religious Doubt among Ultra-Orthodox Jews in New York," *Journal of the Royal Anthropological Institute*, n.s., 23 (2017): 727. See also Ayala Fader, *Hidden Heretics: Jewish Doubt in the Digital Age* (Princeton: Princeton University Press, 2020).
27. Barry Trachtenberg, *The Revolutionary Roots of Modern Yiddish, 1903–1917* (Syracuse, N.Y.: Syracuse University Press, 2008), 57–58.
28. Anna Shternshis, *Soviet and Kosher: Jewish Popular Culture in the Soviet Union, 1923–1939* (Bloomington: Indiana University Press, 2006).
29. See Jeffrey Shandler, *Adventures in Yiddishland: Postvernacular Language and Culture* (Berkeley: University of California Press, 2005), 97.
30. English-language abstract for Khayem Spivak, "Old and New Words in Yehoash's Yiddish Translation of the Bible" [Yiddish], in *Filologishe shriftn* [Philological studies], ed. Max Weinreich and Zalman Rejzen, vol. 2 (Vilna: B. Kletskin, 1928), xv; Yiddish article appears on pp. 55–68.
31. On American secular Yiddish culture, see, e.g., Tony Michels, *A Fire in Their Hearts: Yiddish Socialists in New York* (Cambridge, Mass.: Harvard University Press, 2005).
32. See Baumgarten, *Introduction to Old Yiddish Literature*, 162; Zinberg, *History of Jewish Literature*, 7:50, 51.

33. "Shira fun Yitskhok" [Song of Isaac], Max Weinreich, *Bilder fun der yidisher literaturgeshikhte: Fun di onheybn biz Mendele Moykher-Sforim* [Scenes from the history of Yiddish literature: From its beginnings to Mendele the Bookseller] (Vilna: Tomor, 1928), 134–138; "Akedas Yitskhok" [The binding of Isaac], in *Early Yiddish Texts, 1100–1750*, ed. Jerold Frakes (Oxford: Oxford University Press, 2004), 316–328. A translation of the latter appears in Jerold C. Frakes, ed., *Early Yiddish Epic* (Syracuse, N.Y.: Syracuse University Press, 2014), 149–155. I thank Sylvia Lissner Irwin for this insight; see her dissertation, "The Sacrifice of Isaac in Medieval and Early Modern German and Yiddish Works" (PhD diss., Rutgers University, 2014), ch. 5.
34. *Yudisher Theriak: An Early Modern Yiddish Defense of Judaism*, ed. and trans. Morris M. Faierstein (Detroit: Wayne State University Press, 2016).
35. Elisheva Carlebach, "The Anti-Christian Element in Early Modern Yiddish Culture," *Braun Lectures in the History of the Jews in Prussia* 10 (Ramat Gan, Israel: Bar-Ilan University, 2003), 9.
36. Marvin Herzog et al., eds., *Language and Culture Atlas of Ashkenazic Jewry*, vol. 3: *The Eastern Yiddish–Western Yiddish Continuum* (Tübingen: Max Niemeyer, 2000), 294–297(maps 118, 118S).
37. On *Toledot Yeshu* in Yiddish, see Claudia Rosenzweig, "When Jesus Spoke Yiddish," *PaRDeS: Zeitschrift der Vereinigung für Jüdische Studien* 21 (2015): 199–214; Michael Stanislawski, "A Preliminary Study of a Yiddish 'Life of Jesus' ('Toledot Yeshu'), in *"Toledot Yeshu" ("The Life Story of Jesus") Revisited*, ed. Peter Schäfer et al. (Tübingen: Mohr Siebeck, 2011), 79–87.
38. Aya Elyada, *A Goy Who Speaks Yiddish: Christians and the Jewish Language in Early Modern Germany* (Stanford, Calif.: Stanford University Press, 2012), 24.
39. Yaakov Ariel, *An Unusual Relationship: Evangelical Christians and Jews* (New York: New York University Press, 2013), 26.
40. Elyada, *Goy Who Speaks* Yiddish, 24–27.
41. Ariel, *Unusual Relationship*, 128.
42. As cited in Yaakov Ariel, *Evangelizing the Chosen People: Missions to the Jews in America, 1880–2000* (Chapel Hill: University of North Carolina Press, 2000), 91. For a discussion of this and other New Testament translations, see 88–92.
43. On *The Nazarene* and Asch's other "Christological" novels, see essays by Anita Norich, Hannah Berliner Fischthal, and Matthew Hoffman in *Sholem Asch Reconsidered*, ed. Nanette Stahl (New Haven, Conn.: Beinecke Rare Book and Manuscript Library, 2004), 251–288.
44. Chaim Lieberman, *The Christianity of Sholem Asch: An Appraisal from the Jewish Viewpoint* (New York: Philosophical Library, 1953), 3.
45. See Moshe N. Rosenfeld, "The Origins of Yiddish Printing," in *Origins of the Yiddish Language: Winter Studies in Yiddish*, vol. 1, ed. Dovid Katz (Oxford: Pergamon, 1987), 111–126.
46. See Elisheva Baumgarten, *Mothers and Children: Jewish Family Life in Medieval Europe* (Princeton, N.J.: Princeton University Press, 2004).
47. See, e.g., Kh[ayem] Zhitlovski, "In a Jewish/Yiddish Nation" [Yiddish], *Geklibene verk* [Selected works], ed. Yudl Mark (New York: CYCO, 1955), 321–323. This essay was

first printed in *Yidishe velt* in 1913, with the subtitle "How I Became a Yiddishist"; Sholem Aleichem, "Di groyse behole fun di kleyne mentshelekh" [The great confusion of the little people], in *Ale verk fun Sholem-Aleykhem* [Complete works of Sholem Aleichem], vol. 7 (New York: Forverts oysgabe, 1944), 157–210; Hirsz Abramowicz, *Profiles of a Lost World: Memoirs of East European Jewish Life before World War II*, trans. Eva Zeitlin Dobkin (Detroit: Wayne State University Press, 1999), 66.

48. Both of these phenomena circulate on YouTube; see, e.g., "Cagney Speaks Yiddish," https://www.youtube.com/watch?v=ynpOEcPdjdk, uploaded July 17, 2012; "Colin Powell at Yeshiva University, https://www.youtube.com/watch?v=AX7n-tobc4w, uploaded July 20, 2010.

## Chapter 9

1. Ivan G. Marcus, *Rituals of Childhood: Jewish Acculturation in Medieval* Europe (New Haven, Conn.: Yale University Press, 1996); Diane Roskies, "Alphabet Instruction in the East European Heder: Some Comparative and Historical Notes," *YIVO Annual of Jewish Social Science* 17 (1978): 21–53.
2. Max Weinreich, *History of the Yiddish Language*, ed. Paul Glasser, trans. Shlomo Noble and Joshua A. Fishman, vol. 1 (New Haven, Conn.: Yale University Press, 2008), 270.
3. See Jerold C. Frakes, ed., *Early Yiddish Texts 1100–1750* (Oxford: Oxford University Press, 2004), 187–188, 266–267.
4. Jeffrey A. Grossman, *The Discourse on Yiddish in Germany from the Enlightenment to the Second Empire* (Rochester, N.Y.: Camden House, 2000), 136.
5. See also Ruth H. Sanders, *German: Biography of a Language* (New York: Oxford University Press, 2010), ch. 5.
6. Steven E. Aschheim, *Brothers and Strangers: The East European Jews in German and German Jewish Consciousness, 1800–1923* (Madison: University of Wisconsin Press, 1982), 11.
7. See Isidore Fishman, *The History of Jewish Education in Central Europe: From the End of the Sixteenth to the End of the Eighteenth Century* (London: Edward Goldston, 1944).
8. See Fishman, *History of Jewish Education in Central Europe*, 118–121; Eliyana R. Adler, *In Her Hands: The Education of Jewish Girls in Tsarist Russia* (Detroit: Wayne State University Press, 2011), 133.
9. See Philip Friedman, "Joseph Perl as an Educational Activist and His School in Tarnopol" [Yiddish], *YIVO-bleter* [YIVO pages] 31–32 (1948): 157.
10. Mordechai Zalkin, *Modernizing Jewish Education in Nineteenth Century Eastern Europe: The School as the Shrine of the Jewish Enlightenment* (Leiden: Brill, 2016), 51.
11. See Kh. Sh. Kazdan, *Fun kheyder un "shkoles" biz TSISHO: Dos ruslendishe yidntum in gerangl far shul, shprakh, kultur* [From the *kheyder* and "Russian" school to the CYCO [Central Yiddish School Organization]: Russian Jewry's struggle over schooling, language, culture] (Mexico City: Shloyme Mendelson-fond, 1956), 96.

12. Zalkin, *Modernizing Jewish Education in Nineteenth Century Eastern Europe*, 124.
13. Alice Nakhimovsky and Roberta Newman, *Dear Mendel, Dear Reyzl: Yiddish Letter Manuals from Russia and America* (Bloomington: Indiana University Press, 2014).
14. Cited in Nathan Cohen, "The Bund's Contribution to Yiddish Culture in Poland between the Two World Wars," in *Jewish Politics in Eastern Europe: The Bund at 100*, ed. Jack Jacobs (New York: New York University Press, 2001), 112–113.
15. See Kazdan, *Fun kheyder un "shkoles" biz TSISHO*, 329.
16. See Kalman Weiser, *Jewish People, Yiddish Nation: Noah Prylucki and the Folkists in* Poland (Toronto: University of Toronto Press, 2011), 127–133.
17. On secular Yiddish education in interwar Poland, see Jordana de Bloeme, "Creating a New Jewish Nation: The Vilna Education Society and Secular Yiddish Education in Interwar Vilna," *Polin: Studies in Polish Jewry* 30 (2018): 221–236.
18. See Hirsz Abramowicz, *Profiles of a Lost World: Memoirs of East European Jewish Life before World War II*, trans. Eva Zeitlin Dobkin (Detroit: Wayne State University Press, 1999), 245–247.
19. See Naomi Seidman, *Sarah Schenirer and the Bais Yaakov Movement: A Revolution in the Name of Tradition* (Liverpool: Littman, 2019).
20. Joanna Lisek, "Orthodox Yiddishism in *Beys Yakov* Magazine in the Context of Religious Jewish Feminism in Poland," in *Ashkenazim and Sephardim: A European Perspective*, ed. Andrzej Katny, Izabela Olszewska, and Aleksandra Twardowska (Frankfurt am Main: Peter Lang Edition, 2013), 132, 130.
21. E.g., "Lenin and Stalin" and "Enemies" [Yiddish], in P. Burganski, *Zay greyt!* [Be prepared!], part 1 (Kharkov/Kiev: Melukhe-farlag far di natsyonale minderheytn in USRR, 1932), 39, 60.
22. On Soviet Yiddish schools, see Elias Schulman, *A History of Jewish Education in the Soviet Union* (New York: Ktav, 1971).
23. E.g., Israel Berlin, *Ershtes bukh tsu erlernen di englishe shprakh: A methode far zelbstlerner* [First book for learning the English language: A method for self-study] (New York: A. Wasserman, [1907]); Joseph Bresler, *Esperanto: A laykhte methode tsu lernen di internatsyonale hilfs shprakh* [Esperanto: An easy method to learn the international language] (New York: Sh. Drukerman, 1909); F. Halperin, *Ha-sefer: Lernbukh fun hebreish far yidishe shuln* [The book: Textbook for Hebrew for Jewish schools], part 1 (Vilna: B. Kletskin, 1928); Naftali Hertz Neimanovitch, *Der hoyzlehrer polnish* [The Polish home teacher] (Warsaw: [n.p.], 1901); Hayim Keler, *Lern arabish: A laykhte sisteme tsu erlernen di arabishe shprakh* [Learn Arabic: An easy system for learning the Arabic language] (Tel Aviv: Mitspah, [1935]); M. Meriman, *Portugezish-yidisher lernbukh: Mit a yidish-portugezishn verterbukh; ale gramatishe klolim un di oysshprakh in yidish* [Portuguese-Yiddish textbook: With a Yiddish-Portuguese dictionary: All grammar rules and pronunciation in Yiddish] (Warsaw: A. Gitlin, 1929); Saul Roso, *Der shpanisher lerer: A laykhte metode tsu lernen leyenen, shraybn un reydn shpanish* [The Spanish teacher: An easy method to learn to read, write, and speak Spanish] (New York: Hebrew Publishing Company, 1929); H. Vanel, *Der folks-lehrer: Eyn lehrbukh tsum zelbst-unterrikht in der russishen shprakhe . . .* [The People's teacher: A textbook for self-study of the Russian language . . .] (Vilna: Y.

Pirozshnikov, [1904]); Shebach Walkowski, *Unterrikhtsbrief: Far shprakhen un algemeynes visen . . . daytshe shprakhe* [Study letters: For language and general knowledge of German] (Cracow: Nakładem Autora w Krakowie, [1915]).

24. "The Yiddish School Movement" [Yiddish], *Algemeyne entsiklopedye* [General encyclopedia], vol. *Yidn: giml* (New York: Dubnov-fond fun TSIKO, 1942), cols. 408–424.
25. See Fradle Pomerantz Freidenreich, *Passionate Pioneers: The Story of Yiddish Secular Education in North America, 1910–1960* (Teaneck, N.J.: Holmes & Meir, 2010); Sandra Parker, *Yiddish Schools in North America* (Rowley, Mass.: Newbury House, 1978).
26. Z[almen] Yefroykin, "Yiddish Education in the United States" [Yiddish], *Algemeyne entsiklopedye* [General encyclopedia], vol. *Yidn: hey* (New York: Dubnov-fond, 1957), col. 209.
27. Frank V. Thompson, *Schooling of the Immigrant* (New York: Harper & Bros., 1920), 383, 5.
28. See Jenna Weissman Joselit, *The Wonders of America: Reinventing Jewish Culture, 1880–1950* (New York: Hill & Wang, 1994), 92–93.
29. See Jeffrey Shandler, *Adventures in Yiddishland: Postvernacular Language and Culture* (Berkeley: University of California Press, 2005), 96–97.
30. See, e.g., Leibush Lehrer, *The Objectives of Camp Boiberik in the Light of Its History* ([n.p.]: Camp Boiberik, 1962); Riv-Ellen Prell, *Jewish Summer Camping and Civil Rights: How Summer Camps Launched a Transformation in American Jewish Culture* (Ann Arbor: Jean and Samuel Frankel Center for Judaic Studies, University of Michigan, 2006).
31. Sholem Aleichem College, "Philosophy and Values," http://www.sholem.vic.edu.au/about-us/philosophy-and-values/, accessed January 31, 2018.
32. Josh Nathan-Kazis, "Yiddish Kindergarten May Be Coming to a New York City Public School," *Forward*, April 12, 2019.
33. See Ayala Fader, *Mitzvah Girls: Bringing Up the Next Generation of Hasidic Jews in Brooklyn* (Princeton, N.J.: Princeton University Press, 2009).
34. Uriel Weinreich, *College Yiddish: An Introduction to the Yiddish Language and to Jewish Life and Culture* (New York: YIVO Institute, 1949), 30. My translation.

## Chapter 10

1. UNESCO, *The Plurality of Literacy and Its Implications for Policies and Programmes* (Paris: UNESCO, 2004), 13.
2. See Jerold C. Frakes, *Early Yiddish Texts, 1100–1750* (Oxford: Oxford University Press, 2004); for translations of several epics based on biblical and "secular" sources, see Jerold C. Frakes, ed., *Early Yiddish Epic* (Syracuse, N.Y.: Syracuse University Press, 2014).
3. See Jean Baumgarten, *Introduction to Old Yiddish Literature*, ed. and trans. Jerold C. Frakes (Oxford: Oxford University Press, 2005), chs. 6, 7.
4. See Baumgarten, *Introduction to Old Yiddish Literature*, ch. 3; Moshe N. Rosenfeld, "The Origins of Yiddish Printing," in *Origins of the Yiddish Language: Winter Studies in Yiddish*, vol. 1, ed. Dovid Katz (Oxford: Pergamon, 1987), 111–126.

5. Israel Zinberg, *A History of Jewish Literature*, trans. Bernard Martin, vol. 7: *Old Yiddish Literature from Its Origins to the Haskalah Period* (Cincinnati: Hebrew Union College Press, 1975), 160.
6. Zinberg, *History of Jewish Literature*, 7:185. See also Baumgarten, *Introduction to Old Yiddish Literature*, 298–299.
7. Zinberg, *History of Jewish Literature*, 7:185.
8. Zinberg, *History of Jewish Literature*, 7:217.
9. See Frakes, *Early Yiddish Texts, 1100–1750*, 89–91.
10. See *In Praise of the Baal Shem Tov: The Earliest Collection of Legends about the Founder of Hasidism*, trans. and ed. Dan Ben-Amos and Jerome R. Mintz (Bloomington: Indiana University Press, 1970); *Nahman of Bratslav: The Tales*, trans. Arnold Band (New York: Paulist Press, 1978).
11. See, e.g., introduction to Irving Howe and Eliezer Greenberg, eds., *A Treasury of Yiddish Stories* (New York: Viking, 1954), 24.
12. Max Weinreich, *History of the Yiddish Language*, ed. Paul Glasser, trans. Shlomo Noble and Joshua A. Fishman (New Haven, Conn.: Yale University Press, 2008), vol. 1, ch. 4.
13. Weinreich, *History of the Yiddish Language*, 1:199.
14. Marion Aptroot, "Creating Yiddish Dialogue for 'The First Modern Yiddish Comedy,'" in *Arguing the Modern Jewish Canon: Essays on Literature and Culture in Honor of Ruth R. Wisse*, ed. Justin Cammy, Dara Horn, Alyssa Quint, and Rachel Rubinstein (Cambridge, Mass.: Harvard University Press, 2008), 435–436.
15. See, e.g., Leo Wiener, *The History of Yiddish Literature in the Nineteenth Century* (New York: Charles Scribner's Sons, 1899), 20.
16. See Nancy Sinkoff, *Out of the Shtetl: Making Jews Modern in the Polish Borderlands* (Providence, R.I.: Brown Judaic Studies, 2004), 173–176.
17. Jan Doktór, "Jewish Publishing Houses and the Censorship of Jewish Publications in the Kingdom of Poland before 1862," *Kwartalnik Historii Zydów* [Jewish history quarterly] 262 (2017): 169.
18. David G. Roskies, "An Annotated Bibliography of Ayzik Meyer Dik," in *The Field of Yiddish: Studies in Language, Folklore, and Literature, Fourth Collection*, ed. Marvin I. Herzog, Barbara Kirshenblatt-Gimblett, Dan Miron, and Ruth Wisse (Philadelphia: Institute for the Study of Human Issues, 1980), 117. See also David G. Roskies, *A Bridge of Longing: The Lost Art of Yiddish Storytelling* (Cambridge, Mass.: Harvard University Press, 1995), ch. 3.
19. [Ayzik Meyer Dik], *Di kremerkes, oder Golde Mine di broder agune* [The women shopkeepers, or Golde Mine, the abandoned wife from Brod] (Vilna: Fin-Rozenkrants, 1865), 8, 67.
20. On Goldfaden, see Alyssa Quint, *The Rise of the Modern Yiddish Theater* (Bloomington: Indiana University Press, 2019).
21. See Benjamin Harshav, *The Meaning of Yiddish* (Berkeley: University of California Press, 1990), ch. 5.
22. Dan Miron, *A Traveler Disguised: A Study in the Rise of Modern Yiddish Fiction in the Nineteenth Century* (New York: Schocken, 1973), 18.

23. Miron, *Traveler Disguised*, 12.
24. See Menachem Perry, "Thematic and Structural Shifts in Autotranslations by Bilingual Hebrew-Yiddish Writers: The Case of Mendele Mokher Sforim," *Poetics Today* 2, no. 4 (1981): 181–192.
25. See Gabriella Safran and Steven J. Zipperstein, eds., *The Worlds of S. An-sky: A Russian Jewish Intellectual at the Turn of the Century* (Stanford, Calif.: Stanford University Press, 2006), 361–435.
26. Jeffrey Shandler, "Heschel and Yiddish: A Struggle with Signification," *Journal of Jewish Thought and Philosophy* 2 (1993): 245–299.
27. Naomi Seidman, *The Marriage Plot: Or, How Jews Fell in Love with Love, and with Literature* (Stanford, Calif.: Stanford University Press, 2016).
28. Sarah Abrevaya Stein, *Making Jews Modern: The Yiddish and Ladino Press in the Russian and Ottoman Empires* (Bloomington: Indiana University Press, 2004), 25.
29. Tony Michels, *A Fire in Their Hearts: Yiddish Socialists in New York* (Cambridge, Mass.: Harvard University Press, 2005), 113.
30. The most famous example of this practice is the "Bintl briv" (Packet of letters), a column that appeared during the first seven decades of the twentieth century in the *Jewish Daily Forward*, offering editorial advice in response to readers' letters regarding personal problems. Selected letters are translated in Isaac Metzger, ed., *A Bintel Brief: Sixty Years of Letters from the Lower East Side to the Jewish Daily Forward* (New York: Schocken, 1990).
31. Morris Bassin, *Antologye: Finf hundert yohr yidishe poezye* [Anthlogy: Five Hundred Years of Yiddish Poetry] ([Brooklyn, N.Y.]: Farlag "Dos yidishe bukh," 1917).
32. See, e.g., Ellen Kellman, "Entertaining New Americans: Serialized Fiction in the 'Forverts' (1910–1930)," in *Jews and American Popular Culture*, ed. Paul Buhle, vol. 2 (Westport, Conn.: Praeger, 2007), 199–211.
33. Sholem Aleichem, "The Judgment of Shomer, or The Jury Trial of All of Shomer's Novels," trans. Justin Cammy, in Cammy et al., *Arguing the Modern Jewish Canon*, 129–185.
34. See Nina Warnke, "Immigrant Popular Culture as Contested Sphere: Yiddish Music Halls, the Yiddish Press, and the Processes of Americanization, 1900–1910," *Theatre Journal* 48, no. 3 (1996): 321–335; Nathan Cohen, "'Shund' and the Tabloids: Jewish Popular Reading in Inter-War Poland," *Polin* 16 (2003): 189–211.
35. See Jeffrey Veidlinger, *Jewish Public Culture in the Late Russian Empire* (Bloomington: Indiana University Press, 2009), 105–109.
36. See Veidlinger, *Jewish Public Culture in the Late Russian Empire*, ch. 2.
37. See, e.g., Zalman Shneour, "Newspapers," in *Restless Spirit: Selected Writings of Zalman Shneour*, trans. Moshe Spiegel (New York: Thomas Yoseloff, 1963), 41–52. On cafes, see Shachar M. Pinsker, *A Rich Brew: How Cafés Created Modern Jewish Culture* (New York: New York University Press, 2018).
38. On avant-garde Yiddish poetry, see, e.g., Benjamin Harshav, *The Meaning of Yiddish* (Berkeley: University of California Press, 1990), chs. 7, 8.
39. Farlag un bukhhandlung B. A. Kletskin, *Ilustrirter katalog* [Illustrated catalog], Warsaw, March 1925.

40. Beatrice Lang Caplan, "Shmuel Nadler's *Besht-Simfonye*: At the Limits of Orthodox Literature," in Cammy et al., *Arguing the Modern Jewish Canon*, 599.
41. See Ellen Kellman, "*Dos yidishe bukh alarmirt!* Towards the History of Yiddish Reading in Inter-War Poland," *Polin* 16 (2003): 213–241; Nathan Cohen, "The Yiddish Press as Distributor of Literature," in *The Multiple Voices of Modern Yiddish Literature*, ed. Shlomo Berger, *Amsterdam Yiddish Symposium 2* (Amsterdam: Menasseh ben Israel Institute, 2007), 7–29.
42. On Soviet Yiddish book design, see Margit Rowell and Deborah Wye, *The Russian Avant-Garde Book, 1910–1934* (New York: Museum of Modern Art, 2002).
43. See Gennady Estraikh, *Soviet Yiddish: Language Planning and Linguistic Development* (Oxford: Clarendon, 1999), 62–67.
44. See David Goldberg, "Fantasy, Realism, and National Identity in Soviet Yiddish Juvenile Literature: Itsik Kipnis's Books for Children," in *Field of Yiddish: Studies in Language, Folklore, and Literature, Fifth Collection*, ed. David Goldberg (Evanston, Ill.: Northwestern University Press, 1993), 153–201; David Shneer, *Yiddish and the Creation of Soviet Jewish Culture, 1918–1930* (Cambridge: Cambridge University Press, 2004), ch. 6.
45. See Joshua Rubinstein and Vladimir P. Naumov, eds., *Stalin's Secret Pogrom: The Postwar Inquisition of the Jewish Anti-Fascist Committee* (New Haven, Conn.: Yale University Press, 2001).
46. Harald Haarmann, *Language in Ethnicity: A View of Basic Ecological Relations* (Berlin: Mouton de Gruyter, 1986), 71.
47. See Estraikh, *Soviet Yiddish*, 108–114.
48. Anita Norich, *Discovering Exile: Yiddish and Jewish American Culture during the Holocaust* (Stanford, Calif.: Stanford University Press, 2007), 21, 23.
49. Naomi Prawer Kadar, *Raising Secular Jews: Yiddish Schools and Their Periodicals for American Children, 1917–1950* (Waltham, Mass.: Brandeis University Press, 2017), 156.
50. See Lucy S. Dawidowicz, *From That Place and Time: A Memoir, 1938–1947* (New York: W. W. Norton, 1989), ch. 14; David Fishman, *The Rise of Modern Jewish Culture* (Pittsburgh: University of Pittsburgh Press, 2005), ch. 10.
51. Barry Trachtenberg, *The Revolutionary Roots of Modern Yiddish, 1903–1917* (Syracuse, N.Y.: Syracuse University Press, 2008), 285, 297.
52. Jan Schwarz, *Survivors and Exiles: Yiddish Culture after the Holocaust* (Detroit: Wayne State University Press, 2015), 7.
53. See Jack Kugelmass and Jonathan Boyarin, eds., *From a Ruined Garden: The Memorial Books of Polish Jewry* (New York: Schocken, 1983).
54. See Schwarz, *Survivors and Exiles*, ch. 4.
55. Malena Chinski and Lucas Fiszman, "'A biblyotek vos felt': Planning and Creating the Book Collection *Musterverk fun der yidisher literatur* (Buenos Aires, 1957–1984)," *Journal of Jewish Identities* 10, no. 2 (July 2017): 138.
56. See Shmuel Rozhanski, ed., *Yidish in lid* [Yiddish in verse] (Buenos Aires: Literatur-gezelshaft baym YIVO in Argentine, 1967).

57. Mozny Kohen, "A Letter to the Readers" [Yiddish], in F. Royz, *Der shpion vos iz antlofn* [The spy who escaped] (Monroe, N.Y.: Mozny Kohen, 2000), [4].
58. See Jeffrey Shandler, "Anthologizing the Vernacular: Collections of Yiddish Literature in English Translation," in *The Anthology in Jewish Literature*, ed. David Stern (Oxford: Oxford University Press, 2004), 304–323.
59. See Anita Norich, *Writing in Tongues: Translating Yiddish in the Twentieth Century* (Seattle: University of Washington Press, 2013), ch. 3; Naomi Seidman, *Faithful Renderings: Jewish-Christian Difference and the Politics of Translation* (Chicago: University of Chicago Press, 2006), ch. 6.
60. *Kalevala: Folks epos fun di finen* [Kalevala: The Finnish national epic], trans. Hersh Rosenfeld (New York: Martin Press, 1954), 13. My translation.
61. Barbara Finkelstein, "Why Etgar Keret Wanted His Prizewinning Book Translated into Yiddish," *Forward*, February 4, 2020, https://forward.com/yiddish/439388/why-etgar-keret-wanted-his-prizewinning-book-translated-into-yiddish/?utm_source=PostUp&utm_medium=email&utm_campai. The Yiddish translation appeared in 2019.
62. Jeffrey Shandler, "Enacting Ethnicity: Yiddishkeit Masked and Unmasked on the Contemporary American Stage," *Jewish Social Studies*, n.s., 23, no. 2 (Winter 2018): 12.
63. Dr. Seuss, *Di kats der payats: The Cat in the Hat by Dr. Seuss in Yiddish*, trans. Sholem Berger (New York: Twenty-Fourth Street Books, 2003); Antoine de Saint-Exupéry, *Der kleyner prints: Yidish* [The little prince: Yiddish], trans. Shloyme Lerman (Nidderau, Germany: Verlag Michaeli Naumann, 2000); Wilhelm Busch, *Max und Moritz auf jiddisch: Eine Bubengeshchichte in sieben Streichen / Shmul un Shmerke: A mayse mit vayse-khevrenikes in zibn shpitselekh* [Max and Moritz / Shmul and Shmerke: A tale of pranksters in seven scenes], trans. Charles Nydorf and Elinor Robinson (Nidderau, Germany: Verlag Michaeli Naumann, 2000).
64. Heinrich Hoffman, *Pinye shtroykop: Der Struwwelpeter auf jiddisch* [Pinye Strawhead: Shaggy Peter in Yiddish], trans. Charles Nydorf and Elinor Robinson (Nidderau, Germany: Verlag Michaeli Naumann, 1999); A. A. Milne, *Vini-der-Pu* [Winnie the Pooh], trans. Leonard Wolf (New York: Dutton, 2000), 23.
65. See Jeffrey Shandler, *Adventures in Yiddishland: Postvernacular Language and Culture* (Berkeley: University of California Press, 2005), 116–122.
66. See, e.g., Adrienne Cooper and Zalmen Mlotek, *Ghetto Tango: Wartime Yiddish Theater*, Traditional Crossroads CD 4297, 2000, compact disc; Daniel Kahn and the Painted Bird, *The Butcher's Share*, Oriente Musik RIENCD91, 2017, compact disc.
67. Ross Perlin, "Blitspostn, Vebzaytlekh, Veblogs: The Rise of Yiddish Online," *Slate*, February 27, 2014, https://slate.com/human-interest/2014/02/yiddish-language-the-mame-loshen-has-network-of-adherents-on-the-internet-from-bloggers-to-translators-to-cultural-preservationists.html.
68. Jonathan Boyarin, "Yiddish Science and the Postmodern," trans. Naomi Seidman, in Jonathan Boyarin, *Thinking in Jewish* (Chicago: University of Chicago Press, 1996), 198.

## Chapter 11

1. Jerold C. Frakes, ed., *Early Yiddish Texts, 1100–1750* (Oxford: Oxford University Press, 2004), 52–61, 71–72, 460–462.
2. Nicolas Hatot and Judith Olszowy-Schlanger, eds., *Savants et Croyants: Les Juifs d'Europe du Nord au Moyen Âge* [Scholars and believers: Jews in northern Europe during the Middle Ages] (Ghent: Snoeck, 2018), 163.
3. See Aya Elyada, *A Goy Who Speaks Yiddish: Christians and the Jewish Language in Early Modern Germany* (Stanford, Calif.: Stanford University Press, 2012), 83–98.
4. On eastern European Jewish surnames, see Alexander Beider, *A Dictionary of Jewish Surnames from the Russian Empire* (Teaneck, N.J.: Avotaynu 1993); Alexander Beider, *A Dictionary of Jewish Surnames from the Kingdom of Poland* (Teaneck, N.J.: Avotaynu, 1996).
5. Sholem-Aleykhem, "Stempenyu," in *Yidishe romanen* [Jewish novels] Ale verk fun Sholem-Aleykhem [Complete works of Sholem Aleichem] 2 (New York: Forverts oysgabe, 1944), 136. My translation.
6. See Itzik Nakhmen Gottesman, *Defining the Yiddish Nation: The Jewish Folklorists of Poland* (Detroit: Wayne State University Press, 2003), 129–135.
7. YIVO Institute, *Filologishe shriftn* [Philological studies], vol. 3 (Vilna: B. Kletskin, 1929), xiii.
8. Khayim Khayes and Naftuli Vaynig, *Vos iz azoyns yidishe ethnografye? Hantbikhl farn zamler* [Just what is Jewish ethnography? Handbook for fieldworkers] (Vilna: YIVO, 1929). My translation.
9. H[illel] Aleksandrov, *Forsht ayer shtetl!* [Research your town!] (Minsk: Institut far vaysrusisher kultur, 1926), 8. My translation.
10. See, e.g., Ignatz Bernstein, *Yidishe shprikhverter* [Yiddish proverbs] (Warsaw, 1912).
11. See, e.g., Y. L. Cahan, *Yidishe folkslider nit melodyes* [Yiddish folksongs with melodies], ed. Max Weinreich (New York: YIVO, 1957); Abigail Wood, *And We're All Brothers: Singing in Yiddish in Contemporary North America* (London: Routledge, 2016).
12. On Yiddish in social science scholarship, see, e.g., Gennady Estraikh, "Jacob Lestschinsky: A Yiddishist Dreamer and Social Scientist," *Science in Context* 20, no. 2 (2007): 21–237; Gottesman, *Defining the Yiddish Nation*; Barbara Kirshenblatt-Gimblett, "Coming of Age in the Thirties: Max Weinreich, Edward Sapir, and Jewish Social Science," *YIVO Annual* 23 (1996): 1–103; Deborah Yalen, "Documenting the New Red Kasrilevke: Shtetl Ethnography as Revolutionary Narrative," *East European Jewish Affairs* 37, no. 3 (December 2007): 353–375.
13. See Gabriel Davidson, *Our Jewish Farmers: The Story of the Jewish Agricultural Society* (New York: L. B. Fischer, 1943).
14. On vocational education in the late Russian Empire and interwar Poland, see Hirsz Abramowicz, *Profiles of a Lost World: Memoirs of East European Jewish Life before World War II*, trans. Eva Zeitlin Dobkin (Detroit: Wayne State University Press, 1999), 221–248.

15. "Be a Good Shock Worker!" [Yiddish], in P. Burganski, *Zay greyt!* [Be prepared!], part 1 (Kharkov: Melukhe-farlag far di natsyonale minderheytn in USRR, 1932), 44; L. Frumin, *Vos darf men visn vegn akhtung gebn af a vagranke* [What you need to know to maintain a blast furnace], trans. N. Sakharni (Kharkov: Melukhe-farlag far di natsyonale minderheytn in USRR, 1932); Kolvirttsenter fun FSSR, *Vi azoy organizirn di arbet fun mashin- unferd-stansyes in di kolvirtn* [How to organize work in equipment and horse stations on collective farms] (Moscow: Tsentrfarlag, 1930).
16. Z[almen] Reyzen, *Yidishe gramatik* [Yiddish grammar] (Warsaw: Farlag "progress," 1908).
17. Cited in Barry Trachtenberg, *The Revolutionary Roots of Modern Yiddish, 1903–1917* (Syracuse, N.Y.: Syracuse University Press, 2008), 118.
18. On Lifshits, see essays by Zalman Rejzen, N. Shtif, Mordkhe Schaechter, and David E. Fishman in *Yidishe shprakh* [Yiddish language] 38, nos. 1–3 (1984–1986): 1–58.
19. See Jean Baumgarten, *Introduction to Old Yiddish Literature*, ed. and trans. Jerold C. Frakes (Oxford: Oxford University Press, 2005), 22–23.
20. See Dovid Katz, "Alexander Harkavy and His Trilingual Dictionary," in Alexander Harkavy, *Yiddish-English-Hebrew Dictionary* (1928; repr. New York: Schocken, 1988), xii–xiii.
21. *Sieben-Sprachen-Wörterbuch: Deutsch, Polnisch, Russisch, Weissruthenisch, Litauisch, Lettisch, Jiddisch* [Dictionary of seven languages: German, Polish, Russian, Belorussian, Lithuanian, Latvian, Yiddish] (Leipzig: A. Spamer, [1918]).
22. *Arabish verterbikhel: Mit geshprekhen; mit dem originelen arabishen alefbeys* [Arabic dictionary: With idioms; With the original Arabic alphabet] (Warsaw: Ferlag Altnayland, 1920); David ben Shalom Shakhna Hurvits ha-Levi, *Sefer ha-milim zhargoni-ivri / yudisher loshn-koydesher verter-bukh* [Yiddish-Hebrew dictionary] (Warsaw: Bi-defus ha-ahim Shuldberg, [1893]); *Yidish-portugezisher verter-bukh: Far emigrantn keyn Brazilyen* [Yiddish-Portuguese dictionary: For immigrants to Brazil] (Warsaw: Wydawnictwo Polskiego Komitetu Towarzystwa JCA Jewish Colonization Association, [192-?]); I. Winocur, *Idish-shpanisher verter-bukh* [Yiddish-Spanish dictionary] (Buenos Aires: G. Kaplanski, 1931).
23. Hanoch Rusak, *Entsiklopedisher verterbukh esperanto-yidish* [Encyclopedic dictionary of Esperanto-Yiddish] (Jerusalem: Bet Zamenhof, 1969–1973); Yitskhok Niborski and Bernard Vaisbrot, *Yidish-frantseyzish verterbukh* [Yiddish-French dictionary] (Paris: Medem-Bibliotek, 2002); Henrik Blau, *Idish-ungarish verter-bukh* [Yiddish-Hungarian dictionary] (Budapest: Chábád Lubavics Zsidó Nevelési és Oktatási Egyesület, 1995); Davide Astori, *Parlo Yiddish: Manuele di Conversazione* [I speak Yiddish: Conversation guide] (Milan: Antonio Vallardi, 2000); K. Ueda, *Idisshugo jō yō: 6000-go* [Six thousand commonly used Yiddish words] (Tokyo: Daigaku kan rin, 1993); Lennart Kerbel, *Jiddisch-svensk-jiddisch ordbok* [Yiddish-Swedish-Yiddish dictionary] (Stockholm: Megilla-förlaget, 2005); I. Torchyns'ky, *Kurtser yidish-ukrainisher verterbukh* [Short Yiddish-Ukrainian dictionary] (Kiev: Holovna spetsializovana redaktsiia literatury movamy natsional'nykh menshin Ukraïny, 1996).
24. Katz, "Alexander Harkavy and His Trilingual Dictionary," vii.

25. Uriel Weinreich, *Modern English-Yiddish / Yiddish-English Dictionary* (New York: McGraw-Hill, 1968), xi. On Weinreich's career, see *Journal of Jewish Languages* 5, no. 2 (2017), a special issue devoted to his work.
26. Gitl Schaechter-Viswanath and Paul Glasser, eds., *Comprehensive English-Yiddish Dictionary: Based on the Lexical Research of Mordkhe Schaechter* (Bloomington: Indiana University Press, 2016).
27. Katz, "Alexander Harkavy and His Trilingual Dictionary," xviii; Judah A. Joffe and Yudel Mark, eds., *Groyser verterbukh fun der yidisher shprakh* [Great dictionary of the Yiddish language], vol. 1 (New York: Yiddish Dictionary Committee, 1961), 509.
28. Joffe and Mark, *Groyser verterbukh fun der yidisher shprakh*, 1:510.
29. Additional volumes of the *Groyser verterbukh fun der yidisher shprakh* appeared in 1966 (vol. 2), 1971 (vol. 3), and 1980 (vol. 4).
30. Joffe and Mark, *Groyser verterbukh fun der yidisher shprakh*, 1:509–510.
31. See Max Weinreich, "YIVO during a Year of Mass Murder" [Yiddish], *YIVO-bleter* [YIVO pages] 21 (1943): 88.
32. See Avraham Novershtern, "Between Town and Gown: The Institutionalization of Yiddish at Israeli Universities," in *Yiddish in the Contemporary World*, ed. Gennady Estraikh and Mikhail Krutikov (Oxford: Legenda, 1999), 1–19.
33. David E. Fishman, "The Rebirth of Jewish Scholarship in Russia," *American Jewish Year Book* 97 (1997): 391–400.

## Chapter 12

1. See, e.g., *Der bezim* [The broom], a supplement to *Dos lebn* [Life] (Odessa), April 10, 1906.
2. Tony Michels, *A Fire in Their Hearts: Yiddish Socialists in New York* (Cambridge, Mass.: Harvard University Press, 2005), 79.
3. On Peretz, see Ken Frieden, *Classic Yiddish Fiction: Abramovitsh, Sholem Aleichem, and Peretz* (Albany: State University of New York Press, 1995), 245–249. On "sweatshop poets," see Ori Kritz, *The Poetics of Anarchy: David Edelshtat's Revolutionary Poetry* (New York: Peter Lang, 1997); Marc Miller, *Representing the Immigrant Experience: Morris Rosenfeld and the Emergence of Yiddish Literature in America* (Syracuse, N.Y.: Syracuse University Press, 2007).
4. See David E. Fishman, *The Rise of Modern Jewish Culture* (Pittsburgh: University of Pittsburgh Press, 2005), 53.
5. Fishman, *Rise of Modern Jewish Culture*, 32.
6. See Lewis Glinert, "The First Conference for Hebrew, or When Is a Congress Not a Congress?," in *The Earliest Stage of Language Planning: The "First Congress" Phenomenon*, ed. Joshua A. Fishman, Contributions to the Sociology of Language 65 (Berlin: Mouton de Gruyter, 1993), 85–115; Esther Schor, *Bridge of Words: Esperanto and the Dream of a Universal Language* (New York: Metropolitan, 2016), 85; Holger Nath, "The First International Conference of the Catalan Language in Barcelona (1906): A Spiritual Precursor to Czernowitz (1908)?," in *The Politics of Yiddish: Studies in Language, Literature, and Society*, ed. Dov-Ber Kerler (Walnut Creek, Calif.: AltaMira, 1998), 51–62.

7. Barry Trachtenberg, *The Revolutionary Roots of Modern Yiddish, 1903–1917* (Syracuse, N.Y.: Syracuse University Press, 2008), 121–122.
8. Trachtenberg, *Revolutionary Roots of Modern Yiddish*, 114.
9. Emanuel S. Goldsmith, *Architects of Yiddishism at the Beginning of the Twentieth Century: A Study in Jewish Cultural History* (Rutherford, N.J.: Fairleigh Dickinson University Press, 1976), 168.
10. Goldsmith, *Architects of Yiddishism*, 64.
11. See Ezra Mendelsohn, *The Jews of East Central Europe between the World Wars* (Bloomington: Indiana University Press, 1983).
12. See Gennady Estraikh, *Soviet Yiddish: Language Planning and Linguistic Development* (Oxford: Clarendon, 1999), ch. 3; David Shneer, *Yiddish and the Creation of Soviet Jewish Culture, 1918–1930* (Cambridge: Cambridge University Press, 2004), ch. 2.
13. On the murder of Soviet Yiddish culture leaders, see Joshua Rubinstein and Vladimir P. Naumov, eds., *Stalin's Secret Pogrom: The Postwar Inquisition of the Jewish Anti-Fascist Committee* (New Haven, Conn.: Yale University Press, 2001).
14. See Tony Michels, "Exporting Yiddish Socialism: New York's Role in the Russian Workers' Movement," *Jewish Social Studies* 16, no. 1 (2009): 1–26.
15. The Yiddish *Forward* continued as a weekly and is currently an online publication.
16. See Edna Nahshon, *Yiddish Proletarian Theatre: The Art and Politics of ARTEF, 1925–1940* (Westport, Conn.: Greenwood, 1998); Edward Portnoy, "Modicut Puppet Theatre: Modernism, Satire, and Yiddish Culture," *TDR* 43, no. 3 (1999): 115–134.
17. Raymond Pearson, *National Minorities in Eastern Europe, 1848–1945* (London: Macmillan, 1983), 25.
18. Israel Bartal, "From Traditional Bilingualism to National Monolingualism," in *Hebrew in Ashkenaz: A Language in Exile*, ed. Lewis Glinert (New York: Oxford University Press, 1993), 141–150.
19. See Larry Wolff, *The Idea of Galicia: History and Fantasy in Habsburg Political Culture* (Stanford, Calif.: Stanford University Press, 2010), ch. 1; Pearson, *National Minorities in Eastern Europe*, ch. 3.
20. See Miklós Konrád, "Hungarian Expectations and Jewish Self-Definitions, 1840–1914," in *Modern Jewish Scholarship in Hungary: The "Science of Judaism" between East and West*, ed. Tamás Turán and Carsten Wilke (Berlin: Walter de Gruyter, 2016), 329–348; Szonja Ráhel Komoróczy, "Yiddish in the Hungarian Setting," in *Jewish Languages in Historical Perspective*, ed. Lily Kahn (Leiden: Brill, 2018), 92–107.
21. Marianne Hirsch and Leo Spitzer, *Ghosts of Home: The Afterlife of Czernowitz in Jewish Memory* (Berkeley: University of California Press, 2011), 89.
22. Ahad Ha-'Am, *Selected Essays by Ahad Ha-'Am*, trans. Leon Simon (Philadelphia: Jewish Publication Society of America, 1912), 281, 280, 283.
23. Avraham Novershtern, "Language Wars," in *Critical Terms in Jewish Language Studies*, ed. Anita Norich and Joshua L. Miller (Ann Arbor: Frankel Institute for Advanced Judaic Studies, University of Michigan, 2011), 22–23.
24. Liora R. Halpern, *Babel in Zion: Jews, Nationalism, and Language Diversity in Palestine, 1920–1948* (New Haven, Conn.: Yale University Press, 2015), 58.
25. Shneer, *Yiddish and the Creation of Soviet Jewish Culture*, 49, 51.

26. Yehoshua A. Gilboa, "Hebrew Literature in the USSR," in *The Jews in Soviet Russia since 1917*, ed. Lionel Kochan, 3rd ed. (Oxford: Oxford University Press, 1978), 228.
27. Samuel D. Kassow, *Who Will Write Our History?: Emanuel Ringelblum, the Warsaw Ghetto, and the Oyneg Shabes Archive* (Bloomington: Indiana University Press, 2007).
28. See, e.g., Gila Flam, *Singing for Survival: Songs of the Lodz Ghetto, 1940–45* (Urbana: University of Illinois Press, 1991).
29. United States Holocaust Memorial Museum, "The Yiddish words, 'Jews Revenge!' scrawled in blood on the apartment floor of a Jew murdered in the Slobodka pogrom," Photograph Number: 04640, https://collections.ushmm.org/search/catalog/pa29012, accessed August 25, 2018.
30. Szmerke Kaczerginski, *Dos gezang fun vilner geto* [The song of the Vilna Ghetto] (Paris: Farband fun di vilner in Frankraykh, 1947); Szmerke Kaczerginski, *Lider fun di getos un lagern: Tekstn un melodyes* [Songs of the ghettos and camps: Texts and melodies] (New York: TSIKO, 1948); Yisroel Kaplan, *Dos folks-moyl in natsi-klem: reydenishn in geto un katset* [The voice of the people under Nazi Oppression: Speech in ghettos and concentration camps] (Munich: Tsentraler historisher komisye fun di bafrayte yidn in der amerikaner zone in Daytshland, 1949), translated by Jenny Bell and Dianne Levitin as *The Jewish Voice in the Ghettos and Concentration Camps: Verbal Expression under Nazi Oppression* (Jerusalem: Yad Vashem, 2018).
31. David Slucki, *The International Jewish Labor Bund after 1945: Toward a Global History* (New Brunswick, N.J.: Rutgers University Press, 2012).
32. Diego Rotman, "The 'Tsadik from Plonsk' and 'Goldenyu': Political Satire in Dzigan and Shumacher's Israeli Comic Repertoire," in *A Club of Their Own: Jewish Humorists and the Contemporary World*, ed. Eli Lederhendler, Studies in Contemporary Jewry 29 (Oxford: Oxford University Press, 2016), 167.
33. See Jerome R. Mintz, *Hasidic People: A Place in the New World* (Cambridge, Mass.: Harvard University Press 1994), ch. 26.
34. See Jeffrey Shandler, *Adventures in Yiddishland: Postvernacular Language and Culture* (Berkeley: University of California Press, 2005), 201–202.
35. Ruth Ellen Gruber, *Virtually Jewish: Reinventing Jewish Culture in Europe* (Berkeley: University of California Press, 2002), 194.

## Chapter 13

1. Benjamin Harshav, *The Meaning of Yiddish* (Berkeley: University of California Press, 1990), 91.
2. Endel Markowitz, *The Encyclopedia Yiddishanica: A Compendium of Jewish Memorabilia* (Fredericksburg, Va.: Haymark, 1980), xvii.
3. Leo Rosten, *The Joys of Yiddish* (New York: McGraw-Hill, 1968), xviii.
4. Maurice Samuel, *In Praise of Yiddish* (Chicago: Henry Regnery, 1971), xii, 6, xii.
5. See Jeffrey Shandler, *Adventures in Yiddishland: Postvernacular Language and Culture* (Berkeley: University of California Press, 2005), 22.
6. Samuel, *In Praise of Yiddish*, 97, 99, 103–104.

7. See Nokhem Stutshkov, *Oytser fun der yidisher shprakh* [Thesaurus of the Yiddish Language] (New York: YIVO, 1950), sections 246, 247, 249, 250; Mordkhe Schaechter, *Plant Names in Yiddish: A Handbook of Botanical Terminology* (New York: League for Yiddish, 2005).
8. For example, "Monish" is the opening work in *The Penguin Book of Modern Yiddish Verse*, ed. Irving Howe, Ruth Wisse, and Chone Shmeruk (New York: Viking, 1987), 52–81.
9. Y. L. Perets, "Monish," in *Di verk fun Yitskhok Leybush Perets* [I. L. Peretz's Works], vol. 1: *Lider* [Poems] (New York: Farlag yidish, 1920), 169. My translation. In later versions of the poem, Peretz omitted this section.
10. Mark Zborowski and Elizabeth Herzog, *Life Is with People: The Jewish Little-Town of Eastern Europe* (New York: International Universities Press, 1952), 72–73.
11. See, e.g., Fred Kogos, *A Dictionary of Yiddish Slang and Idioms* (New York: Citadel, 1970); Yosef Guri, *Lomir hern gute bsures: yidishe brokhes un klolim / Let's Hear Only Good News: Yiddish Blessings and Curses* (Jerusalem: Hebrew University Magnes Press, 2004); *Yiddish Wisdom: Humor and Heart from the Old Country* (San Francisco: Chronicle, 2013).
12. James A. Matisoff, *Blessings, Curses, Hopes, and Fears: Psycho-Ostensive Expressions in Yiddish* (Philadelphia: Institute for the Study of Human Issues, 1979), 6, 4.
13. Matisoff, *Blessings, Curses, Hopes, and Fears*, 4, 7, 7.
14. See., e.g., John Murray Cuddihy, *The Ordeal of Civility: Freud, Marx, Levi-Strauss, and the Jewish Struggle with Modernity* (New York: Basic Books, 1974), part 1; Sander Gilman, *Jewish Self-Hatred: Anti-Semitism and the Hidden Language of the Jews* (Baltimore: Johns Hopkins University Press, 1986), 250–269.
15. Christopher Hutton, "Freud and the Family Drama of Yiddish," *Studies in Yiddish Linguistics*, ed. Paul Wexler (Tübingen: Max Niemeyer Verlag, 1990), 16, 21.
16. Hutton, "Freud and the Family Drama of Yiddish," 16.
17. Franz Kafka, "An Introductory Talk on the Yiddish Language," in *Reading Kafka*, ed. Mark Anderson (New York: Schocken, 1990), 263–266.
18. Evelyn Torton Beck, *Kafka and the Yiddish Theater: Its Impact on His Work* (Madison: University of Wisconsin Press, 1971), 28–29.
19. Martin Buber, introduction to *Eisik Schaftel: Ein jüdisches Arbeiterdrama in Drei Akten von David Pinski* [Isaac Schaftel: A Jewish labor drama in three acts by David Pinski] (Berlin: Der jüdische Verlag, 1903), 4f, as cited in Paul Mendes-Flohr, "The Politics of Covenantal Responsibility: Martin Buber and Hebrew Humanism," *ORIM: A Jewish Journal at Yale* 3, no. 2 (Spring 1988): 7.
20. Mendes-Flohr, "Politics of Covenantal Responsibility," 7.
21. Richard Fein, *Dancing with Leah: Discovering Yiddish in America* (Rutherford, N.J.: Fairleigh Dickinson University Press, 1986), 9, 16, 22, 29, 28.
22. Lita Epstein, *If You Can't Say Anything Nice, Say It in Yiddish: The Book of Yiddish Insults and Curses* (New York: Kensington, 2006).
23. Yetta Emmes, *Drek!: The Real Yiddish Your Bubbe Never Taught You* (New York: Plume, 1998); Adrienne Gusoff, *Dirty Yiddish: Everyday Slang from "What's Up?" to "F*%# Off!"* (Berkeley, Calif.: Ulysses, 2012).

24. Martin Marcus, *Yiddish for Yankees: or, Funny, You Don't Look Gentile* (Philadelphia: J. P. Lippincott, 1968); Arthur Naiman, *Every Goy's Guide to Common Jewish Expressions* (New York: Ballantine, 1981).
25. Per a Google search of "Yiddish T-shirts," May 16, 2018. Romanizations per sources.
26. On these resorts, see Stefan Kanfer, *A Summer World: The Attempt to Build a Jewish Eden in the Catskills from the Days of the Ghetto to the Rise and Decline of the Borscht Belt* (New York: Farrar, Straus & Giroux, 1989).
27. Uriel Weinreich, *Languages in Contact: Findings and Problems* (1953; repr. The Hague: Mouton, 1966), 95.

## Chapter 14

1. David Crystal, *Language Death* (Cambridge: Cambridge University Press, 2000), 1.
2. Andrew Dalby, *Language in Danger: The Loss of Linguistic Diversity and the Threat to Our Future* (New York: Columbia University Press, 2003), 275.
3. UNESCO lists Yiddish in Europe and in Israel as "definitely endangered." UNESCO Atlas of the World's Languages in Danger, http://www.unesco.org/languages-atlas/index.php, accessed May 31, 2018.
4. Netta Avineri, "Yiddish Endangerment as Phenomenological Reality and Discursive Strategy: Crossing into the Past and Crossing Out the Present," *Language and Communication* 38 (2014): 18–32.
5. Sarah Bunin Benor, "Hebrew Infusion in American Jewish Life: Tensions and the Role of Israeli Hebrew," in *What We Talk about When We Talk about Hebrew (and What It Means to Americans)*, ed. Naomi B. Sokoloff and Nancy E. Berg (Seattle: University of Washington Press, 2018), 124–138.
6. Anita Norich, *Discovering Exile: Yiddish and Jewish American Culture during the Holocaust* (Stanford, Calif.: Stanford University Press, 2007), 5.
7. Jeffrey Shandler, *Holocaust Memory in the Digital Age: Survivors' Stories and New Media Practices* (Stanford, Calif.: Stanford University Press, 2017), 94, 122.
8. Cynthia Ozick, "Envy; or, Yiddish in America," in *Jewish Literature in America: A Norton Anthology*, ed. Jules Chametzky, John Felstiner, Hilene Flanzbaum, and Kathryn Hellerstein (New York: W. W. Norton, 2001), 859.
9. Celia Stopnicka Heller, *On the Edge of Destruction: Jews of Poland between the Two World Wars* (New York: Columbia University Press, 1977), 66. See also John Myhill, *Language in Jewish Society: Towards a New Understanding* (Clevedon, UK: Multilingual Matters, 2004), 136–140.
10. Samuel Kassow, "Polish Jewish, Yiddish Jewish: Language Angst in Interwar Jewish Poland," seminar presentation, American Academy for Jewish Research Fellows Retreat, University of California Berkeley, May 22, 2012. On Yiddish in postwar Poland, see Joanna Nalewajko-Kulikov, "Yiddish Form, Socialist Content: Yiddish in Postwar Poland, 1945–1968," in *Yiddish after 1945*, ed. Marion Aptroot, Amsterdam Yiddish Symposium 11 (Amsterdam: Menasseh Ben Israel Institute, 2018), 29–44.

11. Joshua A. Fishman, ed., *Never Say Die!: A Thousand Years of Yiddish in Jewish Life and Letters* (The Hague: Mouton, 1981).
12. Joshua A. Fishman, "The Lively Life of a 'Dead' Language or 'Everyone Knows That Yiddish Died Long Ago,'" *Judaica Book News* 13, no. 1 (Fall/Winter 1982–1983): 10.
13. Avrom Sutskever, "Yidish" [Yiddish], in *Yidish in lid* [Poems on Yiddish], ed. Shmuel Rozhanski (Buenos Aires: YIVO, 1967), 186–187. My translation.
14. Yankev Glatshteyn, "A Lively Decline: A Language for Eternity, Not for the Meantime" [Yiddish], in Fishman, *Never Say Die!*, 610. Reprinted from Yankev Glatshteyn, *In der velt mit yidish: Eseyen* [In the world with Yiddish: Essays] (New York: Congress for Jewish Culture, 1972). My translation; in the original, the words *good time* are in English, rendered in the *alef-beys*.
15. Ahad Ha-'Am, "The Spiritual Revival," in *Selected Essays by Ahad Ha-'Am*, trans. Leon Simon (Philadelphia: Jewish Publication Society, 1912), 282. The essay was "originally an address delivered before the general meeting of Russian Zionists at Minsk, in the summer of in 1902" (253).
16. Leo Wiener, *The History of Yiddish Literature in the Nineteenth Century*, 2nd ed. (New York: Herman, 1972), 24, 10–11.
17. Cited in Ezekiel Lifschutz, "Morris Rosenfeld's Attempts to Become an English Poet," *America Jewish Archives* (1970): 124. Rosenfeld was writing to Leo Wiener, who arranged for the English-language publication of Rosenfeld's poetry.
18. Norich, *Discovering Exile*, 5.
19. Janet Hadda, "Yiddish in Today's America," *Jewish Quarterly* 170 (Summer 1998): 34–35.
20. E.g., Aaron Lansky, *Outwitting History: The Amazing Adventures of a Man Who Rescued a Million Yiddish Books* (Chapel Hill, N.C.: Algonquin, 2004).
21. Adrienne Cooper and Joyce Rosenzweig, *Dreaming in Yiddish*, Adrienne Cooper AC 8432, 1997, compact disc liner notes.
22. Interview with Alicia Svigals, New York, November 14, 2000, cited in Jeffrey Shandler, *Adventures in Yiddishland: Postvernacular Language and Culture* (Berkeley: University of California Press, 2005), 144.
23. As cited in Paul Kresh, *Isaac Bashevis Singer: The Magician of West 86th Street* (New York: Dial, 1979), 418.
24. Isaac Bashevis Singer, *Nobel Lecture* (New York: Farrar, Straus & Giroux, 1978), 9.
25. Amram Nowak, dir., *Isaac in America: A Journey with Isaac Bashevis Singer* (documentary film), 1986. My transcription.
26. Simon Rawidowicz, *Israel, the Ever-Dying People, and Other Essays*, ed. Benjamin C. I. Ravid (Rutherford, N.J.: Fairleigh Dickinson University Press, 1986), 61, 63.
27. Irving Saposnik, "A Canticle for Isaac: A Kaddish for Bashevis," in *The Hidden Isaac Bashevis Singer*, ed. Seth L. Wolitz (Austin: University of Texas Press, 2001), 3.
28. See, e.g., "Daniel Kahn and The Painted Bird," https://www.paintedbird.de/index.php?option=com_content&view=featured&Itemid=101&lang=en, accessed August 16, 2018.
29. "Sala-Manca Group," http://www.sala-manca.net/salamancagroup.htm. See Jeffrey Shandler, "Sala-Manca: Mediating the Poetics of Translation," *AJS Perspectives*, Spring 2006, 38–39.

30. "Yevgeniy Fiks: Books," https://yevgeniyfiks.com/artwork/4191033-Soviet-Moscow-s-Yiddish-Gay-Dictionary.html, accessed January 1, 2019.
31. Michael Cooper, "A Yiddish-Cuban Opera to Have Its Premiere in Havana in March," *New York Times*, February 19, 2017, https://www.nytimes.com/2017/02/19/arts/music/a-yiddish-cuban-opera-to-have-its-premiere-in-havana-in-march.html.
32. "The Company," New Yiddish Rep, http://www.newyiddishrep.org/The%20Company.html, accessed Aug. 28, 2016.
33. Corey Kilgannon, "A Gentile Who Lives for Yiddish," *New York Times*, January 29, 2012, https://www.nytimes.com/2012/01/29/nyregion/shane-baker-raised-episcopalian-lives-for-yiddish-theater.html.
34. Yermiyahu Ahron Taub, "Why I Write in Yiddish," Jewish Book Council blog, March 12, 2018, https://www.jewishbookcouncil.org/_blog/The_ProsenPeople/post/why-i-write-in-yiddish/.
35. The online periodical *In geveb* (In the network) publishes annual bibliographies of Yiddish studies scholarship in English, https://ingeveb.org).
36. "Voices of the Holocaust," http://voices.iit.edu, accessed June 3, 2018.
37. "The Ruth Rubin Legacy Archive of Yiddish Folksongs," https://exhibitions.yivo.org/exhibits/show/ruth-rubin-sound-archive/home, accessed December 24, 2018; "The Stonehill Jewish Song Collection," http://www.ctmd.org/stonehill.htm, accessed June 3, 2018.
38. "EYDES: Evidence of Yiddish Documented in European Studies," http://www.eydes.de/, accessed June 3, 2018; "Language and Culture Atlas of Ashkenazic Jewry," http://library.columbia.edu/locations/global/jewishstudies/lcaaj.html, accessed June 3, 2018.
39. Avraham Novershtern, "Between Town and Gown: The Institutionalization of Yiddish at Israeli Universities," in *Yiddish in the Contemporary World: Papers of the First Mendel Friedman International Conference on Yiddish*, ed. Gennady Estraikh and Mikhail Krutikov (Oxford: Legenda, 1999), 16.
40. "AHEYM: The Archives of Historical and Ethnographic Yiddish Memories," http://www.iub.edu/~aheym/, accessed June 3, 2018.
41. See Shandler, *Holocaust Memory in the Digital Age*, ch. 3.
42. Jeffrey Shandler, "Queer Yiddishkeit: Practice and Theory," *Shofar: An Interdisciplinary Journal of Jewish Studies* 25, no. 1 (Fall 2006): 112, 122, 113.
43. Jerold C. Frakes, "Yiddish in Italia: Yiddish Manuscripts and Printed Books from the 15th to the 17th Century" (review), *Shofar: An Interdisciplinary Journal of Jewish Studies* 24, no. 3 (2006): 154–156.
44. Ricardo Otheguy, Ofelia García, and Wallis Reid, "Clarifying Translanguaging and Deconstructing Named Languages: A Perspective from Linguistics," *Applied Linguistics Review* 6, no. 3 (2015): 281. See also Ofelia García and Li Wei, *Translanguaging: Language, Bilingualism and Education* (New York: Palgrave Macmillan, 2013).
45. Sarah Bunin Benor, "Towards a New Understanding of Jewish Language in the Twenty-First Century," *Religion Compass* 2, no. 6 (2008): 1068.

46. Sarah Bunin Benor, "Echoes of Yiddish in the Speech of Twenty-First-Century American Jews," in *Choosing Yiddish: Studies in Language, Culture, and History*, ed. Lara Rabinovitch, Shiri Goren, and Hannah Pressman (Detroit: Wayne State University Press, 2012), 319–323.
47. See, e.g., Marc van Oostendorp, "How Yiddish Dissolved into the Dutch Dialects," in *Dutch in Yiddish, Yiddish in Dutch*, ed. Marion Aptroot (Amsterdam: Menasseh Ben Israel Institute, 2016), 39–56; Lutz Edzard, "Hebrew and Hebrew-Yiddish Terms and Expressions in Contemporary German: Some (Socio-)Linguistic Observations," in *Proceedings of the Oslo-Austin Workshop in Semitic Linguistics: Oslo, May 23 and 24, 2013*, ed. Lutz Edzard and John Huehnergard, Abhandlungen für die Kunde des Morgenlandes 88 (Wiesbaden: Harrassowitz Verlag, 2014): 127–143.
48. Ghil'ad Zuckermann, "Hybridity versus Revivability: Multiple Causation, Forms and Patterns," *Journal of Language Contact* 2 (2009): 45.

# Glossary

***alef-bet*** The Jewish alphabet, used to write Hebrew, Yiddish, and most other Jewish languages. Pronounced *alef-beys* in Yiddish.

**Arbeter Ring (Workers Circle)** A secular Jewish organization, founded in New York in 1900, committed to promoting socialist values and Yiddish culture.

**Ashkenaz** Originally used to name the German lands of medieval Europe, the adjective Ashkenazic (in Yiddish, *ashkenazish*) now describes the Jewish people and culture generally understood as originating in this region.

**Ashkenazim** The diaspora Jewish people generally understood as originating in northern Europe in the late Middle Ages.

***brivnshteler(s)*** Manuals offering instruction in writing business and personal correspondence.

**Bund** See Yidisher Arbeter Bund.

***daytshmerish*** The perceived overuse in Yiddish of loanwords from modern German.

***doikeyt*** Literally, "hereness," a political principle of Jewish diaspora nationalists, who asserted the right and the value of Jews to live "here"—that is, wherever they found themselves—as citizens of their respective countries and as Jews.

**Farband** Yidish-natsyonaler Arbeter Farband (Jewish National Workers Alliance), a Labor Zionist organization founded in North America in 1912. Affiliated with the Labor Zionist party Poale Zion, the Farband ran Yiddish and Hebrew schools, summer camps, publications, a mutual aid society, and a cooperative apartment.

**Folkspartey (Folkists)** A political party, founded in 1905 in Russia, which advocated for Jewish national autonomy in the diaspora. The Folkspartey was active in politics in interwar Poland, Lithuania, and Latvia.

**Gemara** A section of the Talmud providing analysis and commentary on the Mishna, the oldest section of the Talmud. The term *gemara* is sometimes used to refer to the Talmud as a whole.

**Haggadah** The text of the ritual service performed in Jewish homes at the beginning of Passover.

***haredim*** "God-fearing people," refers to Jews, sometimes termed "ultra-Orthodox," who are most stringently observant of traditional practices and most resistant to mainstream culture; *haredi* is the adjectival form.

**Haskalah** Conventionally translated as the "Jewish Enlightenment," this intellectual movement, which began in German states in the mid-eighteenth century, advocated for

Jews' integration into the mainstream of western European culture and society through reforms of Jewish education, worship, and language use.

**Hasidism** A Jewish spiritual movement initiated in small towns in western Ukraine in the mid-eighteenth century, characterized by its commitment to popularizing esoteric mystical teachings and practices through vernacular practices, such as storytelling, singing, dancing, and feasting. Hasidism quickly gained followers throughout eastern Europe, especially in the southern half. The movement is distinguished by charismatic leaders, known as *rebeyim* or *tsadikim*, each of whom oversees a community of followers as their spiritual leader.

**Internatsyonaler arbeter-ordn (International Workers' Order)** A mutual aid organization founded in 1930, which oversaw a variety of secular Yiddish educational and cultural programs and publications. Allied with the Communist Party, it became the target of American anti-Communist activism and was shut down in 1954.

***ivre*** Yiddish term for a reading knowledge of the Hebrew of the Bible and other sacred texts, such as the prayer book.

***ivre-taytsh*** The version of Yiddish used in word-for-word translations of sacred Hebrew texts.

***jüdeln*** See *mauscheln*.

**Judezmo** The vernacular of Sephardic Jews following their expulsion from Iberia in the fifteenth century, sometimes also called Ladino or Spaniol. Its components include Old Spanish, *leshon ha-kodesh*, Ottoman Turkish, Arabic, Greek, Italian, and French.

**Khazars** A Turkic people who established a major empire in the region north of and between the Black Sea and the Caspian Sea, from the seventh through tenth centuries. The population of the Khazar Empire was both multiethnic and multilingual, including Jews; some claim that the Khazar ruling class converted to Judaism in the eighth century.

***kheyder*** Privately run school providing traditional elementary education in *ivre*.

**Knaanic** A Western Slavic Jewish language, now extinct.

***kulturshprakh*** A register of language used in high culture, such as works of literature and scholarship.

**Ladino** See Judezmo.

***leshon ha-kodesh*** Literally, "the language of holiness," refers collectively to the Hebrew and Aramaic of traditional Jewish worship and devotional study. Pronounced *loshn-koydesh* in Yiddish.

**Loez** A term from Biblical Hebrew that subsequently came to mean "foreign language," used to refer collectively to Old French and Old Italian.

***loshn-koydesh*** See *leshon ha-kodesh*.

***mahzor*** Holiday prayer book.

***mame-loshn*** Literally, "mother tongue," a term often used to refer affectionately to Yiddish.

***maskil* (plural, *maskilim*)** An advocate of the Haskalah.

***mauscheln*** A German-language term, coined in the nineteenth century, to disparage the distinct way that Jews spoke German, with traces of Yiddish idioms or intonation. The word is generally described as derived from *Moshe*, i.e., Moses. *Jüdeln* is a synonym for this phenomenon.

**Mishna** The earliest section of rabbinic laws and commentaries that make up the Talmud to be codified, ca. 200 CE.

***nekudes*** Diacritical marks, used in Hebrew and Yiddish orthography to indicate vowel signs. Pronounced *nekudot* in Modern Hebrew.

**Poale Zion** Literally, "Workers of Zion," a Labor Zionist movement organized in eastern Europe at the turn of the twentieth century. Poale Zion supported both the international workers' movement and the creation of a Jewish state, though factions disagreed on how to achieve both ends. In interwar Poland, Poale Zion ran candidates for public office and sponsored publications and educational programs.

***rebeyim*** Literally, "masters," a term for the charismatic leaders of Hasidic communities.

**Romaniote** The vernacular of Romaniote Jews, who have lived in the eastern Mediterranean since the Byzantine era, also known as Yavonic or Judeo-Greek.

***Rotwelsch*** A German term for the secret language used by criminals in southern Germany and Switzerland.

***shtetl* (plural, *shtetlekh*)** The Yiddish word for "town," often used in other languages, especially in the post–World War II era, to refer to provincial towns in eastern Europe with sizeable Jewish populations before the war.

***shprakhnkamf*** Literally, "language war," referring to the ideological clashes that took place, primarily during the first decades of the twentieth century, between advocates for Yiddish and for Modern Hebrew as the preferred Jewish national language.

***shund*** Sensational, lowbrow fiction and drama.

***taytsh*** A word originally used to refer to the vernacular of either Ashkenazim or their neighbors in German lands. In modern Yiddish, *taytsh* means "meaning, sense."

**Territorialism** A Jewish political movement that advocated creating a large-scale Jewish settlement in an unpopulated site somewhere in the diaspora, as opposed to the political Zionist agenda to create a Jewish state in Palestine. Beginning in 1903, the Jewish Territorialist Organization pursued multiple possibilities for securing territory for Jewish settlement. The organization's efforts were superseded by the Frayland-lige, which was established in 1935.

***tkhines*** Supplicatory prayers, written in Yiddish, primarily for and sometimes by women.

***tsadik* (plural, *tsadikim*)** Literally, "saintly man," a term for the charismatic leader of a Hasidic community.

***Tsene-rene*** A Yiddish rendering of the liturgical Hebrew Bible, imbricated with narrative expansions and commentaries from a range of rabbinic sources, compiled by Rabbi Jacob ben Isaac Rabbino of Janova. First published in the early seventeenth century, *Tsene-rene* became the most frequently reprinted Yiddish work. The name by which it is known, which means literally "Go forth and see," is a citation from Song of Songs 3:11.

***vaybertaytsh*** The distinctive typeface used for most Yiddish publications from the sixteenth to eighteenth centuries. The name implies that these publications were particularly intended for women, though their readership also included men.

**Wissenschaft des Judentums** A movement to undertake the "scientific study of Judaism," initiated in 1819 by Jewish scholars living in German states, who employed modern Western methodologies to analyze the development of Jewish texts and practices since ancient times.

**Yiddishism** A movement that emerged at the turn of the twentieth century in eastern Europe, committed to promoting Yiddish language and culture as central to facilitating Jewish cultural autonomy and sustaining a sense of Jewish nationhood.

**Yidisher Arbeter Bund (Jewish Labor Bund)** Jewish socialist political party, founded in Vilna in 1897, as the first workers' mass movement organization in Russia. In interwar Poland, the Bund ran officers for political elections and sponsored periodicals, youth movements, schools, and children's camps. The Bund supported the international workers' movement and championed Jewish diaspora nationalism.

***yidishkeyt*** Literally, "Jewishness," a term that can variously refer to Jewish practice, culture, or sensibility, whether in general or specifically among Ashkenazim. When this term appears in English it is often spelled Yiddishkeit, where its meaning can refer specifically to Yiddish culture.

***yizker-bikher*** Memorial books that commemorate destroyed eastern European Jewish communities.

***zhargon*** Literally, "jargon," originally a derogatory term for Yiddish that some of its speakers and writers adopted as a legitimate name for the language.

# Index

Note: Page numbers in italic type indicate illustrations.